*From
Confederation
to Nation*

BERNARD SCHWARTZ

From Confederation to Nation

THE AMERICAN CONSTITUTION, 1835-1877

THE JOHNS HOPKINS UNIVERSITY PRESS

BALTIMORE & LONDON

Copyright © 1973 by The Johns Hopkins University Press
All rights reserved. No part of this book may
be reproduced or transmitted in any form or by
any means, electronic or mechanical, including
photocopying, recording, xerography, or any
information storage and retrieval system, without permission
in writing from the publisher.
Manufactured in the United States of America

The Johns Hopkins University Press, Baltimore, Maryland 21218
The Johns Hopkins University Press Ltd., London

Library of Congress Catalog Card Number 72-12353
ISBN 0-8018-1464-2

Library of Congress Cataloging in Publication data
will be found on the last printed page of this book.

for Aileen

Contents

Preface

In 1827 Henry Hallam published his now-classic *Constitutional History of England*—the first work to bear the title of constitutional history. In his preface, Hallam stated that his was not a general history, but rather a history of the progress of the English Constitution: "The title which I have adopted appears to exclude all matter not referrible to the state of government, or what is loosely denominated the constitution." The present work is a constitutional history in the Hallam sense. It is not a general history of the United States during the period covered, though (as Hallam himself pointed out) "constitutional and general history . . . at some periods, nearly coincide," nor is it a history of American law, a history of the Supreme Court, or even a history of constitutional thought during the nineteenth century, though all of these areas are touched upon.

The author has attempted to analyze the development of the American Constitution from 1835 to 1877, much as Hallam did for the English Constitution from the accession of Henry VII to the death of George II. In its essentials, this means an examination of the federal Constitution in operation during the years covered. Though emphasis is placed on the work of the Supreme Court, attention is also given to the executive and legislative branches, and, during the latter part of this period, the stress is on the activities of the political departments, since it was they, rather than the Court, which made the most important contributions to the developing Constitution.

The study begins with the death of John Marshall in 1835 and concludes with 1877, the year which is usually cited as the end of Reconstruction and which almost coincides with the centennial of the nation itself. These were the years when the American system was put to the test of fire and survived—if anything, stronger than it had been before. The Constitution that emerged from this crucible was, in many ways, very different from what had originally been drafted. The four decades after Marshall's death can be considered as a virtual continuing constitutional convention, during which a second Constitution developed and took its place side by side with the Constitution of 1787 and the Bill of Rights of 1791. The most important amendments to the Constitution, except for the Bill of Rights itself, were added, and drastically altered the organic framework. They provided for basic new rights and for their federalization. Enforcement of civil rights now became a national rather than exclusively a state function; in the process, the great guarantees of life, liberty, and property were made operative against all governments throughout the land.

The result was a major shift in constitutional emphasis. The primary constitutional concern had been to draw the line between the authority of the nation and the power remaining to the states. The Bill of Rights protected only against the federal government, and complaints of violation had been most rare. There was to be a new constitutional focus, testing state action by the standard of the postbellum amendments. The Constitution now contained guarantees of individual rights enforceable against the states as well as the nation, and the stress during the next century would be increasingly on the protection of individual rights from all governmental power.

This book begins in the Golden Age of American law and ends in the era of the Crédit Mobilier and the Whiskey Ring. The early nineteenth century was the age of giants at the bench and bar, men who appeared larger than life, particularly in comparison with their successors. In politics, both ends of Pennsylvania Avenue could boast leaders of comparable distinction. The White House for the first time assumed its place as the vital center of government; Jackson's presidency revealed, albeit briefly, the potential inherent in the office. But even the "hero in the White House" could not completely overshadow the men who sat in the legislature, men like Clay, Calhoun, Webster, and Benton, who, for all their faults, towered over their successors even more than they did over their contemporaries.

In 1835, when the judge who had the greatest influence in our constitutional history, Chief Justice John Marshall, died, his Court had laid the doctrinal foundations of our constitutional law. It was the task of later courts to adapt that foundation to the needs of the day. The task was begun by Marshall's successor, Roger B. Taney, and it is with the work of the Taney Court that this volume begins. Under Taney, the Supreme Court mirrored the Jacksonian emphasis upon public power as a counterweight to the property rights stressed by the Marshall Court.

Concern shifted from federal to state power, not because the justices had become extreme exponents of states' rights doctrine but because they saw state authority as the instrument for redressing the balance which they felt the Marshall Court had tipped unduly against the public interest in favor of constitutional protection of property.

But now a new threat to constitutional doctrine appeared, and it could be resolved only by extra-constitutional means. The most significant constitutional decision of the period was that delivered at Appomattox courthouse. It settled what had become the most crucial question of all—whether the constitutional system itself could survive. Yet Appomattox did more than ensure the continuance of the nation: it placed the imprimatur of arms upon the nationalist construction of the Constitution expounded by Hamilton, Marshall, and, to a lesser extent (as we shall see), even by Taney himself.

The Constitution which emerged from the Civil War and Reconstruction established a federal predominance which dwarfed even the doctrine of national supremacy developed by Marshall. The United States was now emphatically a nation, and not a mere confederation of states. The full potential of national power was not realized in the reaction that followed Reconstruction, yet it was clearly established by the northern victory. Extreme states' rights was dead as a matter of constitutional law. When the issue of national power arose again with the Interstate Commerce Act of 1887, constitutional doctrine was able to reflect the changed nation-state balance, at first grudgingly and then, half a century later, at an increasingly accelerated pace.

Along with the supremacy of the federal government, the postwar Constitution placed increased emphasis on protection of individual rights. The postbellum amendments furnished the stuff of the constitutional law of the future, particularly in their provision of an equal protection guarantee and extension of due process protection to those injured by state, as well as federal, action. Here too, the post-Reconstruction reaction obscured the potential latent in the constitutional changes. What had been intended as great guarantees of human rights became transformed into the Great Charter of corporate expansion. This reaction also proved temporary, though it persisted for over half a century. During the 1950s the postbellum amendments began to be interpreted as their framers had intended. It is, indeed, not too much to say that the changes in the Constitution during the 1835–1877 period have become the dominant themes of the Constitution as it functions today.

CHAPTER ONE

The Taney Court

MARSHALL'S SUCCESSOR

The new chief justice was tall and impressive. He was, said an 1838 magazine article, "full six feet high: spare, but yet so dignified in deportment that you are at once impressed with an instinctive reverence and awe."[1] As he led the Supreme Court into its chamber on January 9, 1837, he looked the picture of a model judge. On that day Roger Brooke Taney first took his seat in the Court's central chair[2] and began a new era in the constitutional history of the nation.

One familiar with the marble temple in which the highest bench now sits will find it hard to picture the dingy quarters which that tribunal occupied during its early years. When the Capitol was built, the high Court was completely overlooked and no chamber provided for it: "When the seat of government was transferred to Washington, the court crept into an humble apartment in the basement beneath the Senate Chamber."[3] It was in that odd-shaped chamber, "on the lower floor in a dark room almost down cellar,"[4] that the Court sat until the end of 1860. "A stranger," wrote an 1824 newspaper account, "might traverse the dark avenues of the Capitol for a week, without finding the remote

---

[1] Quoted in W. Lewis, *Without Fear or Favor: A Biography of Chief Justice Roger Brooke Taney* 250 (1965).

[2] Actually, Taney presided over the Court on August 1, 1836, but no other justice was present and the Court was adjourned until the January term. *See* F. Frankfurter, *The Commerce Clause under Marshall, Taney and Waite* 46 (1964).

[3] 3 A.G. Beveridge, *The Life of John Marshall* 121 (1919).

[4] Charles Sumner, quoted in 2 C. Warren, *The Supreme Court in United States History* 252 (1924).

corner in which Justice is administered to the American Republic."[5]
According to the sardonic comment of a contemporary, housing the
Court underneath the Senate was "an arrangement wholly unjustifiable
unless perhaps by the idea that Justice should underlie legislation."[6]

When Benjamin F. Butler (Taney's successor as attorney general)
visited a Supreme Court session with his son, the latter recalled that his
"boyish attention was fastened upon the seven judges as they entered
the room—seven being the number then composing the Court. It was a
procession of old men—for so they seemed to me—who halted on
their way to the bench, each of them taking from a peg hanging on the
side of the wall near the entrance a black robe and donning it in full
view of the assembled lawyers and other spectators."[7]

It was just such a session over which Taney first presided as chief
justice at the beginning of 1837. The courtroom itself had been
refurbished (at least as much as was possible in such "a potato hole of a
place"[8]), but the essentials were the same as they had been in John
Marshall's day. Taney's great predecessor had headed the high court for
thirty-four years—longer than any man before or since. Nor was it
mere length of tenure alone that enabled Marshall to mold the Supreme
Court in the shape of his intense convictions. When he came to the
central judicial chair, the Court was but a shadow of what it has since
become. When he died on July 6, 1835, it had been transformed into
the head of a fully coordinate department, endowed with the ultimate
authority of safeguarding the ark of the Constitution.

Marshall it was who gave to the Constitution the impress of his own
mind, and the form of our constitutional law is still what it is because
he shaped it.[9] "Marshall," declared John Quincy Adams at news of his
death, "by the ascendancy of his genius, by the amenity of his deportment, and by the imperturbable command of his temper, has given a
permanent and systematic character to the decisions of the Court, and
settled many great constitutional questions favorably to the continuance of the Union." It was under Marshall's leadership that the Supreme Court transmuted the federal structure created by the Founders
into a nation strong enough to withstand even the shock of civil war.
To quote Adams' not unbiased view again, "Marshall has cemented the
Union which the crafty and quixotic democracy of Jefferson had a
perpetual tendency to dissolve."[10]

5 Quoted in *id.* at 461.

6 *C.H. Butler, A Century at the Bar of the Supreme Court of the United States* 29 (1942).

7 *Id.* at 29–30.

8 New York Tribune, Mar. 16, 1859, quoted in *Warren, supra* note 4, at 84.

9 *Compare Selected Writings of Benjamin Nathan Cardozo* 179 (M.E. Hall ed. 1947).

10 9 *Memoirs of John Quincy Adams* 243 (C.F. Adams ed. 1876).

The void created by Marshall's death can scarcely be overestimated. Wrote Joseph Story (who, as senior associate justice, had to "act as *locum tenens* of the Chief Justiceship"), "I miss the Chief Justice at every turn. . . . the room which he was accustomed to occupy . . . wears an aspect of desolation."[11] The dejection of Marshall's admirers was compounded by apprehension with regard to his potential successor. "It is much to be feared," gloomily wrote Adams, "that a successor will be appointed of a very different character. The President of the United States now in office . . . has not yet made one good appointment. His Chief Justice will be no better than the rest."[12]

Marshall himself had expressed misgivings about the future of the Supreme Court toward the end of his life. The advent of Jacksonian democracy, with its "enormous pretentions of the Executive," appeared but a portent of the fate that awaited both his constitutional labors and the strong national government which he sought to construct through them. "To men who think as you and I do," he wrote Story during the last year of his life, "the present is gloomy enough; and the future presents no cheery prospect."[13] Toward the end of his career, the great chief justice saw the Supreme Court defied, both by the State of Georgia and the president himself. "Georgia," complained Adams, "has planted the Standard against the Supreme Court of the United States—and I hear the twenty-fifth Section of the Judiciary Law is to be repealed. To these proceedings there is an apparent acquiescence of the People in all Quarters."[14] President Jackson, too, was the author of a vehement attack upon the very basis of the Supreme Court's review power in his famous 1832 message vetoing a bill to extend the charter of the Bank of the United States.[15] Well might Marshall feel that his long effort to construct judicial power as the cornerstone of an effective and enduring Union had been all but in vain.

Now it was Jackson himself who, on Marshall's death, was given the occasion to remold the Court in the feared Locofoco image. He had an opportunity denied to most presidents. He was able to place more men on the Supreme Court than any president before him except Washington or after him except Franklin D. Roosevelt. Not unnaturally, Jackson chose his six appointees from men of his own party, whom he felt he could trust. Not unnaturally, the Whigs attacked the packing of the

[11] Letter from Joseph Story to Harriet Martineau, Feb. 8, 1836, in 2 *Life and Letters of Joseph Story* 227, 226 (W. Story ed. 1851).

[12] *Adams, supra* note 10, at 243–44.

[13] Letter from John Marshall to Joseph Story, Oct. 6, 1834, *supra* note 11, at 173.

[14] Letter from J.Q. Adams to General P. Porter, Jan. 11, 1831, Parke-Bernet Galleries, Sale No. 3103, Item 3 (1970).

[15] 2 *J.D. Richardson, A Compilation of the Messages and Papers of the Presidents 1789–1897,* at 576–91 (1896).

Court with Democrats and southerners (by 1837, when Jackson went out of office, a majority of the high tribunal, newly enlarged to nine, came from below the Mason-Dixon Line). Such a bench, its opponents were convinced, would be all too ready to write the principles of Jacksonian democracy into the law. Above all, the opposition was apprehensive about Jackson's choice of a new chief justice. To Marshall's admirers, it must be admitted, no selection Jackson might have made (except perhaps Justice Story) would have been satisfactory. Jackson's choice, asserted Story himself, "will follow a man who cannot be equalled and all the public will see . . . the difference."[16]

The apprehension of men like Story appeared justified when, on December 28, 1835, Jackson nominated Roger B. Taney as chief justice of the United States. It was Taney who had drafted the key portions of the 1832 Veto Message and who had been the instrument for carrying out the president's plan for the removal of government deposits from the Bank of the United States. The veto had questioned the very review power of the Supreme Court, asserting that "the opinion of the judges has no more authority over Congress than the opinion of Congress has over the judges, and on that point the President is independent of both. The authority of the Supreme Court must not, therefore, be permitted to control the Congress or the Executive."[17] The choice of the author of these words to head a bench dominated by Jacksonian Democrats appeared to presage the virtual undoing of all that the Marshall Court had accomplished. Wrote Daniel Webster soon after the Taney nomination, "Judge Story . . . thinks the Supreme Court is *gone* and I think so too."[18]

Despite the bitterness of the opposition—"the pure ermine of the Supreme Court," acridly affirmed one Whig newspaper, "is sullied by the appointment of that political hack"[19] —and the fact that Taney had, during the preceding two years, been turned down by the Senate as secretary of the treasury and as a justice of the Supreme Court, this time his nomination was confirmed by the upper house, on March 15, 1836, by a vote of 29 to 15. The nearly two-to-one majority in Taney's favor is somewhat surprising since the Jackson and anti-Jackson forces were equally divided in the forty-eight-member Senate. When John Tyler received his "walking papers from the [Virginia] Legislature"[20]

16 Letter from Joseph Story to Richard Peters, July 24, 1835, *supra* note 11, at 202.

17 *Richardson, supra* note 15, at 582.

18 Quoted in *Warren, supra* note 4, at 284.

19 Quoted in *Warren, supra* note 4, at 290.

20 Letter from John Tyler to Mrs. Mary Jones, Jan. 20, 1836, Charles Hamilton, Auction No. 12, Item 190 (1966).

and, the day before the vote, was replaced by a Democrat the Jackson forces still had only the slimmest of majorities.

Apparently, what happened was that most of the Senate opposition abstained from the proceedings, largely because they felt that the administration now had the votes necessary for the nomination. As Francis Scott Key tells it in a letter to his sister (Taney's wife), "Taney, Kendall & Barbour have all passed. . . . —those who did not choose to vote for them went off, knowing it was of no use to stay." Therefore, concluded Key, "I must greet you as Mrs. *Chief Justice Taney*."[21]

TANEY AND JACKSONIAN DEMOCRACY

Taney first sat with his brethren when he was just under sixty years old. He was to serve until he was eighty-seven, a tenure as chief justice second only to that of Marshall. He was the first chief justice to wear trousers; his predecessors had always given judgment in knee breeches.[22] There was something of portent in his wearing democratic garb beneath the judicial robe,[23] for, under Taney and the new majority appointed by Jackson, the Supreme Court for the first time mirrored the Jacksonian emphasis upon public power as a counterweight to the property rights stressed by the Federalists and then the Whigs.

Taney had been one of the foremost exponents of Jacksonian democracy; it has been asserted that the Jacksonian political theory is more completely developed and more logically stated in Taney's writings and speeches than anywhere else.[24] This assertion may be extreme, but it cannot be denied that Taney's years on the Court marked growing judicial concern for safeguarding of the rights of the community as opposed to property rights—of the public, as opposed to private welfare. "We believe property should be held subordinate to man, and not man to property," declared a leading Jacksonian editor, "and therefore that it is always lawful to make such modifications of its constitution as the good of Humanity requires."[25] The Taney Court was to elevate this concept to the constitutional plane.

Taney himself was well aware of the crucial part played in his career

---

[21] Letter from Francis Scott Key to Mrs. R.B. Taney, Mar. 15, 1836, Charles Hamilton, Auction No. 24, Item 183 (1968). Amos Kendall was nominated as postmaster general and Philip P. Barbour as a supreme court justice.

[22] See 2 *B.P. Poore, Perley's Reminiscences of Sixty Years in the National Metropolis* 85 (1886).

[23] *See C.B. Swisher, Roger B. Taney* 359 (1935).

[24] *C.W. Smith, Roger B. Taney: Jacksonian Jurist* 3 (1936).

[25] Orestes A. Brownson, quoted in *A.M. Schlesinger, Jr., The Age of Jackson* 312 (1945).

by his relationship to Jackson. When the Senate approved his nomination, Taney wrote the president expressing warm gratitude, saying he would rather owe the honor to Jackson than to any other man in the world. It was a particular gratification, he declared, that "it will be the lot of one of the rejected of the panic Senate, as the highest judicial officer of the country to administer in your presence and in the view of the whole nation, the oath of office to another rejected of the same Senate, when he enters into the first office in the world."[26]

It is hard to understand Taney and his judicial work without awareness of his constant concern with the rejections that occurred during different stages of his career, from his early defeats in elections for Congress and the Maryland legislature[27] to the refusals of the Senate in 1834 and 1835 to confirm his nomination by Jackson as secretary of the treasury and then as associate justice of the Supreme Court. In this respect, Taney is one of the most difficult judicial historical subjects, much more so than Marshall, for his character was far more complex than that of his relatively straightforward predecessor. Like Marshall, he left an autobiographical sketch, but it is longer, rambling and abstruse, and unfinished.[28] It does clearly reveal his more complicated character —a constant emphasis on what he himself termed "morbid sensibility."[29] This sensibility, exaggerated perhaps by his delicate health and the fact that he was a Catholic in the Know-Nothing era, was to remain an essential part of the true Taney, beneath the stern façade shown to contemporaries. "I do not exactly understand why *Friday* has become the fashionable day for dinners here," he plaintively complained in an 1845 letter to his son-in-law, indicating his acute susceptibility to supposed slights at his religion.[30]

Taney was not only overly sensitive but had an exaggerated conception of himself as the very paragon of rectitude, an attitude that was to lead directly to the judicial fall that followed the *Dred Scott* decision. When he was first appointed to Jackson's cabinet, he served briefly as both attorney general and acting secretary of war. During that period he drew the salaries of both positions—something which strikes the observer as unethical. Yet he stoutly defended his action in an 1841

26 Letter from Roger B. Taney to Andrew Jackson, Mar. 17, 1836, in 5 *J.S. Bassett, Correspondence of Andrew Jackson* 390 (1933). The reference at the end of the letter is to Martin Van Buren, whom the Senate had refused to confirm as minister to England in 1831.

27 Taney states that he was "mortified" by one of these early defeats. *Lewis, supra* note 1, at 38.

28 His autobiography is contained in S. Tyler, *Memoir of Roger Brooke Taney, LL.D.* 17–95 (1872).

29 *Id.* at 78, 79.

30 Letter from Roger B. Taney to James M. Campbell, Dec. 21, 1845, Parke-Bernet Galleries, Sale No. 2310, Item 125 (1964).

letter, declaring that "as I performed the duties of both offices, I received the salaries of both. I thought then and still think that it was right."[31]

Even at Marshall's death, it should have been evident that the doctrines of national power the great chief justice had espoused were bound to prevail. Contemporary admirers of the Marshall constitutional edifice might look upon Taney as the instrument chosen for its destruction, but Taney was not the man to preside at the liquidation of the tribunal he was called upon to head. On the contrary, the Supreme Court under him continued the essential thrust of constitutional development begun by Marshall and his colleagues. In fact, if we look at Taney's constitutional work, avoiding the tendency to compare his accomplishments with the colossal structure erected by his predecessor, we find it far from a mean contribution. The shadow of the *Dred Scott* decision, it is now generally recognized, for too long cast an unfair pall over his judicial stature. To be sure, there was an inevitable reaction after Marshall's death, but it was not as great as has often been supposed. Chief Justice Taney may not have been as nationalistic in his beliefs as his predecessor, but his greater emphasis on states' rights should not obscure the continuing theme of his Court: that of formulating the principles needed to ensure effective operation of the Constitution.

In addition, it should be borne in mind that, however far-reaching Jacksonian democracy might have seemed to its contemporary opponents, it was, by present-day conceptions, quite limited. The Jacksonians did, it is true, go further than the Founders in the direction of both political and economic equality, but their notion of the democratic ideal as providing both liberty and equality for all must be sharply distinguished from the twentieth-century conception of the meaning of the word "all."[32] The Jacksonians, like the Framers before them, did not understand the ideal of liberty and equality *for all men* to require the abolition of slavery, the emancipation of women from legal and political subjection, or the eradication of all constitutional discriminations based on wealth, race, or previous condition of servitude.[33] Yet, though the Jacksonian conception was limited, one should not underestimate its significance: it made substantial contributions to both the theory and practice of equality.

When the occasion demanded it, indeed, the Jacksonians could

[31] Letter from Roger B. Taney to James M. Campbell, Jan. 18, 1841, Parke-Bernet Galleries, Sale No. 2310, Item 125 (1964).

[32] *Compare M.J. Adler,* The Great Ideas: A Syntopicon, *2 Great Books of the Western World* 305 (1952).

[33] *Compare id.* at 221, 305.

eloquently articulate the concept of equality and the premises upon which it was based. "In the full enjoyment of the gifts of Heaven and the fruits of superior industry, economy, and virtue," declared Jackson in his 1832 veto of the bill rechartering the Bank of the United States,

> every man is equally entitled to protection by law; but when the laws undertake to add to these natural and just advantages artificial distinctions, to grant titles, gratuities, and exclusive privileges, to make the rich richer and the potent more powerful, the humble members of society—the farmers, mechanics, and laborers—who have neither the time nor the means of securing like favors to themselves, have a right to complain of the injustice of their Government. . . . If it would confine itself to equal protection, and, as Heaven does its rains, shower its favors alike on the high and the low, the rich and the poor, it would be an unqualified blessing.[34]

The language quoted (which may have been written by Taney himself) is a statement, in positive terms, of the equal right of all persons to the equal protection of equal laws, in terms that are comparable to the negative version in the Fourteenth Amendment which was adopted over thirty-five years later.[35]

THE *CHARLES RIVER BRIDGE* CASE

We need not, in Justice Frankfurter's phrase, subscribe to the hero theory of history to recognize that great men do make a difference, even in the law.[36] Certainly, it made a difference that the 1837 term of the Supreme Court was presided over by Taney instead of Marshall. In all likelihood Marshall would have decided differently at least two of the three key decisions rendered in 1837.[37] The three cases had been argued while Marshall was still chief justice, but the Court had been unable to reach a workable decision. The cases were inherited by the Taney Court, and the new chief justice galvanized the Court into speedy action; the cases were all reargued and decided within less than a month after Taney first sat with his brethren.

---

34 Quoted in *Richardson, supra* note 15, at 590.

35 Compare *R.J. Harris, The Quest for Equality* 17 (1960).

36 *Frankfurter, supra* note 2, at 4.

37 *See* Story, J., dissenting, in New York v. Miln, 11 Pet. 102, 161 (U.S. 1837); Briscoe v. Bank of Kentucky, 11 Pet. 257, 328, 350 (U.S. 1837). It is probable that Marshall, after the first argument, had opted in favor of constitutionality in the Charles River Bridge case, the third of the key 1837 decisions. *S.I. Kutler, Privilege and Creative Destruction: The Charles River Bridge Case* 172–79 (1971); *G.T. Dunne, Justice Joseph Story and the Rise of the Supreme Court* 364 (1970).

The Marshall Court had been concerned with strengthening the power of the fledgling nation so that it might realize its political and economic destiny. Like the Framers themselves, it stressed the need to protect property rights as the prerequisite to such realization. To Jacksonians like Taney, private property, no matter how important, was not the be-all and end-all of social existence. "While the rights of property are sacredly guarded," declared the new chief justice in his first important opinion, "we must not forget that the community also have rights, and that the happiness and well being of every citizen depends on their faithful preservation."[38] The opinion was delivered in *Charles River Bridge* v. *Warren Bridge,*[39] a case which was a *cause célèbre* in its day, both because it brought the Federalist and Jacksonian views on the place of property into sharp conflict and because stock in the corporation involved was held by Boston's leading citizens and Harvard College.

The Charles River Bridge had been operated as a toll bridge by a corporation set up under a charter obtained by John Hancock and others in 1785. Each year £200 was paid from its profits to Harvard. The bridge, opened on a day celebrated by Boston as a "day of rejoicing," proved so profitable that the value of its shares increased tenfold and its profits led to public outcry. The bridge became a popular symbol of monopoly, and, in 1828, the legislature incorporated the Warren Bridge Company to build and operate another bridge near the Charles River Bridge. The second charter provided that the new bridge would become a free bridge after a short period of time. This would, of course, destroy the business of the first bridge, and its corporate owner sued to enjoin construction, alleging that the contractual obligation contained in its charter had been impaired.

The case was elaborately argued on January 24, 1837, with Daniel Webster appearing for the Charles River Bridge, "and at an early hour all the seats within and without the bar . . . filled with ladies, whose beauty and splendid attire and waving plumes gave to the Court-room an animated and brilliant appearance such as it seldom wears."[40] Less than three weeks later, the Court was ready for decision. On February 11, Justice Story wrote to his Harvard colleague, Professor Greenleaf (who had argued in opposition to Webster), "tomorrow . . . the opinion of the Court will be delivered in the Bridge case. You have triumphed."[41]

---

[38] Charles River Bridge v. Warren Bridge, 11 Pet. 420, 548 (U.S. 1837).

[39] 11 Pet. 420 (U.S. 1837).

[40] *Warren, supra* note 4, at 295–96.

[41] *Supra* note 11, at 267.

The new chief justice delivered the opinion of the Court. Taney's opinion refused to hold that there had been an invalid infringement upon the first bridge company's charter rights. There was no express provision in the charter making the franchise granted exclusive or barring the construction of a competing bridge, and the basic principle is "that in grants by the public, nothing passes by implication."[42] Since there is no express obligation not to permit a competing bridge nearby, none may be read in.

In deciding as it did, the Taney Court laid down what has since become a legal truism—that the rights of property must, where necessary, be subordinated to the needs of the community. The Taney opinion declined to rule that the charter to operate a toll bridge granted a monopoly in the area. Instead, the charter should be construed narrowly to preserve the rights of the community: where the rights of private property conflict with those of the community, the latter must be paramount. "The object and end of all government," Taney declared in words virtually setting forth the theme of Jacksonian democracy in the economic area, "is to promote the happiness and prosperity of the community by which it is established, and it can never be assumed that the government intended to diminish its power of accomplishing the end for which it was created." Governmental power in this respect may not be transferred, by mere implication, "to the hands of privileged corporations."[43]

Writing to his wife, Justice Story, who delivered a characteristically learned thirty-five-thousand-word dissent, bitterly attacked the majority decision, asserting that "a case of grosser injustice, or more oppressive legislation, never existed."[44] In his dissent, he declared that the Court, by impairing the sanctity of property rights, was acting "to alarm every stockholder in every public enterprise of this sort, throughout the whole country."[45] Yet, paradoxical though it may seem, it was actually the Taney decision, not the Story dissent, which ultimately was the more favorable to the owners of property, particularly those who invested in corporate enterprise. Though in form the *Charles River Bridge* decision was a blow to economic rights, it actually facilitated economic development by providing the legal basis for public policy choices favoring technological innovation and economic change, even at the expense of some vested interests.[46] The case itself arose when the

[42] 11 Pet. at 546.
[43] *Id.* at 547, 548.
[44] Letter from Joseph Story to Mrs. Joseph Story, Feb. 14, 1837, *supra* note 11, at 268.
[45] 11 Pet. at 608.
[46] *Kutler, supra* note 37, at 161.

corporate form was coming into widespread use as an instrument of capitalist expansion. In the famous *Dartmouth College* case,[47] the Marshall Court had ruled the grants of privileges in corporate charters to be contracts and, as such, beyond impairment by government. The Marshall approach here would have meant the upholding of the first bridge company's monopoly. Such a result would have had most undesirable consequences, for it would have meant that every bridge or turnpike company was given an exclusive franchise which might not be impaired by the newer forms of transportation being developed:

> Let it once be understood, that such charters carry with them these implied contracts, and give this unknown and undefined property in a line of travelling; and you will soon find the old turnpike corporations awakening from their sleep, and calling upon this court to put down the improvements which have taken their place. The millions of property which have been invested in railroads and canals, upon lines of travel which had been before occupied by turnpike corporations, will be put in jeopardy.[48]

To read monopoly rights into existing charters would be to place modern improvements at the mercy of existing corporations and defeat the right of the community to avail itself of the benefits of scientific progress.

Those who believed as Story did refused to see the beneficial implications of Taney's decision. Like all those wedded to the old order, they knew only that a change had been made in the status quo, and that was sufficient for their condemnation. "I stand upon the old law," plaintively affirmed the Story dissent, "upon law established more than three centuries ago . . . not . . . any speculative niceties or novelties." [49] In a letter written several weeks later, he dolefully declared, "I am the last of the old race of Judges."[50] To men like Story, Taney and the majority had virtually "overturned . . . one great provision of the Constitution."[51]

The truth, of course, is that the Taney Court had only interpreted the Contract Clause in a manner that coincided with the felt needs of the era of economic expansion upon which the nation was entering. Because of the Taney decision, that expansion could proceed unencumbered by inappropriate legal excrescences. By 1854, a member of the

---

47 Dartmouth College v. Woodward, 4 Wheat. 518 (U.S. 1819).

48 11 Pet. at 552–53, per Taney, C.J.

49 *Id.* at 598.

50 Letter from Joseph Story to Harriet Martineau, Apr. 7, 1837, *supra* note 11, at 277.

51 Letter from Daniel Webster to Joseph Story, n.d., *supra* note 11, at 269.

highest court could confidently assert, with regard to the *Charles River Bridge* decision, "No opinion of the court more fully satisfied the legal judgment of the country, and consequently none has exerted more influence upon its legislation."[52]

STATE POWER

Two other cases decided by the Taney Court during its first term received much public attention. They too had been inherited from the Marshall Court and were decided differently than they would have been before Taney's accession. Both *Briscoe* v. *Bank of Kentucky* and *New York* v. *Miln*[53] dealt with the question of reserved state power—an issue crucial in a federal system such as ours in which national and state governments coexist, each endowed with the complete accoutrements of government, including the full apparatus of law enforcement, both executive and judicial. Marshall, with his expansive nationalistic tenets, had perhaps tilted the scale unduly in favor of federal power. The Taney Court sought to redress the balance by shifting the emphasis to the reserved powers possessed by the states.

In the *Briscoe* case, the Court held that the issuance by a state-owned bank of small-denomination notes which circulated as currency did not violate the constitutional prohibition against issuance by the states of bills of credit. According to the majority opinion of Justice McLean, the notes were not bills of credit put out by the state since they were issued by the bank, not the state, even though the state owned the bank. Again Justice Story dissented. He tells us that Marshall himself— "a name never to be pronounced without reverence"—would not have been with the majority: "Had he been living, he would have spoken in the joint names of both of us."[54] As it was, Story was alone in his effort to preserve the reign of the dead hand.[55]

The *Briscoe* decision is today of purely historical significance since the problem of state power at issue there has long been academic. Yet the decision does show the willingness of the Taney Court to uphold state action if at all possible, even though it involved a refusal to look behind the form to the substance of the challenged action. Perhaps the best explanation of *Briscoe* is to be found in the Jacksonian fear of the growing power of finance, particularly as exemplified by "the power

---

[52] Campbell, J., dissenting, in Piqua Branch v. Knoop, 16 How. 369, 409 (U.S. 1853).

[53] 11 Pet. 257 (U.S. 1837); 11 Pet. 102 (U.S. 1837).

[54] Briscoe v. Bank of Kentucky, 11 Pet. at 328, 350.

[55] *Compare Swisher, supra* note 23, at 375.

which the moneyed interest derives from a paper currency which they are able to control."[56] To avoid the evils of financial monopoly, the state was ruled able to regulate its circulating medium through the issue of notes by its own bank.[57]

More interesting to the present-day observer is *New York* v. *Miln*, for it dealt with an aspect of state power that is still most pertinent, namely, the police power and its impact upon commerce. At issue in *Miln* was a New York law which required masters of vessels to report the names, places of birth, ages, health, occupations, and last legal residence of all passengers landing in New York City and to give security to the city against their becoming public charges. The city was seeking to collect the statutory penalty against the ship *Emily* because of its master's failure to file the report required by the statute. Defendant contended that the statute involved an invalid state regulation of foreign commerce since the power over such commerce was vested exclusively in Congress by the Constitution.

The opinion of the Court in *Miln* was written by Justice Barbour (characterized by John Quincy Adams as that "shallow-pated wild-cat . . . fit for nothing but to tear the Union to rags and tatters"[58]), who had been appointed to the Court at the same time as Taney himself. The Barbour opinion avoided the Commerce Clause issue, holding that the statute was valid as a matter of "internal police." The state's powers with regard to such "internal police" were not surrendered or restrained by the Constitution; on the contrary, "in relation to these, the authority of a state is complete, unqualified, and exclusive." The law at issue was passed by the state "to prevent her citizens from being oppressed by the support of multitudes of poor persons, who come from foreign countries, without possessing the means of supporting themselves. There can be no mode in which the power to regulate internal police could be more appropriately exercised."[59]

Perhaps the most significant aspect of *New York* v. *Miln* is its role in the development of the police power concept. That subject is so important that it deserves separate treatment. Here let us note another phase of the decision, which plainly appears anomalous today, yet is useful to illustrate the restricted scope of the Jacksonian notions of freedom and equality. The *Miln* opinion asserts a general power in the states to exclude undesirables. "We think it," declared the opinion, "as competent and as necessary for a state to provide precautionary measures against the moral pestilence of paupers, vagabonds, and possibly

[56] Jackson, Farewell Address, 3 *Richardson, supra* note 15, at 305.
[57] *Compare Frankfurter, supra* note 2, at 69.
[58] 8 *Adams, supra* note 10, at 315–16.
[59] 11 Pet. at 139, 141.

convicts; as it is to guard against the physical pestilence, which may arise from unsound and infectious articles imported."[60] Similar language, it should be noted, was repeated in other high bench decisions down to the turn of the century.[61]

Relying upon these Supreme Court dicta, many states enacted laws restricting the movement of indigent persons. Those laws were consistent with the historical common law tradition of restricting the liberty of the pauper. To the judges of a century ago, to strike down such a restriction would be to include in citizenship "a right of the indigent person to live where he will although the crowding into one State may be a menace to society. No such right exists."[62]

This justification for a statutory restriction upon the poor person's freedom of movement is wholly inconsistent with our concepts of personal liberty. In 1941 the Supreme Court itself ruled that the power to restrict freedom of movement may never be based upon the economic status of those restricted. The Court then stated that it did not consider itself bound by the contrary language in the *Miln* case, emphasizing that *Miln* was decided over a century ago: "Whatever may have been the notion then prevailing, we do not think that it will now be seriously contended that because a person is without employment and without funds he constitutes a 'moral pestilence.' "[63]

POLICE POWER

Taney's leading biographer asserts that more credit has been given Taney in recent years for the development of the police power than he is entitled to or than he himself would have been willing to accept. [64] This assertion unduly denigrates the contribution of Taney and his brethren in the development of what has become so seminal a concept in our public law. It was the Taney Court which first gave to the notion of police power something like its modern connotation. In his opinion in the *Charles River Bridge* case, Chief Justice Taney affirmed the existence of police power in the states: "We cannot . . . by legal intendments and mere technical reasoning, take away from them any portion of that power over their own internal police and improvement, which is

---

60 *Id.* at 142.

61 The cases are cited in Edwards v. California, 314 U.S. 160, 176–77 (1941).

62 *Matter of* Chirillo, 283 N.Y. 417, 436 (1940) (dissenting opinion).

63 Edwards v. California, 314 U.S. 160, 177 (1941). For a more recent case, *see* Shapiro v. Thompson, 394 U.S. 618 (1969).

64 *Swisher, supra* note 23, at 309.

so necessary to their well-being and prosperity."[65] And, as noted above, the decision in *New York* v. *Miln* turned expressly upon the police power concept.

In the 1847 *License Cases* Taney himself gave to the police power the broad connotation that has been of such influence in molding the development of constitutional law. "But what," he asked there, "are the police powers of a State? They are nothing more or less than the powers of government inherent in every sovereignty to the extent of its dominions. And whether a State passes a quarantine law, or a law to punish offenses, or to establish courts of justice, or requiring certain instruments to be recorded, or to regulate commerce within its own limits, in every case it exercises the same power; that is to say, the power of sovereignty, the power to govern men and things within the limits of its dominion."[66]

In the Taney conception, police powers and sovereign powers are the same.[67] In this sense, the states retain all powers necessary to their internal government which are not prohibited to them by the federal Constitution. Of course, such a broad conception of state power over internal government may be inconsistent with the fullest exertion of individual rights. Taney saw the inconsistency as inherent in the very nature of the police power. Indeed, it was his chief contribution to recognize and articulate the superior claim, in appropriate cases, of public over private rights. The Taney Court developed the police power as the basic instrument through which property might be controlled in the public interest. Community rights were thus ruled "paramount to all private rights . . . , and these last are, by necessary implication, held in subordination to this power, and must yield in every instance to its proper exercise."[68]

It was the Taney opinion in the *License Cases* which gave currency to the phrase "police power." In 1851 was decided the first case in the state courts to speak of the police power, the now classic Massachusetts case of *Commonwealth* v. *Alger*,[69] with its oft-cited definition of the term by Chief Justice Shaw. Only four years later, a Missouri court could say of this power that it was "known familiarly as the police power."[70] By the time of the Civil War, certainly, the term was in common use throughout the land.

65 11 Pet. at 552.
66 5 How. 504, 583 (U.S. 1847).
67 *See* Passenger Cases, 7 How. 283, 424 (U.S. 1849).
68 West River Bridge v. Dix, 6 How. 507, 532 (U.S. 1848).
69 7 Cush. 53 (Mass. 1851).
70 State v. Searcy, 20 Mo. 489, 490 (1855).

The Taney Court's articulation of the police power concept was a necessary complement to the expansion of governmental power that was an outstanding feature of the Jacksonian period. During that period "the demand went forth for a large governmental programme: for the public construction of canals and railroads, for free schools, for laws regulating the professions, for anti-liquor legislation."[71] In the police power concept, the law developed the constitutional theory needed to enable the states to meet the public demand. The Taney Court could thus clothe the states with the authority to enact social legislation for the welfare of their citizens. Government was given the "power of accomplishing the end for which it was created."[72] Through the police power a state might, "for the safety or convenience of trade, or for the protection of the health of its citizens,"[73] regulate the rights of property and person. Thenceforth, a principal task of the Supreme Court was to be determination of the proper balance between individual rights and the police power.

COMMERCE REGULATION

One of the most difficult tasks of the Taney Court was that of determining the reach of the Commerce Clause and the proper scope of concurrent state power over commerce. In *New York* v. *Miln*,[74] it will be recalled, the justices had avoided direct resolution of the question of whether the commerce power was exclusively vested in the federal government. The question came before the Supreme Court with increasing frequency because of the growing resort by the states to regulatory legislation.

Taney and his colleagues vacillated on the commerce issue, confirming, in the 1847 *License Cases*,[75] the power of the states to regulate the sale of liquor which had been imported from abroad, and then, in the 1849 *Passenger Cases*,[76] striking down state laws imposing a tax on foreign passengers arriving in state ports. The confusion in the Court was shown by the plethora of judicial pronouncements to which it gave rise. Nine opinions were written in the first case and eight in the second; in neither was there an opinion of the Court in which a majority was willing to concur.

[71] *Corwin, The Doctrine of Due Process of Law before the Civil War*, 24 *Harv. L. Rev.* 460, 461 (1911).

[72] Charles River Bridge v. Warren Bridge, 11 Pet. at 547.

[73] License Cases, 5 How. at 579.

[74] *Supra* note 53.

[75] 5 How. 504 (U.S. 1847).

[76] 7 How. 283 (U.S. 1849).

To understand the problem presented in these cases involving commerce regulation, we should bear in mind that the Commerce Clause itself is, as Justice Rutledge tells us, a two-edged sword.[77] One edge is the positive affirmation of congressional authority; the other, not nearly so smooth or keen, cuts down state power by negative implication. By its very inferential character, the limitation is lacking in precise definition. The clause may be a two-edged blade, but the question really posed is the swath of the negative cutting edge.[78] To put it more specifically, did the Commerce Clause, of its own force, take from the states any and all authority over interstate and foreign commerce, so that state laws on the subject automatically dropped lifeless from the statute books for want of the sustaining power that had been wholly relinquished to Congress?[79] Or was the effect of the clause less sweeping, so that the states still retained at least a portion of their residual powers over commerce?

According to Justice Story's dissent in *New York* v. *Miln,* the Marshall Court had rejected the notion that the congressional power was only concurrent with that of the states. Marshall, said Story, held that the power given to Congress was full and exclusive: "Full power to regulate a particular subject implies the whole power, and leaves no residuum; and a grant of the whole to one, is incompatible with the grant to another of a part."[80] In actuality, despite the Story statement to the contrary, the Marshall view of the commerce power was not that of unequivocal federal exclusiveness, as shown by his opinion in *Willson* v. *Black Bird Creek Marsh Co.*[81] In that case, a state law had authorized the construction of a dam across a small navigable creek for the purpose of draining surrounding marshland. It was claimed that the law was repugnant to the federal commerce power. Marshall rejected this contention, emphasizing in his opinion the benefits to be derived from draining the marsh in enhanced land values and improved health. "Measures calculated to produce these objects," he said, "provided they do not come into collision with the powers of the general government, are undoubtedly within those which are reserved to the states."[82]

The *Willson* opinion indicates that Marshall's interpretation of the negative aspect of the Commerce Clause was not as far from that of Taney as is generally believed. "It appears to me to be very clear," declared Taney in an 1847 opinion, "that the mere grant of power to

---

[77] *W.B. Rutledge, A Declaration of Legal Faith* 33 (1947).

[78] *Id.* at 45.

[79] *Compare* Gibbons v. Ogden, 9 Wheat. 1, 226 (U.S. 1824).

[80] 11 Pet. at 158.

[81] 2 Pet. 245 (U.S. 1829).

[82] *Id.* at 251.

the general government cannot, upon any just principles of construction, be construed to be an absolute prohibition to the exercise of any power over the same subject by the States."[83] Yet the *Willson* case indicates that Marshall also shared this view as far as the commerce power was concerned. Both Marshall and Taney, then, refused to follow the notion of complete exclusiveness of federal power under which the Commerce Clause, of its own force, removed from the states any and all power over interstate and foreign commerce.

Where Marshall and Taney really differed was in their conception of just how much power over commerce remained in the states. Taney followed his rejection of the complete exclusiveness theory to the opposite extreme and asserted in the states a concurrent power over commerce limited only by the Supremacy Clause of the Constitution. The states, in his view, might make any regulations of commerce within their territory, subject only to the power of Congress to displace any state law by conflicting federal legislation.[84] His concurrent power theory (under which the states possess, concurrently with Congress, the full power to regulate commerce) is, however, incompatible with the basic purpose which underlies the Commerce Clause—that of promoting a system of free trade among the states protected from state legislation inimical to that free flow. For that goal to be achieved, the proper approach to the commerce power lies somewhere between the antagonistic poles of extreme exclusiveness and coextensive concurrent power.

Such an approach was urged by Daniel Webster in the greatest of his legal arguments in the Supreme Court,[85] that made in *Gibbons* v. *Ogden.*[86] He contended that the federal power to regulate commerce was, "to a certain extent necessarily exclusive."[87] What he meant by this was "not that all the commercial powers are exclusive, but that those powers being separated, there are some which are exclusive in their nature."[88] Webster's conception was based upon acute perception. To those who urged that the commerce power had to be either entirely exclusive or concurrent, he posed the query: "is not the subject susceptible of division, and may not some portions of it be exclusively vested in Congress?"[89] In other words, some, but not all, areas of commercial regulation are absolutely foreclosed to the states by the

83 License Cases, 5 How. 504, 579 (U.S. 1847).

84 *Id.*

85 So characterized in 4 *Beveridge, supra* note 3, at 424–25.

86 9 Wheat. 1 (U.S. 1824).

87 *Id.* at 9

88 *Id.* at 181.

89 *Id.* at 180. The actual quote is from the argument of Webster's colleague William Wirt.

Commerce Clause. Here was a doctrine of what might be termed "selective exclusiveness," with the Supreme Court determining, in specific cases, the areas in which Congress possessed exclusive authority over commerce. Its great advantage was that of flexibility. Since it neither permitted nor foreclosed state power in every instance in advance, it might serve as a supple instrument to meet the needs of the future.

THE *COOLEY* CASE

It was not until *Cooley* v. *Board of Port Wardens*[90] that the Supreme Court was to adopt the middle approach urged by Webster to the question of state power to regulate commerce. Before that case (as already indicated), the Taney Court had vacillated in its answer to that question. Taney had urged the existence of a commerce power in the states coextensive with that of Congress, to yield only where state regulation was in conflict with federal law, but he could not induce a majority to acquiesce in his view. A compromise was necessary if the question was to be resolved in a way which rejected the opposite extreme of exclusive congressional authority, urged by the "high-toned Federalists on the bench."[91]

The *Cooley* opinion was delivered by Justice Benjamin R. Curtis, best remembered for his dissent in the *Dred Scott* case. Curtis had a keen legal mind and was regarded as one of the leading lawyers of the day (Webster, who had urged his appointment to the Supreme Court, wrote that he "is in point of legal attainment and general character in every way fit for the place"[92]). Curtis had taken his seat on the high bench only two months before the *Cooley* case was argued and was thus an ideal judge to write a compromise opinion between the extremes of exclusive congressional power advocated by Justices McLean and Wayne (who dissented in *Cooley*) and the Taney view of coextensive concurrent power.

Taney himself concurred silently in the Curtis *Cooley* opinion. Why he did so has always been a matter for speculation. As chief justice, he could, if he chose, make himself spokesman for the Court. That he did not do so shows that he could not carry a majority for his own approach.[93] If he did not accept the *Cooley* compromise, it would have

[90] 13 How. 299 (U.S. 1852).

[91] Letter from Benjamin R. Curtis to Mr. Ticknor, Feb. 29, 1852, 1 *Memoir of Benjamin Robbins Curtis, LL.D.* 168 (1879).

[92] Letter from Daniel Webster to President Millard Fillmore, Sept. 10, 1851, *id.* at 154.

[93] *Compare Frankfurter, supra* note 2, at 57.

meant the same fragmented resolution of the commerce issue that had occurred in the *License* and *Passenger Cases*. Taney's concurrence in the *Cooley* compromise made it possible for the law at last to be settled with some certainty on the matter (it was only after *Cooley*, asserts the Court's historian, "that a lawyer could advise a client with any degree of safety as to the validity of a State law having any connection with commerce between the States"[94]) and, what is more, settled along lines that, in many cases at least, would be favorable to the existence of concurrent state power.

Taney's biographer asserts that the author of the *Cooley* opinion "brought to the Court no new ideas on the subject of the interpretation of the commerce power."[95] The assertion is unfair. Of course, Justice Curtis followed the time-honored judicial technique of pouring new wine into old bottles. He based his opinion on Webster's "selective exclusiveness" doctrine,[96] but he went beyond Webster's argument to make a truly original contribution which has since controlled the law on the matter. Well could Curtis write, just before the *Cooley* decision was announced, "I expect my opinion will excite surprise. . . . But it rests on grounds perfectly satisfactory to myself . . . , although for twenty years no majority has ever rested their decision on either view of this question, nor was it ever directly decided before."[97]

The *Cooley* case arose out of a Pennsylvania law requiring vessels using the port of Philadelphia to engage local pilots or pay a fine, amounting to half the pilotage fee, to go to the Society for the Relief of Distressed and Decayed Pilots. Since there was no federal statute on the subject, the question for the Supreme Court was that of the extent of state regulatory power over commerce where the Congress was silent on the matter. It was contended that the pilotage law was repugnant to the Constitution because the Commerce Clause had vested the authority to enact such a commercial regulation exclusively in Congress. To the question whether the power of Congress was exclusive, Justice Curtis answered, "Yes and No"—or, to put it more accurately, "Sometimes Yes and sometimes No." There remained the further inquiry: "When and why, Yes? When and why, No?"[98]

With regard to that query, too, Webster had pointed the way. The words of the Commerce Clause, said he, in his *Gibbons* v. *Ogden*

---

94 *Warren, supra* note 4, at 429.

95 *C.B. Swisher, American Constitutional Development* 205 (1943).

96 Which had also been followed by Woodbury, J., dissenting, in Passenger Cases, 7 How. at 559.

97 *Supra* note 91.

98 *Compare T.R. Powell, Vagaries and Varieties in Constitutional Interpretation* 152–53 (1956).

argument, "must have a reasonable construction, and the power should be considered as exclusively vested in Congress, so far, and so far only, as the nature of the power requires."[99] This was the basic approach followed in *Cooley*. If the states are excluded from power over commerce, Justice Curtis said, "it must be because the nature of the power, thus granted to Congress, requires that a similar authority should not exist in the States."[100] If that be true, the states must be excluded only to the extent that the nature of the commerce power requires. When, Curtis asked, does the nature of the commerce power require that it be considered exclusively vested in Congress? This depends not upon the abstract "nature" of the commerce power itself but upon the nature of the "subjects" over which the power is exercised, for "when the nature of a power like this is spoken of, when it is said that the nature of the power requires that it should be exercised exclusively by Congress, it must be intended to refer to the subjects of that power, and to say they are of such a nature as to require exclusive legislation by Congress."[101]

Having thus transferred the focus of inquiry from the commerce power in the abstract to the subjects of regulation in the concrete, Curtis then examined them pragmatically. If we look at the subjects of commercial regulation, he said, we find that they are exceedingly various and quite unlike in their operation. Some imperatively demand a single uniform rule, operating equally on commerce throughout the United States; others as imperatively demand that diversity which alone can meet local necessities. "Either absolutely to affirm, or deny," said Curtis, "that the nature of this power requires exclusive legislation by Congress, is to lose sight of the nature of the subjects of this power, and to assert concerning all of them, what is really applicable but to a part." Whether the states may regulate depends upon whether it is imperative that the subjects of the regulation be governed by a uniform national system. As the *Cooley* opinion put it, "Whatever subjects of this power are in their nature national, or admit only of one uniform system, or plan of regulation, may justly be said to be of such a nature as to require exclusive legislation by Congress."[102] On the other hand, where national uniformity of regulation is not necessary, the subject concerned may be reached by state law. That is the case with a law for the regulation of pilots like that at issue in *Cooley*.

Almost two decades after the *Cooley* decision, Justice Miller, speaking for the Supreme Court, stated, "Perhaps no more satisfactory

[99] 9 Wheat. at 14.
[100] 12 How. at 318.
[101] *Id.* at 319.
[102] *Id.*

solution has ever been given of this vexed question than the one furnished by the court in that case."[103]   A century later, much the same comment can be made, despite attempts by the high bench since *Cooley* to formulate other tests. Such tests have proved unsatisfactory, and the Court has basically continued to follow the *Cooley* approach in cases involving the validity of state regulations of commerce.

CORPORATE EXPANSION

Justice Frankfurter once said that the history of our constitutional law in no small measure is the history of the impact of the modern corporation upon the American scene.[104]   While the Taney Court sat, new economic forces were bringing new issues for judicial resolution; the corporate device and the concentrations of economic power made possible by it began to come before the justices with increasing frequency.

If there was one tenet common to advocates of Jacksonian democracy, it was that of opposition to "the rich and powerful [who] too often bend the acts of government to their selfish purposes."[105]   They deeply distrusted corporations as aggregations of wealth and power—the "would-be lordlings of the Paper Dynasty"[106] —which posed a direct danger to the democratic system. In his 1837 Farewell Address, Jackson had warned of the perils posed by "the great moneyed corporations": "unless you become more watchful . . . and check this spirit of monopoly and thirst for exclusive privileges you will in the end find that the most important powers of Government have been given or bartered away, and the control over your dearest interests has passed into the hands of these corporations."[107]

The Jacksonian view of corporate power was shared by Taney and most of his colleagues on the bench. Taney himself had been a leader in the war against the Bank of the United States—the corporate monster, "citadel of the moneyed power,"[108] which the Jacksonians had finally overthrown. An 1834 Taney speech affirmed that "in every period of the world . . . history is full of examples of combinations among a *few* individuals, to grasp all power in their own hands, and wrest it from the

103 Crandall v. Nevada, 6 Wall. 35, 42 (U.S. 1868).

104 *Frankfurter, supra* note 2, at 164.

105 Jackson Bank Veto Message, *Richardson, supra* note 15, at 590.

106 William Leggett, quoted in *H.S. Commager, The Era of Reform, 1830–1860,* at 94 (1960).

107 3 *Richardson, supra* note 15, at 305–6.

108 Speech by Taney, Aug. 6., 1834, quoted in *Swisher, supra* note 23, at 297.

hands of the many." [109] Certainly Taney subscribed to the view that "the extent of the wealth and power of corporations among us, demands that plain and clear laws should be declared for their regulation and restraint." [110]

In theory at least, the Jacksonians on the bench shared the agrarian persuasion of their most extreme member, Justice Peter V. Daniel, who wrote in 1841 that, though he perceived the spread of banks and corporations to every hamlet, he still hoped that they might be weeded completely out of society. [111] In practice, however, even the Jacksonian justices had to recognize that the corporation had a proper place in the legal and economic systems. The result was that, as Jacksonians, men like Taney might fear its abuses, but as practical men of affairs they had to recognize its utility in an expanding nation. To the United States of the first half of the nineteenth century, the corporate device was an indispensable adjunct of the nation's growth. The corporation enabled men to establish the pools of wealth and talent needed for the economic conquest of a continent. Even these Jacksonian judges realized the relationship between the corporation and economic development and made decisions favorable to the corporate personality—notably the 1839 decision in *Bank of Augusta* v. *Earle*. [112]

The question presented in that case has been characterized by the high court's historian as "of immense consequence to the commercial development of the country—the power of a corporation to make a contract outside of the State in which it was chartered." [113] It should be borne in mind that the corporation itself is entirely a creation of law; its very existence and legal personality have their origin in some act of the law. Corporations themselves, of course, appear at an early stage of American history, for chartered companies first settled the colonies of Virginia and Massachusetts Bay. Yet, though the corporation as a legal person was developed under English law and recognized from the beginning in American law (especially in the classic 1819 *Dartmouth College* case), it was not until the decision in *Bank of Augusta* v. *Earle* that it could really be made to serve the needs of the burgeoning American economy.

In the *Bank of Augusta* case two banks and a railroad, incorporated respectively in Georgia, Pennsylvania, and Louisiana, brought an action

[109] Quoted in *Smith, supra* note 24, at 67.

[110] Corporations, 4 *American Jurist* 298 (1830), in *The Golden Age of American Law* (C. Haar ed. 1965).

[111] Letter from Peter V. Daniel to Martin Van Buren, Dec. 16, 1841, quoted in *J.P. Frank, Justice Daniel Dissenting: A Biography of Peter V. Daniel, 1784–1860,* at 164 (1964).

[112] 13 Pet. 519 (U.S. 1839).

[113] *Warren, supra* note 4, at 324.

in the federal court in Alabama on bills of exchange purchased by them in that state; the makers had refused to pay on the ground that the corporations had no power to do business in Alabama, or, indeed, outside their own states. Their contention was upheld by Justice McKinley, sitting in the Circuit Court. As explained in an oft-quoted letter of Justice Story to Charles Sumner, "He has held that a corporation created in one State has no power to contract (or, it would seem, even to act) in any other State, directly or by an agent."[114]

The McKinley ruling was characterized by Story as "a most sweeping decision . . . which has frightened half the lawyers and all the corporations of the country out of their proprieties.[115] Its practical effect was to limit corporate business to the states in which they were chartered, which would have rendered all but impossible the growth of interstate enterprises of any consequence. Well might Webster, in his argument, characterize McKinley's decision as "anti-commercial and anti-social . . . and calculated to break up the harmony which has so long prevailed among the States and people of this Union."[116]

The Supreme Court opinion in the *Bank of Augusta* case was delivered by the chief justice. Taney rejected the notion that a corporation could have no existence beyond the limits of the state in which it was chartered. He held that a corporation, like a natural person, might act in states where it did not reside. Comity among the states provided a warrant for the operation throughout the Union of corporations chartered in any of the states: "We think it is well settled that by the law of comity among nations, a corporation created by one sovereignty is permitted to make contracts in another, and to sue in its courts; and that the same law of comity prevails among the several sovereignties of this Union."[117]

Taney did not go as far as Webster had urged in his argument. Though he upheld the power of corporations to act outside their domiciliary states, he also recognized the power of a state to legislate against the entrance of outside corporations. Corporations could operate nationwide, but each state was given the authority to regulate corporate activities within its own borders.[118]

In this respect, the *Bank of Augusta* opinion is a clear reflection of the mixed attitude of judges like Taney toward the corporation. Taney gave legal recognition to the fact that a corporation has the same

114 *Id.*
115 *Id.*
116 13 Pet. at 567.
117 *Id.* at 592.
118 *Compare Lewis, supra* note 1, at 292.

practical capacity for doing business outside its home state as within its borders. But he refused to go further and adopt the Webster theory of citizenship for the corporation within the protection of the Privileges and Immunities Clause of the Constitution. Instead, he carefully circumscribed the basis of their constitutional rights.[119]

Historically speaking the most important aspect of the decision is the stimulus it provided to economic expansion. The view of the rising capitalist class was expressed by Story, when he wrote to Taney, "Your opinion in the corporation cases has given very general satisfaction to the public; . . . it does great honor to yourself as well as to the Court."[120] Because of the Taney decision, said Webster, "we breathe freer and deeper."[121] *Bank of Augusta* v. *Earle* was the first step in what the Supreme Court in 1898 was to term "the constant tendency of judicial decisions in modern times . . . in the direction of putting corporations upon the same footing as natural persons."[122] This tendency has been the essential jurisprudential counterpart of the economic unfolding of the nation. Looked at this way, the *Bank of Augusta* decision was as nationalistic as those rendered by Marshall himself.

TANEY AND JUDICIAL POWER

In 1842 John J. Crittenden, recently resigned as Tyler's attorney general, was commenting about a case he had just lost before the highest bench. "If it was not a decision of the *Supreme Court,*" he declared, "I should say it was *Supremely* erroneous [*sic*]—It is thoroughly against us on all the questions of law and evidence. . . . *Sic Transit* &c."[123] The Crittenden complaint is one which has been directed against the Supreme Court throughout its history, and not only on behalf of disappointed litigants or their counsel. At times the propensity of the high tribunal toward error has even been animadverted upon by justices themselves. "There is no doubt," caustically commented Justice Jackson over a century after the Crittenden reproof, "that if there were a super-Supreme Court, a substantial proportion of our reversals . . . would also be reversed. We are not final because we are infallible, but we are infallible only because we are final."[124]

[119] *Compare Frankfurter, supra* note 2, at 64–65.

[120] Quoted in *Tyler, supra,* note 28, at 288.

[121] Quoted in *Warren, supra* note 4, at 332.

[122] Barrow Steamship Co. v. Kane, 170 U.S. 100, 106 (1898).

[123] Letter from John J. Crittenden to J. Meredith, 1842, Charles Hamilton, Auction No. 19, Item 340 (1967).

[124] Concurring, in Brown v. Allen, 344 U.S. 443, 540 (1953).

That the Taney Court was far from infallible is apparent to even a casual student of its work. Yet it is amazing to note how, once Taney had established his imprint upon the Court, the opposition that had greeted his appointment was quickly stilled. Even his bitterest enemies soon saw, from his work on the bench, that their partisan censures were unjustified. Until the *Dred Scott* case, the stature of the Supreme Court compared favorably with what it had been under Marshall, and, if anything, its decisions were more generally accepted. Criticisms by disappointed litigants and political opponents, of course, continued, but its prestige as an institution never stood higher than in Taney's first twenty years.

It was doubtless of Taney, who had been a Federalist before he became a supporter of Andrew Jackson,[125] that James K. Polk was thinking when, in 1845, he wrote in his diary, "I have never known an instance of a Federalist who had after arriving at the age of 30 professed to change his opinions, who was to be relied on in his constitutional opinions. All of them who have been appointed to the Supreme Court Bench, after having secured a place for life became very soon broadly Federal and latitudinarian in all their decisions involving questions of Constitutional power."[126]

To accuse Taney of a "relapse into the Broad Federal doctrines of Judge Marshall and Judge Story"[127] was unfair. The Taney Court did make important doctrinal changes, particularly in shifting the judicial emphasis from private to community rights and stressing the existence of state power to deal with internal problems. That the Court's reaction after Marshall's death was not as great as has often been supposed does not alter the fact that there was a real change.

Even with the changes in constitutional law which it continuously made, however, the Taney Court did not (Justice Story to the contrary notwithstanding) seek to destroy the constitutional structure built by Marshall and his colleagues. Instead, it used that structure as the base for its own jurisprudence, making only such modifications as it deemed necessary to meet the needs of the day. In no respect was this more apparent than in its decisions on the place of judicial power in the governmental system.

In the 1832 Veto Message on the bill to recharter the Bank of the United States, President Jackson had denied the authority of the Supreme Court to make decisions binding upon the political branches. The implication was that the Court's review power could not control the president. Jackson's opponents charged (as Taney put it years later)

---

[125] Taney had been a leader of the Federalist Party in Maryland before the War of 1812.
[126] 4 *The Diary of James K. Polk during His Presidency* 137 (M.M. Quaife ed. 1910).
[127] *Id.* at 138.

that he was, in effect, asserting "that he, as an executive officer, had a right to judge for himself whether an Act of Congress was constitutional or not, and was not bound to carry it into execution, even if the Supreme Court had decided otherwise."[128] Writing Martin Van Buren in 1860, Taney denied that the Veto Message meant any such thing: "no intelligent man who reads the message can misunderstand the meaning of the President. He was speaking of his rights and duty when acting as part of the legislative power, and not his right or duty as an executive officer."[129] If all Jackson meant was that the president could veto bills on constitutional grounds despite Supreme Court decisions going the other way, the Veto Message was far from heretical doctrine, despite the contrary view of Jackson's Whig opponents.

Whether Taney's later justification of the words he wrote for Jackson in the heat of political battle was valid is not as relevant as the fact that almost three decades as chief justice gave ample proof of his full adherence to the notion of judicial power expounded by the Marshall Court. In the very first case in which he sat, even before he presided over a Supreme Court session, he declared (in an 1836 charge to a Circuit Court grand jury), "In a country like ours, blessed with free institutions, the safety of the community depends upon the vigilant and firm execution of the law; every one must be made to understand, and constantly to feel, that its supremacy will be steadily enforced by the constituted tribunals, and that liberty cannot exist under a feeble, relaxed or indolent administration of its power."[130]

The Taney Court was just as insistent as the tribunal headed by Marshall in vindicating the position of the Supreme Court as guardian of the Constitution and ultimate interpreter of its provisions. The judiciary, in the Taney view, was plainly the *sine qua non* of the constitutional machinery—draw out this particular bolt and the machinery falls to pieces: "For the articles which limit the powers of the Legislative and Executive branches of the Government, and those which provide safeguards for the protection of the citizen in his person and property, would be of little value without a Judiciary to uphold and maintain them which was free from every influence, direct or indirect, that might by possibility, in times of political excitement, warp their judgments."[131]

---

[128] Letter from Roger B. Taney to Martin Van Buren, May 8, 1860, quoted in *Lewis, supra* note 1, at 164.

[129] *Id. See Swisher, supra* note 23, at 197.

[130] Charge to the grand jury, Circuit Court of the U.S., April Term, 1836, Taney's Circuit Court Reports 615, 616.

[131] Letter from Roger B. Taney to the secretary of the treasury, Feb. 16, 1863, quoted in *Tyler, supra* note 28, at 433.

The point is illustrated most clearly by *Ableman* v. *Booth* [132] —a case which, during the 1850s, excited an interest comparable to that aroused by *Dred Scott* itself. The *Booth* case arose out of the prosecution of an abolitionist newspaper editor in Milwaukee for his part in rescuing a fugitive slave from federal custody. After his conviction in a federal court early in 1855 for violating the Fugitive Slave Act, Booth secured a writ of habeas corpus in the Wisconsin courts on the ground that the act was unconstitutional. A writ of error was taken to the United States Supreme Court, but the highest state court directed its clerk to make no return, declaring that its judgment in the matter was final and conclusive.

In effect, the Wisconsin judges were asserting a power to nullify action taken by the federal courts. In Taney's characterization, "the supremacy of the State courts over the courts of the United States, in cases arising under the Constitution and laws of the United States, is now for the first time asserted and acted upon in the Supreme Court of a State." To uphold the power thus asserted would, he said, "subvert the very foundations of this Government." [133] If the state courts could suspend the operation of federal judicial power, "no one will suppose that a Government which has now lasted nearly seventy years, enforcing its laws by its own tribunals, and preserving the union of the States, could have lasted a single year, or fulfilled the high trusts committed to it." The Constitution itself, in its very terms, refutes the claimed state power; its language, in this respect, "is too plain to admit of doubt or to need comment." [134] The federal supremacy "so carefully provided in . . . the Constitution . . . could not possibly be maintained peacefully, unless it was associated with this paramount judicial authority." In affirming its authority to set federal judicial action at naught, Wisconsin really "has reversed and annulled the provisions of the Constitution itself . . . and made the superior and appellate tribunal the inferior and subordinate one." [135]

The Court's decision (correct though it was in law) was the subject of bitter political attack. To the public, the legal issues were inextricably intertwined with the slavery controversy. More than a century later, we are scarcely concerned with the partisan censures of Taney's day, and *Ableman* v. *Booth* stands as a ringing affirmation of federal judicial power, as strong as any made by Marshall himself.

[132] 21 How. 506 (U.S. 1859).
[133] *Id.* at 514, 525.
[134] *Id.* at 515, 517.
[135] *Id.* at 518, 522–23.

JUDICIAL SELF-RESTRAINT

Just after Andrew Jackson took office Secretary of War Eaton informed him that "the Cherokees have filed here a protest against the laws of Georgia being extended over them. As it is a delicate matter will you think as to the course of the reply, to be given." Jackson took note of the problem thus presented and wrote on the address leaf of Eaton's letter, "the answer to be well considered on constitutional grounds."[136] Despite his realization that Georgia was acting in violation of federal treaties, the president declined to support the Indians. Instead, he upheld Georgia and helped induce the "voluntary" removal of most of the Indians across the Mississippi.[137] The Indians then sought a judicial remedy, and the Supreme Court held that the Constitution barred Georgia from extending its laws over Indian lands and ruled invalid the arrest and imprisonment by the state of two missionaries working with the Cherokees.[138]

Georgia defied the Court's mandate and refused to release the imprisoned missionaries. "The Constitution, the laws and treaties of the United States," declared John Quincy Adams, "are prostrate in the State of Georgia. Is there any remedy for this state of things? None. Because the Executive of the United States is in league with the State of Georgia."[139] Jackson is reported to have said that Marshall had made his decision, now let him enforce it, but this may be only apocryphal.[140] Even so, it accurately describes Jackson's actions.[141] He did not seek in any way to enforce the judgment. Instead, he stated, "The decision of the supreme court has fell still born, and they find that it cannot coerce Georgia to yield to its mandate."[142]

This example of judicial impotence in the face of refusal by the political departments and the state to carry out the Supreme Court judgment is one that inevitably had great influence upon Taney, at least during most of his tenure on the high bench. He developed a strong

[136] Letter from J.H. Eaton to Andrew Jackson, Apr. 13, 1829, Charles Hamilton, Auction No. 25, Item 141 (1968).

[137] *See Richardson, supra* note 15, at 458.

[138] Worcester v. Georgia, 6 Pet. 515 (U.S. 1832).

[139] 8 *Adams, supra* note 10, at 262–63.

[140] *Compare Warren, supra* note 4, at 219, *with M. James, The Life of Andrew Jackson* 603–4 (1938).

[141] *See W.W. Freehling, Prelude to Civil War: The Nullification Controversy in South Carolina, 1816–1836,* at 233 (1966).

[142] Letter from Andrew Jackson to John Coffee, Apr. 7, 1832, 4 *Bassett, supra* note 26, at 430.

tendency to restrict the area of judicial discretion in constitutional decision.[143] Judicial self-restraint became for the first time an essential element of Supreme Court doctrine. With the Cherokee Indian example before him, Taney strove to steer the Court away from unduly political issues.

Speaking of Taney, Dean Acheson has said that "judicial self-restraint . . . was his great contribution to the law and custom of the Constitution. . . . the giant stature which Taney assumes in the history of the Supreme Court is due chiefly to his insistence that the judge, in applying constitutional limitations, must restrain himself and leave the maximum of freedom to those agencies of government whose actions he is called upon to weigh."[144] The concept of self-restraint cuts across the work of the Taney Court and distinguishes it most sharply from its predecessor. Where Marshall and his colleagues did not hesitate to involve themselves in issues that were essentially political in character, the Taney Court was more cautious. Until the *Dred Scott* case, Taney was largely successful in keeping the Court out of the "political thicket"[145] of party controversies. The basic Taney philosophy was to leave every opportunity for the solving of political problems elsewhere than in the courtroom. "In taking jurisdiction as the law now stands," he asserted in one case, "we must exercise a broad and indefinable discretion, without any certain and safe rule to guide us. . . . such a discretion appears to me much more appropriately to belong to the Legislature than the Judiciary."[146]

This statement was made in *Pennsylvania* v. *Wheeling & B. Bridge Co.,* [147] a case which shows both the Taney approach and the danger of departing from it. "The stupendous structure that spans the Ohio at Wheeling . . . ," wrote a contemporary of the bridge involved in the case, "strikes the eye of the traveller passing beneath it, as it looms above him in the darkness, as one of the great architectural wonders of the age."[148] When it had been dedicated, Henry Clay had declaimed, "You might as well try to take down the rainbow."[149] But Pennsylvania sought to do just that by a suit in the Supreme Court[150] for an injunction directing the removal of the bridge on the ground that it

---

[143] *Compare Frankfurter, supra* note 2, at 71.

[144] *Acheson, Roger Brooke Taney: Notes upon Judicial Self Restraint,* 31 *Ill. L. Rev.* 705 (1937).

[145] The famous term of Frankfurter, J., in Colegrove v. Green, 328 U.S. 549, 556 (1946).

[146] Dissenting, in Pennsylvania v. Wheeling & B. Bridge Co., 13 How. 518 (U.S. 1852).

[147] 13 How. 518 (U.S. 1852).

[148] Quoted in *Warren, supra* note 4, at 509.

[149] Quoted in *Frank, supra* note 111, at 198.

[150] The Court had original jurisdiction over such an action brought by a state.

blocked river traffic. The majority of the Court was willing to order that the rainbow at least be raised to meet minimum ship clearances.[151]   Taney dissented, urging (as the quote from his opinion already given indicates) that the matter was one for Congress, not the Court, to regulate under the commerce power. The Court's acceptance of jurisdiction was, however, short-lived. Congress passed a statute declaring the bridge to be a lawful structure and not an obstruction to navigation.[152]   The Court then upheld the congressional power to enact such law,[153]   and the ultimate result was thus precisely what Taney had urged in his original dissent—though only at the cost of congressional intervention to, in effect, reverse a Supreme Court decision.

Most of the time, Taney was able to carry the Court with him in adherence to the self-restraint doctrine,[154]   particularly in cases involving judicial attempts to dictate action by the other branches. "The interference of the courts with the performance of the ordinary duties of the executive departments of the government," he once affirmed, "would be productive of nothing but mischief."[155]   In line with this view, he refused to order a state governor to extradite a fugitive from another state: "if the governor of Ohio refuses to discharge this duty, there is no power delegated to . . . the judicial department . . . to use any coercive means to compel him."[156]   At the back of Taney's mind must have been the need to avoid a clash such as that involved in the *Cherokee Indian* case.

The most famous case in which the Taney Court applied the self-restraint doctrine was *Luther* v. *Borden.* [157]   It arose out of the only revolution that occurred in a state of the Union after the Revolutionary War itself, the so-called Dorr Rebellion in Rhode Island in 1841. That state was then still operating under the royal charter granted in 1663. It provided for a very limited suffrage and, worse still from the point of view of those who considered it completely out of date, no procedure by which amendments might be made. Popular dissatisfaction led to mass meetings in 1841, which resulted in the election of a convention to draft a new constitution. It was drawn up and provided for universal suffrage. Elections were held under it, and Thomas Wilson Dorr was elected governor. All these acts were completely unauthorized by the exsiting charter government, which declared martial law and called out

---

151 *Compare Frank, supra* note 111.

152 10 Stat. 112 (1852).

153 Pennsylvania v. Wheeling & B. Bridge Co., 18 How. 421 (U.S. 1856).

154 *But see* Rhode Island v. Massachusetts, 12 Pet. 657 (U.S. 1838).

155 Decatur v. Paulding, 14 Pet. 497, 516 (U.S. 1840).

156 Kentucky v. Dennison, 24 How. 66, 109–10 (U.S. 1861).

157 7 How. 1 (U.S. 1949).

the militia to repel the threatened attack. In addition, it appealed to the federal government for aid, and President Tyler, expressly recognizing the charter government as the rightful government of the state, took steps to extend the necessary help, declaring that he would use armed force if that should prove necessary. The announcement of the president's determination caused Dorr's Rebellion to die out. *Luther* v. *Borden,* decided several years later, was left as its constitutional legacy.

The actual case arose out of the efforts of the charter government to suppress the Dorr Rebellion. When one of its agents broke into the house of a strong Dorr supporter and arrested him, the latter brought an action of trespass. Defendant justified his action by the plea that he was acting under the authority of the legal government of the state. Plaintiff countered with the contention that the charter government was not republican in form, as required by the Constitution. Therefore, he asserted, that government had no valid legal existence and the acts of its agents were not justified in law. Essentially, he was claiming that the action of the charter government violated his constitutional right to live under a republican government and that that claim was cognizable in a court.

The Supreme Court rejected the claim, denying that it was within judicial competence to apply the constitutional guarantee. On the contrary, the enforcement of the guarantee is solely for the Congress. Under Article IV, section 4, declares the opinion of Chief Justice Taney, "it rests with Congress to decide what government is the established one in a State . . . , as well as its republican character." Moreover, the congressional decision in the matter is not subject to any judicial scrutiny: "its decision is binding on every other department of the government, and could not be questioned in a judicial tribunal."[158]

Likewise, it is up to the Congress "to determine upon the means proper to be adopted to fulfill this guarantee."[159] Under an act of 1795,[160] that body had delegated to the president the responsibility of determining when the federal government should interfere to effectuate the constitutional guarantee, and, in this case, as we saw, the president acted to support the charter government. After such action by the president, asked Taney, "is a circuit court of the United States authorized to inquire whether his decision was right? Could the court, while the parties were actually contending in arms for the possession of the government, call witnesses before it and inquire which party represented a majority of the people? . . . If the judicial power extends so

---

[158] *Id.* at 42.
[159] *Id.* at 43.
[160] Now 10 U.S.C. § 331.

far, the guarantee contained in the Constitution of the United States is a guarantee of anarchy, and not of order."[161]

In *Luther* v. *Borden,* Taney refused to go into the issue of the legal authority of the government actually in power, holding that the questions involved were political and beyond the sphere of judicial competence. The overriding consideration was to steer clear of political involvement; the question of governmental legitimacy was left exclusively to the political departments. The wisdom and authority of Taney's restraint in this respect has not been generally questioned.[162]

The judicial reluctance to approach too close to the founts of sovereignty was a dominant characteristic of the Taney Court. The soundness of such an attitude was amply demonstrated when the Court itself refused to follow the rule of abnegation and sought instead to resolve in the judicial forum the basic controversy over slavery which had come to tear the nation apart. Even masterful judges are not always restrained by the wisdom of self-denial:[163] the *Dred Scott* case was the one occasion when Taney yielded to the temptation, always disastrous, to save the country, and put aside the judicial self restraint which was one of his chief contributions to our constitutional law.[164]

TANEY AND HIS COURT

It is customary to point to the drastic change that occurred in constitutional jurisprudence when Taney succeeded Marshall. The traditional historical view was summarized a generation ago by Justice Frankfurter: "even the most sober historians have conveyed Taney as the leader of a band of militant 'agrarian,' 'localist,' 'pro-slavery' judges, in a strategy of reaction against Marshall's doctrines. They stage a dramatic conflict between Darkness and Light: Marshall, the architect of a nation; Taney, the bigoted provincial and protector of slavery."[165]

Such an approach is based upon ignorance of the manner in which a tribunal like the Supreme Court functions. It is incorrect to suppose that Taney accomplished a wholesale reversal of Marshall's doctrines. He did not and could not do so: the institutional traditions of the Supreme Court have always exercised an overpowering influence. Even the Jacksonian neophytes on the bench were molded, more than is

---

[161] 7 How. at 43.

[162] *See Acheson, supra* note 144, at 714. *But see* Douglas, J., concurring, in Baker v. Carr, 369 U.S. 186, 242 (1962).

[163] *Compare Frankfurter, supra* note 2, at 72.

[164] *Compare Acheson, supra* note 144, at 705.

[165] *Frankfurter, supra* note 2, at 48.

generally realized, into the Court's institutional pattern. To be sure, with Taney's accession, the supreme bench was now safely in the hands of the Democrats. That fact alone implies much.[166]   The judges appointed by Jackson and Van Buren inevitably had a different outlook than their predecessors, themselves products of an earlier day. As already emphasized, Taney and his colleagues shared the Jacksonian belief that property rights must be subject to control by the community. Acting on that belief, they sought to redress the balance of constitutional protection which they felt the Marshall Court had thrown unfairly against the public interest in favor of property.[167]

Yet, as indicated above, it is an error to assume that the Taney Court translated wholesale the principles of Jacksonian democracy into constitutional law. The performance of the Jacksonian justices shows, as well as anything, the peril of predicting in advance how new appointees to the Supreme Court will behave after they don the robe. "One of the things that laymen, even lawyers, do not always understand," Justice Frankfurter has stated, "is indicated by the question you hear so often: 'Does a man become any different when he puts on a gown?' I say, 'If he is any good, he does.'"[168]   Certainly, Taney and his brethren must have seemed in many cases altogether different men as judges than they had been off the bench. Paradoxically, perhaps, the erstwhile Jacksonian politicians did as much as Marshall and his colleagues to promote economic development and the concentrations of wealth and financial power that were its inevitable concomitants. Taney may have had the strong Jacksonian bias against "the multitude of corporations with exclusive privileges which [the moneyed interest] have succeeded in obtaining in the different States," [169] but it was his opinions in cases like *Charles River Bridge* v. *Warren Bridge* and *Bank of Augusta* v. *Earle* which opened the door to the greatest period of corporate expansion in our history. The corporation first became common in the 1820s and 1830s [170] —stimulated both by the *Dartmouth College* case and the decisions favorable to corporate personality rendered during the early years of the Taney Court.[171]   The statistics underline the stimulus given to economic expansion by the decisions of the high tribunal. In the 1830s and 1840s there was a sharp increase in the number of corpora-

---

166 *Compare A.C. McLaughlin, A Constitutional History of the United States* 456 (1935).

167 *Compare Frankfurter, supra note 2, at 71.*

168 F. *Frankfurter, Of Law and Men: Papers and Addresses, 1939–1956,* at 133 (P. Elman ed. 1956).

169 Jackson, Farewell Address, 3 *Richardson, supra note 15,* at 306.

170 *C.W. Wright, Economic History of the United States* 388 (1941).

171 An important decision along this line was that in Louisville, C. & C.R. Co. v. Letson, 2 How. 497 (U.S. 1844), holding that for purposes of suit in a federal court a corporation should be treated as a citizen of the state of incorporation.

tions, particularly those engaged in manufacturing.[172] Before Taney, only $50 million was invested in manufacturing; that figure had grown to $1 billion by 1860.[173]

Perhaps the major change in the jurisprudence of the Taney Court arose from its tendency, in doubtful cases, to give the benefit of the doubt to the existence of state power far more than had been the case in Marshall's day, but this is far from saying that he and his confreres were ready to overturn the edifice of effective national authority constructed so carefully by their predecessors. On the contrary, like Jackson himself, they were firm believers in national supremacy where there was a clear conflict between federal and state power. When state authorities acted to interfere with federal power, Taney and his colleagues were firm in upholding federal supremacy. Hence, despite its greater willingness to sustain state authority, it is unfair to characterize the Taney Court as concerned only with states' rights.

When the occasion demanded, Taney could assert federal power in terms characterized by Chief Justice Hughes as "even more 'national' than Marshall himself."[174] This is shown dramatically by the 1852 case of *The Genesee Chief* v. *Fitzhugh*,[175] which arose out of a collision between two ships on Lake Ontario. A damage suit was brought in a federal court under an 1845 statute extending federal admiralty jurisdiction to the Great Lakes and connecting navigable waters. The constitutionality of this law was upheld in *The Genesee Chief*. In an earlier case,[176] the Supreme Court had confined the territorial extent of federal admirality jurisdiction substantially to that followed under English doctrine, namely, to the high seas and to rivers only as far as the ebb and flow of the tide extended. In a small island like Britain, where practically all streams are tidal, such a limitation might be adequate, but it hardly proved so in a country of continental extent.

The Taney opinion in the *Genesee Chief* well illustrates the manner in which the law changes to meet changed external conditions. When the basic document went into operation, the English "tidal flow" test of admiralty jurisdiction may well have sufficed. In the original thirteen states, as in England, almost all navigable waters were tidewaters. With the movement of the nation to the west and the consequent growth of commerce on the inland waterways, the English test became inadequate. "It is evident," says the Taney opinion, "that a definition that would at this day limit public rivers in this country to tide water rivers

---

[172] *G.H. Evans, Business Incorporations in the United States* 13 (1948).

[173] *H.U. Faulkner, American Economic History* 243 (D.L. Spriggs ed. 8th ed. 1960).

[174] *Hughes, Roger Brooke Taney, 17 A.B.A.J.* 787 (1931).

[175] 12 How. 443 (U.S. 1852).

[176] *The Thomas Jefferson,* 10 Wheat. 428 (U.S. 1825).

is utterly inadmissible. We have thousands of miles of public navigable waters, including lakes and rivers in which there is no tide. And certainly there can be no reason for admiralty power over a public tide water, which does not apply with equal force to any other public water used for commercial purposes."[177]

An inexorable advocate of states' rights would scarcely have written the *Genesee Chief* opinion. In fact, the extreme Jacksonian on the Court, Justice Daniel, flatly refused to countenance the revolutionary[178] enlargement of federal jurisdiction approved by the decision and delivered a stinging dissent. But Daniel's opinion was (as he himself conceded) "contracted and antiquated, unsuited to the day in which we live."[179] The Taney opinion was dictated by sound common sense; it was a legitimate nationalizing decision brought on by the changed conditions resulting from the geographic growth of the nation. As Ralph Waldo Emerson put it, in commenting on the case, "The commerce of rivers, the commerce of railroads, and who knows but the commerce of air balloons, must add an American extension to the pondhole of admiralty."[180]

A decision like *The Genesee Chief* shows how difficult it is to pigeonhole judges like Taney. His states' rights heritage did not blind him to the need for effective governmental power. His distrust of corporations did not make him disregard the practical possibilities of the corporate device and its utility in an expanding economy. His Jacksonianism was at bottom only an ethical conception of the social responsibilities of private property.[181] To translate that conception into decisions like that in the *Charles River Bridge* case was the great constitutional contribution of the Taney Court.

Henry Clay, who had led the fight against Taney's confirmation, was later to tell the new chief justice that "no man in the United States could have been selected, more abundantly able to wear the ermine which Chief Justice Marshall honored."[182] The judgment of history has confirmed the Clay estimate. The pendulum has shifted from the post-*Dred Scott* censures by men like Charles Sumner to the more sober estimate of those who sat with Taney on the bench or argued before him at the bar. According to a vituperative denunciation published at his death, Taney "was, next to Pontius Pilate, perhaps the worst that

---

177 12 How. at 457.

178 The term used in *Warren, supra* note 4, at 513.

179 12 How. at 465.

180 Quoted in *B.C. Steiner, Life of Roger Brooke Taney* 292 (1922).

181 *Frankfurter, supra* note 2, at 71.

182 Quoted in *Warren, supra* note 4, at 290.

ever occupied the seat of judgment,"[183] but today we reject such partisan bias. "The devastation of the Civil War for a long time obliterated the truth about Taney. And the blaze of Marshall's glory will permanently overshadow him. But the intellectual power of his opinions and their enduring contribution to a workable adjustment of the theoretical distribution of authority between two governments for a single people, place Taney second only to Marshall in the constitutional history of our country."[184]

[183] Quoted in *Lewis, supra* note 1, at 477.
[184] *Frankfurter, supra* note 2, at 72–73.

CHAPTER TWO

The Presidency

THE PRE-CIVIL WAR PRESIDENCY

One of the most dramatic and interesting scenes in our history, Woodrow Wilson tells us, was that enacted when Andrew Jackson was sworn into the presidency by John Marshall, the aged chief justice at whose hands the law of the nation had received both its majesty and its spirit of ordered progress. "The two men," he writes, "were at the antipodes from one another both in principle and in character; had no common insight into the institutions of the country which they served; represented one the statesmanship of will and the other the statesmanship of control."[1]

Jackson's inauguration marked a definite turning point in the constitutional history of the presidency—every bit as consequential as Taney's succession to the central judicial chair in the Supreme Court. The day before the new president left the Hermitage for his inauguration, Daniel Webster wrote, "Nobody knows what he will do when he does come. . . . My opinion is, that when he comes he will bring a breeze with him."[2]

"The Aristocracy and the Democracy of the country are arrayed against each other" was how a leading Democrat described the election that sent Jackson to the White House.[3] Constitutionally speaking, what was at stake were two theories of the presidency which have competed

[1] *W. Wilson, Constitutional Government in the United States* 160 (1911).

[2] Quoted in *L.D. White, The Jacksonians: A Study in Administrative History, 1829–1861,* at 1 (1954).

[3] Letter from Michael Hoffman to Azariah Flagg, Nov. 8, 1828, quoted in *G.G. Van Deusen, The Jacksonian Era: 1828–1848,* at 28 (1959).

with each other throughout American history. In operation, the out-standing feature of the highest office has been the fluctuation between these competing conceptions with now one and now the other domi-nant, reflecting the ebbs and flows of presidential power. From a historical point of view, the presidency has been an accordian-like office, able to expand or contract to meet changing needs.

Like so much else in our political theory, the competing theories on the presidency can be traced to the opposing views of Hamilton and Jefferson. The former urged a broad theory of presidential prerogative. Jefferson had a more limited conception. "Nothing shall be wanting on my part . . . ," he declared in his first annual message, "to carry [the legislative judgment] into faithful execution."[4] Though Jefferson in practice may have been far from a weak president, he gave substance to Marshall's 1800 prediction that he would weaken the office,[5] and under his successors, the concept of presidential autonomy gave way to that of legislative supremacy.

For twenty years after Jefferson, the presidency was virtually in commission. Nomination to the office was by "King Caucus" (a meet-ing of party congressional leaders). Once elected, the new chief execu-tive was only *primus inter pares* in a cabinet continued in large part from his predecessor. The president became what the stricter Whig theorists in Britain had wished the king to be: the *legal* executive, with powers of a negative sort alone, armed with the veto as solely a "check"—a power of restraint, not of guidance.[6]

All this was completely altered under Jackson, who made the presi-dent a "tribune of the people"; he converted the veto into a nine-teenth-century counterpart of the Roman tribune's weapon for protect-ing the common man. As De Tocqueville noted, to Jackson "the veto . . . is sort of an appeal to the people. The executive power . . . adopts this means of pleading its cause and stating its mo-tives."[7] Elected as a popular leader, Jackson resolved to use the "Executive Power" to achieve those ends in which he believed, such as the destruction of the Bank of the United States. He saw clearly that the stature of the nation rose and fell with that of the president. Under his administration, for the first time, the highest office became the personification of national prestige and power.

It is, all the same, erroneous to assume that Jackson, for all the force he brought to the highest office, succeeded in immediately remaking

---

[4] 1 *J.D. Richardson, A Compilation of the Messages and Papers of the Presidents 1789–1897*, at 331–32 (1896–99).

[5] 2 *A.G. Beveridge, The Life of John Marshall* 537 (1916).

[6] *Compare Wilson, supra* note 1, at 59.

[7] 1 *A. de Tocqueville, Democracy in America* 126 (P. Bradley ed. 1954).

the presidency in his own image. In an acute passage based upon personal observation, De Tocqueville affirmed, "The power of General Jackson perpetually increases, but that of the President declines; in his hands the Federal Government is strong, but it will pass enfeebled into the hands of his successor."[8] Things turned out as the perceptive Frenchman predicted. To many contemporaries, after eight years of "King Andrew" it might have seemed that the power of the president could scarcely be restrained, but the balance speedily shifted. From Van Buren's administration to the Civil War (with the exception of Polk's four years of strong leadership) the presidency went through a period of rapid and sustained decline, during which weakness and indecision became its outstanding characteristics. If the period began with the remaking of the office under Jackson, it ended with the virtual abdication of presidential power toward the close of Buchanan's term.

Of the chief executives during the pre-civil War generation, only Jackson himself and Polk are now remembered as effective leaders; the others have been relegated to the obscurity reserved for the Tylers, Buchanans, and other lesser lights who failed to measure up to the country's conception of what a proper president should be. Who now knows or cares to know anything about the personality of Franklin Pierce or Millard Fillmore? "The only thing remarkable about them is that being so commonplace they should have climbed so high."[9]

Certainly the post-Jackson presidency gives point to Bryce's celebrated observation that great men are not chosen to be president. It is not wholly accurate to assume, as Americans have done in answer to the Bryce aphorism, that while mediocrity all too frequently characterizes the office in periods of normalcy, in times of emergency it has been occupied by men of stature. The decades before the Civil War may not seem years of crisis to a century in which global and domestic emergencies have become part of the normal way of life. On its own terms, nevertheless, from the Panic of 1837, to the first rumblings of the distant drum, to the breakdown of the Union itself, it was a time of constant crises. The call for a strong executive went unanswered for almost the entire period, and one may well ask whether sectional strife would have magnified as it did if the popular wish for an Old Hickory to supply the strength shown in the Nullification Crisis had actually been fulfilled in the 1850s. "The 'one hour of Dundee,' " declared an 1862 article, "was not more wanting to the Stuarts than the one month of Jackson was wanting to us two years ago."[10]

---

[8] *Id.* at 432.

[9] 1 *J. Bryce, The American Commonwealth* 77 (1917).

[10] *Hazewell, The Hour and the Man, Atlantic Monthly* 623, 625 (November, 1862).

"KING ANDREW I"

In a much-quoted letter written to a friend in 1834, Justice Story declared, "the truth, which cannot be disguised, [is] that though we live under the form of a republic we are in fact under the absolute rule of a single man."[11] Jackson's opponents concurred in this estimate. An 1834 letter of Chancellor James Kent (the American Eldon, who, like his English model, was a bigoted adversary of all reform, who "believed in everything which it is impossible to believe in"[12]) characterized the political system under Jackson as "This American Elective Monarchy."[13] A famous cartoon of the 1832 election depicts Jackson as "King Andrew I," regally attired with crown and scepter—"a King . . . possessing as much power as his Gracious Brother William IV. . . . A King who has placed himself above the laws."[14]

Arch-conservatives like Story and Kent were so blinded by fear of the consequences of "the reign of King 'Mob' "[15] that they could scarcely perceive the affirmative nature of Jackson's contribution to the constitutional system. A truer estimate is that of William Cullen Bryant at the end of 1836: "he was precisely the man for the period in which he well and nobly discharged the duties demanded of him by the times."[16] His greatness consisted in his transformation of the highest office from a negative to an affirmative position, showing, for the first time, what the president might become as the leader of the nation. His presidency was no mere revival of the office; it meant the ultimate remaking of it. From a constitutional point of view, the Jackson contribution arose primarily out of his actions with regard to two essential presidential powers: the veto power and the removal power. In addition, and even more important perhaps, was his notion of the president as a direct representative of the people, one who alone spoke for all the people rather than for a limited class or constituency, and, as such, one of the three *equal* departments of government.[17]

[11] Letter from Joseph Story to Judge Fay, Feb. 18, 1834, 2 *Life and Letters of Joseph Story, Associate Justice of the Supreme Court of the United States* 154 (W.W. Story ed. 1851).

[12] Walter Bagehot, quoted in 13 *W. Holdsworth, A History of English Law* 606 (1952).

[13] Letter from James Kent to Joseph Story, Apr. 11, 1834, quoted in 4 *Beveridge, supra* note 5, at 535.

[14] *See Van Deusen, supra* note 3, illustrations facing 110.

[15] Letter from Joseph Story to Mrs. Story, Mar. 7, 1829, *Story, supra* note 11, at 563.

[16] Quoted in *M. James, The Life of Andrew Jackson* 721 (1938).

[17] *E.S. Corwin, The President: Office and Powers* 20 (4th ed. 1957). The president, said Jackson, "is the direct representative of the American people" and in that respect "is the coequal of the other two [departments], and all are servants of the American people, without power or right to control or censure each other in the service of their common superior," Protest, Apr. 15, 1834, in 3 *Richardson, supra* note 4, at 90, 71.

THE VETO POWER

"The Constitution in giving the President a qualified negative over legislation—commonly called a veto," the Supreme Court has declared, "entrusts him with an authority and imposes upon him an obligation that are of the highest importance."[18] It was not until Jackson's day that the full potential of the veto power became apparent. Before then, there had been no effective use of the authority to negative laws. In 1830 John Quincy Adams could state that "the Presidential veto has hitherto been exercised with great reserve."[19] That was true because the early presidents, following the view expressed by Jefferson, had acted on the assumption that the veto power was to be used only as a defense against unconstitutional legislation.

Jackson brushed aside this restrictive theory, and acted instead on the belief that the president might interpose his negative on any grounds deemed by him desirable. In his Second Annual Message, he affirmed that he would use his veto "in matters of deep interest, when the principle involved may be justly regarded as next in importance to infractions of the Constitution itself."[20] The chief executive himself would, of course, determine when such an occasion for use of the veto on non-constitutional grounds arose.

Jackson employed the veto power more freely than any of his predecessors. John Quincy Adams wrote in his diary after Jackson's first vetoes, "Not more than four or five[21] Acts of Congress have been thus arrested by six Presidents, and in forty years. He has rejected four in three days. The overseer ascendancy is complete."[22] From his first exercise of the authority to negative laws, Jackson's vetoes were based upon grounds of expediency. This was particularly the case with regard to his most famous veto—that of the bill to recharter the Bank of the United States. Though the constitutional argument is used there, it is secondary to the main theme of opposition to the policy behind the bank. "The Bank is trying to kill me, but I will kill it," Jackson told Van Buren just after he sent his veto message,[23] and that, as well as anything, explains the rejection of the bill. Jackson's opponents caustically complained that his vetoes were "contrary to the spirit of the

---

18 Pocket Veto case, 279 U.S. 655, 677 (1929).

19 8 *Memoirs of John Quincy Adams* 230 (C.F. Adams ed. 1876).

20 2 *Richardson, supra* note 4, at 512.

21 The actual number was nine.

22 *Adams, supra* note 19, at 231.

23 Quoted in *James, supra* note 16, at 601.

Constitution—a usurpation of the judiciary power, and susceptible of great abuse."[24] Yet they clearly put to rest the legal issue and settled the power of the president to veto bills deemed objectionable for whatever reasons might commend themselves to him.

Since Jackson's time, his veto practice has been consistently followed. Particularly significant were the vetoes of President Tyler, who had been elected as part of a Whig ticket which attacked the negativing of bills "upon the ground of their being inexpedient or not as well adapted as they might be to the wants of the people."[25] Tyler, like Jackson, did not hesitate to reject bills on his conception of "the soundest considerations of public policy."[26] Though Tyler may have thought of himself as "an agent of Providence to accomplish [the] restoration . . . of old fashioned republican principles,"[27] he used the veto in Jackson's, not Jefferson's, image.

The Whig leaders, of course, bitterly resented the apostate course of the "Judas Iscariot"[28] whom they had placed in the line of succession to the highest office. After the most important of Tyler's vetoes (that of the "Little Tariff" bill of 1842), the matter was referred to a select House committee chaired by John Quincy Adams. The committee called for a constitutional amendment giving Congress the power to override a veto by a simple majority, and even went so far as to recommend impeaching Tyler—a move that even Adams knew was "impracticable, or a cracked gun-barrel, fit only to explode in the hand of him who would use it."[29] Tyler wrote a strong protest attacking the committee's report,[30] but the House refused to enter it on its journal. Yet the veto stood; the Whigs could not muster a two-thirds majority to override the president or to impeach him.

It was also under Tyler that the veto's potential as a positive tool for the assertion of legislative leadership became apparent. It has become an ever-present threat to promoters of bills and has tended to become an instrument of bargaining for desired legislation. In 1841, Henry Clay agreed to an amendment that took the heart out of his distribution bill[31] only because he knew that Tyler would use the veto unless the

---

24 *Adams, supra* note 19, at 230.

25 William Henry Harrison, Inaugural Address, in 4 *Richardson, supra* note 4, at 10.

26 Tyler Veto Message, Aug. 9, 1842, in 4 *Richardson, supra* note 4, at 189. For a good discussion of Tyler's use of the veto power, *see* R.J. Morgan, *A Whig Embattled: The Presidency under John Tyler* ch. 2 (1954).

27 Letter from John Tyler to William L. Hellfienstein, June 22, 1842, Charles Hamilton, Auction No. 17, Item 247 (1967).

28 *Van Deusen, supra* note 3, at 167.

29 *Adams, supra* note 19, at 37.

30 4 *Richardson, supra* note 4, at 190.

31 So characterized in *Van Deusen, supra* note 3, at 162.

amendment were included. "The question," as Clay once put it, "is no longer what laws will Congress pass, but what will the Executive not veto?"[32] It was his vetoes, more than anything else, that led the Whigs to "a just conception of Mr. Tyler's perfidy,"[33] but it was clear by then that no real constitutional objection could be interjected, though Polk did go out of his way to make a gratuitous defense of the Jackson conception in his last Annual Message.[34] The Jackson conception of the veto power became confirmed by presidential practice. Polk, Pierce, and Buchanan all vetoed bills on grounds of expediency,[35] and no president since has hesitated to use the veto when his judgment of the public good has been seriously at issue with that of the Congress.[36] Through the veto power the president acts legislatively under the Constitution, though he is not a constituent part of the Congress.[37] In this sense, acceptance of the Jackson veto practice has all but made the president a coordinate branch of the legislature. May we not, indeed, go further and state that, in our system, the legislature itself is, in fact, though not in form, composed of three distinct parts, the Senate, the House of Representatives, and the president?

ADMINISTRATIVE CHIEF

In 1848 a new constitution was adopted in Switzerland. Though the Swiss imitated the American document in several respects, they took pains to steer clear of the presidency because they felt it favorable to dictatorship.[38] The Swiss fear could scarcely have arisen under the negative conception of the presidency that prevailed prior to Jackson. The Framers conceived of the president as primarily a political leader. It was intended that his powers should be essentially political and military, as enumerated in the Constitution, and that he should not have the direction of administrative affairs. This narrow conception was, however, wholly incompatible with the notion of the office upon which presidents like Jackson and Polk acted. Jackson, for the first time, gathered together all the executive power vested in the govern-

---

[32] *Reg. of Deb.*, 23d Cong., 1st Sess. 94.

[33] Letter from Henry Clay to Henry Dearborn, July 13, 1842, Charles Hamilton, Auction No. 17, Item 26 (1967).

[34] 4 *Richardson, supra* note 4, at 662–70.

[35] *See White, supra* note 2, at 30. For an example not there cited, *see* 4 *Richardson, supra* note 4, at 466.

[36] *Compare Wilson, supra* note 1, at 73.

[37] Edwards v. United States, 286 U.S. 482, 490 (1932).

[38] *See Corwin, supra* note 17, at 22–23.

ment—both the political and the administrative functions which pertain to executive power, a combination which doubtless gave rise to the Swiss fears mentioned above.

Though it was under Jackson that the practical leadership of the president in administrative matters was first fully asserted, it was based upon a crucial vote of the very first Congress on the bills setting up the new executive departments. In setting up the Department of Foreign Affairs, Congress, after lengthy debate on the matter, provided that the president might remove its head from office. Similar provisions were included in the laws setting up the Treasury and War departments. According to the Supreme Court, the "decision of 1789"[39] (as the vote in the first Congress on the removal power is usually referred to) was, and was intended to be, a legislative declaration that the power to remove department heads was vested in the president alone.[40] Even Webster, who opposed the power, conceded, in an 1835 speech, that it was "a settled point; settled by construction, settled by precedent, settled by the practice of the Government, and settled by statute."[41] The power thus recognized has enabled the president to ensure that administrative action would be taken only in accordance with his directions. Since he may remove from office at will department heads who do not follow his instructions, he can, in practice, dictate the policies to be followed by the administration.

The use of the removal power to compel compliance with presidential directions was strikingly demonstrated in 1833 by President Jackson. He had ordered Secretary of the Treasury Duane to transfer federal funds from the Bank of the United States. Duane refused to comply "without the action of congress."[42] He was forthwith removed from office by the president. His successor, Roger Taney, immediately ordered the fund transfer that Jackson had directed.

Jackson's removal of Duane has had more value as a precedent than even a score of decisions from the law reports. It all but conclusively settled the position of the president as the administrative chief of the government. The president, as Jackson showed, has the practical power in all matters to force any department head to carry out any act which that official has authority to do. He can dictate in all matters because of his unfettered power of instant dismissal. As Webster put it, with regard to Jackson's removals, "it is generally true that he who controls

---

[39] So termed by Webster in 1835, *Reg. of Deb.*, 23d Cong., 2d Sess. 465.

[40] Myers v. United States, 272 U.S. 52, 114 (1926).

[41] *Reg. of Deb.*, 23d Cong., 2d Sess. 462.

[42] Letter from William Duane to Hugh Hamilton, 1833, Charles Hamilton, Auction No. 15, Item 121 (1966). Duane's predecessor, Louis McLane, had also opposed the fund transfer and had, in consequence, been shifted from the Treasury to the State Department.

another man's means of living controls his will."[43] As a purely legal proposition, a department head who refuses to follow a presidential directive may not be violating any law, but the practical realities are quite another thing. He can be dealt with as summarily as was Duane in 1833, and the mere knowledge that such is the case is enough to ensure the president's administrative leadership. When Tyler's veto of the second bank bill in 1841 caused an irreparable breach between him and his cabinet, the latter took the path of resigning rather than putting presidential authority to the acid test.[44]

That the president can thus control the administrative work of the departments was recognized even before the Duane removal. In 1831 Taney wrote an opinion as attorney general on the question of whether the president had the legal power to direct a federal district attorney to discontinue a prosecution. According to Taney, the district attorney might refuse to obey the president's direction, and, if he did, the prosecution would continue while he remained in office. On the other hand, the district attorney held his office at the president's pleasure, [45] "and if that officer still continue a prosecution which the President is satisfied ought not to continue, the removal of the disobedient officer and the substitution of one more worthy in his place would enable the President through him faithfully to execute the law. And it is for this among other reasons that the power of removing the District Attorney resides in the President."[46] The removal power is, in other words, the sanction provided by the Constitution to enable the president to control the departments in all their official actions of public consequence.[47] It has been this sanction that has led to the development of the notion of the president as the effective head of the administration.

WHIG PRESIDENTS

The Whigs (doctrinal descendants of the Federalists though they were in many ways) were all but forced, as the party of opposition to Jackson, into the position of adherents of the negative theory of the presidency. Clay, Webster, and the other Whig leaders consistently looked with alarm on the growth of executive power under Jackson. "We are in the midst of a revolution," asserted the "*Judas of the*

[43] *Reg. of Deb.*, 23d Cong., 2d Sess., 458.

[44] Except for Webster. *See R. Seager, And Tyler Too* 160 (1963); *G.R. Poague, Henry Clay and the Whig Party* 100–103 (1936).

[45] That the president may remove a United States attorney at will is shown by Parsons v. United States, 167 U.S. 324 (1897).

[46] 2 *Op. Att'y Gen.* 482 (1831).

[47] *Corwin, supra* note 17, at 84.

West"[48] in a famous Senate speech, "hitherto bloodless, but rapidly tending towards a total change of the pure republican character of the Government, and to the concentration of all power in the hands of one man."[49]

The Whigs did not limit themselves to mere denunciations of the "rapid and alarming"[50] expansions of presidential power which "put the whole [Constitution] at imminent peril."[51] When they captured the presidency in 1840, they sought to translate their limited conception of the highest office into actual practice. Harrison's 1841 Inaugural Address (written with the help of Webster and Clay) sought to spell out Whig doctrine with regard to the presidency; its main theme was to lament the recent concentration of power in executive hands. "To this danger to our republican institutions . . . ," Harrison declared, "I propose to apply all the remedies which may be at my command."[52] In particular, he promised to curb the veto power so that it would be "used only with the forbearance and in the spirit which was intended by its authors."[53] In addition, it was "a great error" in the Framers not to have made the head of the Treasury "entirely independent of the Executive."[54] He further promised never to remove a secretary of the treasury without communicating his reasons to both houses—this was the Whig doctrine urged unsuccessfully at the time of the Duane removal.

The Whig leaders tried to use the new president to push their theory of limited executive powers almost to its limits by reducing the president to the status of a figurehead. The plan, apparently, was to bind Harrison by the majority vote of the cabinet (most of whose members had been chosen by the Whig leaders themselves). The cabinet, supported by the opinion of Attorney General Crittenden, took the position that it was the president's duty to take such action as they chose to direct.[55] Similarly, Clay, as the recognized leader of the Whig Party

[48] Clay was so characterized by Jackson in an 1825 letter, quoted in 3 *J.S. Bassett, Correspondence of Andrew Jackson* 276 (1933).

[49] *Reg. of Deb.*, 23d Cong., 1st Sess. 59.

[50] *Id.* at 94.

[51] Letter from Henry Clay to F.T. Brooke, Nov. 24, 1827, speaking of the need to preserve the country "from the calamity of the election of Genl. Andrew Jackson," Charles Hamilton, Auction, No. 15, Item 30 (1966).

[52] 4 *Richardson, supra* note 4, at 12-13. Harrison took a similar restrictive view of congressional power. In a letter written while he was a senator, he said, "I will never vote for the Exercise of a power by Congress that is not expressly given or which is not Necessary and proper to carry into effect the powers which are given," W. H. Harrison to ___, Dec. 9, 1825, Parke-Bernet Galleries, Sale No. 2988, Item 76 (1970).

[53] 4 *Richardson, supra* note 4, at 9.

[54] 4 *Richardson, supra* note 4, at 13.

[55] See B.P. Poore, *Perley's Reminiscences of Sixty Years in the National Metropolis* 258 1886).

(though he was outside the cabinet), sought to dictate the decisions of the new administration. He virtually forced the reluctant Harrison to call a special session of Congress and expected that he, not the president, would control the administration.

The second Whig president came into office publicly committed to the limited concept of presidential power. Just before his election, Taylor wrote that "for many years past . . . the Executive have exercised undue and injurious influence upon the Legislative Department of the government."[56] In his first (and only) Annual Message, he deplored "every claim or tendency of one coordinate branch to encroach upon another." For himself, he rejected the view that the president has more than "authority to recommend (not to dictate) measures to Congress." The veto was characterized as "an extreme measure," and he committed himself to using it "only in extraordinary cases."[57] The Taylor approach in this respect hardly bespoke the energy and direction of a Hamiltonian or a Jacksonian chief executive.[58] On the contrary, as his predecessor put it, it indicated that Taylor "will be in the hands of others, and must rely wholly upon his Cabinet to administer the Government."[59]

It is, of course, a matter of conjecture whether the Whig doctrine of presidential power would have been consistently followed even by presidents elected under the Whig banner. Harrison and Taylor both died too soon for the doctrine really to be put to the test. Yet, even during their short-lived tenures, there were signs that no president after Jackson could be reduced to the position of a Merovingian monarch. Harrison himself, pliant instrument though the Whig leadership considered him, gave clear indications that he—not Clay or his cabinet—was going to exercise the power of his office. Against the opposition of the cabinet, he held his ground on an important appointment, saying, when told by Webster that the cabinet had decided on another man, "and William Henry Harrison, President of the United States, tells you, gentlemen, that, by ＿＿, John Chambers shall be Governor of Iowa."[60] When Clay sought to dictate various appointments, there was a stormy scene at the White House, which led to a formal letter from the president requesting that any further communications from Clay be in writing.[61]

---

[56] Quoted in *H. Hamilton, Zachary Taylor: Soldier in the White House* 80 (1966).

[57] 5 *Richardson, supra* note 4, at 23–24. *Compare* the view expressed in Fillmore's First Annual Message, 5 *Richardson, supra* note 4, at 79.

[58] *White, supra* note 2, at 48.

[59] 4 *The Diary of James K. Polk during His Presidency* 376 (M.M. Quaife ed. 1910).

[60] *White, supra* note 2, at 48. For another version *see* Poore, *supra* note 55, at 258.

[61] *See* Poage, *supra* note 44, at 30–31 (1936); *Poore, supra* note 55, at 259.

Comparable hints of independence appeared during Taylor's brief incumbency. In 1850 he strongly opposed the terms of the proposed slavery compromise sponsored by the leaders of his party. The president's independence on the matter—what, asks his biographer, had become of Whig "weak executive" theories?[62] —threatened a major crisis (when Taylor said that, if necessary, "he would take command of the army" and hang "traitors," his opponents threatened to impeach him[63]). The crisis was averted only by Taylor's death and the subsequent passage of a modified compromise.

Looking back at it, we can see that the Whig notion of a negative presidency was utterly inconsistent with the concentration of executive power contained in Article II. After Jackson, that notion could never be translated into complete political reality, regardless of the doctrines of the Whig leadership. In theory, at least, the Whig leaders were asserting an American equivalent of the cabinet system of government— something they were closest to achieving during Harrison's month in office. Yet even Harrison, as we saw, was not willing to have the cabinet take over the reins of government completely.

As it turned out, Harrison's death all but ended any possibility of an importation of the cabinet system. At Tyler's first cabinet meeting, Webster informed the new chief executive that it had been the practice under Harrison for matters relating to administration to be brought before the cabinet and decided by majority vote, with the president having one vote. Tyler categorically refused to consent to such a system: "I, as President, shall be responsible for my administration. I hope to have your hearty co-operation in carrying out its measures. So long as you see fit to do this, I shall be glad to have you with me. When you think otherwise, your resignations will be accepted."[64]

Any effort to implant the cabinet system into our constitutional structure was bound to be stillborn, for it lost sight of the reality of power as it is distributed under the basic document. As Bryce put it, in now-classic terms, "An American administration resembles not so much the cabinets of England and France as the group of ministers who surround the Czar or Sultan, or who executed the bidding of a Roman emperor like Constantine or Justinian."[65] The fundamental fact about the legal relation of the president to the cabinet is his complete predominance. The attorney general of even so weak a president as Pierce recognized that such was the constitutional posture: "the

[62] *Hamilton, supra* note 56, at 384.

[63] *See Hamilton, supra* note 56, at 300, 383.

[64] Quoted in *White, supra* note 2, at 86; *Seager, supra* note 44, at 149.

[65] 1 *Bryce, supra* note 9, at 94.

determination of all executive questions belongs, in theory and by constitutional right, to the President."[66] The members of the cabinet are merely the instruments by which the policy of their chief is carried out: "the Head of Department is subject to the direction of the president. . . . no Head of Department can lawfully perform an *official* act against the will of the President."[67]

By the close of the pre-Civil War period, the president's dominance over the Cabinet could not be altered even by the breakdown of presidential effectiveness at the close of Buchanan's term. The cabinet as an institution sharply declined during the late 1840s and 1850s, with the decline, if anything, accelerating under the weak presidents after Polk. It became a body of counselors, not a council of colleagues with whom the president had to work and upon whose approval he depended. Even consultation, as the experience after Jackson established, was not a duty owed to the cabinet. The practice that has ever since prevailed was well stated by Polk with regard to an 1846 veto: "I did not consult the Cabinet to ascertain their opinions on the subject. Having made up my mind that I could not sign the Bill under any circumstances, it was unnecessary to consult the Cabinet on the subject."[68] The power of the cabinet turned solely upon the will of the president himself and varied with the personality of the particular White House incumbent. A president might depend heavily upon his cabinet, as did Pierce, or very little, as did Jackson. All in all, the history of the post-Jackson cabinet is a history of the growth of presidential power.

"HIS ACCIDENCY"

On March 3, 1845, John Quincy Adams wrote in his diary, "Close of the Twenty-Eighth Congress, and of the Administration of John Tyler, Vice-President of the United States, acting as President—memorable as the first practical application of the experimental device in the Constitution of the United States, substituting the Vice-President as the Chief Executive Magistrate of this Union in the event of the decease of the President."[69] When, after but one month in office, William Henry Harrison went shopping in unseasonably cold spring weather, seeking White House provender, and contracted the pneumonia which led to his death on April 4, 1841, it put to the test the organic provision relating

---

66 7 *Op. Att'y Gen.* 480 (1855).

67 *Id.* at 469–70.

68 2 *Polk, supra* note 59, at 58. *See,* similarly, 4 *Polk* at 130–31.

69 12 *Adams, supra* note 19, at 176.

to presidential succession, "that provision of the Constitution which places in the Executive chair a man never thought of for it by anybody."[70] Article II plainly provided that the vice president was to become the new White House tenant. But what was it that Tyler was to succeed to at that time, "the Powers and Duties of the said Office" or the office of president itself? There is reason to believe that the Framers never intended the vice president to succeed to the presidency. The debates of 1787 indicate that it was expected that he would exercise the powers and duties of the president but would remain as vice president until a new president was elected. In this view, the vice president would become at most acting president upon his chief's death.

The approach just outlined was the one John Quincy Adams thought correct. Writing on the day of Harrison's death, Adams wrote that it made Tyler "Acting President of the Union."[71] The Adams view was also that taken by the cabinet. Informing Tyler of Harrison's death, it still addressed him as "Vice-President of the United States."[72] The members had arrived at the conclusion that Tyler should be styled "Vice-President of the United States, acting President."[73] Tyler himself, however, decided immediately that he was now president, not merely acting president. With Chief Justice Taney absent, he summoned Chief Justice Cranch of the District of Columbia Supreme Court to his parlour at the Indian Queen Hotel. It was in that hostelry (distinguished by a large swinging sign depicting Pocahontas in lurid colors[74]) that Tyler took the oath of office prescribed in the Constitution for the president. He declared his belief that he was "qualified to perform the duties and exercise the powers and office of President on the death of William Henry Harrison," and explained that he took the oath only "for greater caution."[75]

Tyler's taking of the oath (superfluous as it probably was under the Constitution) has caused practical difficulty, as shown, for example, in the confusion over Lyndon Johnson's taking of the oath after the assassination of President Kennedy. In other respects, however, Tyler's attempts to establish his succession were forthright and consistent. On April 9 he published an "inaugural address," in which he declared that he had been "called to the high office of President of this Confed-

---

[70] 10 *Adams, supra* note 19, at 457.
[71] 10 *Adams, supra* note 19, at 456.
[72] 4 *Richardson, supra* note 4, at 22.
[73] *Poore, supra* note 55, at 269.
[74] *Poore, supra* note 55, at 42.
[75] 4 *Richardson, supra* note 4, at 31–32.

eracy."[76] He also speedily convinced the cabinet that he meant to be president. At his first cabinet meeting (as already noted), he indicated categorically that he, as president, was responsible for his administration. If the cabinet disagreed, he said, their resignations would be accepted. When it came to the test some months later, the entire cabinet (except for Webster) resigned in order to avoid dismissal by the now-acknowledged chief executive.

When the Congress convened weeks later in response to Harrison's call for a special session, the usual resolutions were introduced to inform "the president" that they were in session. Amendments were proposed to substitute the term "vice president," but they were resoundingly defeated. The congressional approval of Tyler's succession all but settled the matter. It is true that the original resolution for Andrew Johnson's impeachment designated him as "Vice-President and acting President of the United States," but this language was soon changed and it was as president that Johnson was impeached. Since that impeachment, the Tyler precedent has never been questioned. The most complete legal discussion of it is contained in an opinion of the attorney general prepared, poignantly enough, for President Kennedy. According to it, "although President Tyler's action might readily have been questioned had historical materials on the framers' intent been at hand, the fact remains that it has been relied on for the proposition that the Vice President becomes President when the elected President dies—a proposition scarcely to be questioned today."[77]

COMMANDER IN CHIEF

Not too long ago James K. Polk was considered anything but a great president. Bryce, classifying him among the post-Jackson *fainéant* presidents, used him to illustrate his assertion that great men are not chosen for that office. The Bryce estimate was shared by the country when Polk was nominated as the first "dark horse" by the 1844 Democratic convention. When news of the nomination reached Washington by the telegraph, just invented, Democrats in the capital went shouting "Hurrah for Polk," only pausing now and then to ask "Who the hell is Polk?"[78]

As it turned out, Polk proved to be the strongest president between Jackson and Lincoln; he displayed a brand of leadership the country

---

[76] 4 *Richardson, supra* note 4, at 37.

[77] 42 *Op. Att'y Gen.* No. 5, at 17 (1961). The Twenty-Fifth Amendment now expressly confirms that the vice president becomes president upon the president's death.

[78] W. *Binkley, The Man in the White House: His Powers and Duties* 87 (1958).

would not see again until the Civil War.[79] Indeed, if a president's quality is measured by attainment of the goals outlined in his Inaugural Address, he should be rated among the most successful incumbents of the White House. Bryce rated him as insignificant as Pierce only because his judgment was formed before the publication of Polk's diary in 1910. Until then Polk remained true to the sentiment he expressed just before his election: "as a general rule I have been of the opinion that the less I write the better."[80] His diary shows in revealing detail that his theory of the presidency was that of Hamilton and Jackson and that he, not his cabinet or even the military, was responsible for the successes of his term. Lack of personal magnetism alone kept him from recognition for over half a century.

Interestingly enough, Jackson himself had no doubts about the capacity of "Young Hickory." He wrote gleefully from the Hermitage just after the 1844 election that "Polk and Dallas are elected and the Union is safe." With his loyal supporter in the White House, the Old Hero, who was racked with pain in the last year of his life ("my health continues feeble, and my afflictions great"), could conclude with satisfaction, "I am now like Simeon of old having seen my country safe, I am prepared to depart in peace."[81]

Polk's great contribution to the presidency was to demonstrate, for the first time, the potential inherent in the constitutional provision which makes the highest officer "Commander in Chief of the Army and Navy." During the previous war, that of 1812, the Commander in Chief Clause had largely lain dormant. The conduct of our worst-planned war was mostly out of Madison's control from its beginning, and confusion prevailed even with regard to the chain of military command—a confusion, if anything, compounded by the "withered little Applejohn" [82] who occupied the presidency.

Madison may have been too much the scholar to prove a strong war leader. The same was not true of Polk, who had determined, even before he set out for Washington in February, 1845, that he was going to be the president. After the war with Mexico broke out, he made it equally evident that he intended to be the commander in chief.[83] "I am held responsible for the conduct of the War," he wrote,[84] and he

[79] *Compare C. Sellers, James K. Polk: Continentalist, 1843–1846,* at 310 (1966).

[80] Letter from James K. Polk to George M. Dallas, Sept. 17, 1844 (marked "Confidential"), Parke-Bernet Galleries, Sale No. 2988, Item 101 (1970).

[81] Letter from Andrew Jackson to Andrew J. Donelson, Nov. 18, 1844, 6 *Bassett, supra* note 48, at 329–30.

[82] The term used by Washington Irving, quoted in *Binkley, supra* note 78, at 228.

[83] *White, supra* note 2, at 50.

[84] 2 *Polk, supra* note 59, at 355–56.

exercised that responsibility to the very limit of his physical capacity. He did so by acting on the Jacksonian concept of the president as an affirmative leader, under the war power as under the other authority delegated in Article II. "He succeeded," said George Bancroft (who had been Polk's navy secretary) in 1888, "because he insisted on being [the administration's] center and in overruling and guiding all of his secretaries so as to produce unity and harmony."[85] Polk, for the first time, showed that the Commander in Chief Clause was the fount and origin of vast presidential power. The president does normally delegate the power of actual command to the relevant military officers, but, under the Constitution, he is not required to do so. He may even assume personal command of the forces in the field, as Washington did when he accompanied the troops dispatched to suppress the so-called Whiskey Rebellion.

A president possessed of superior military talents might, in an extraordinary emergency, still see fit to follow Washington's example. Yet possessed of military ability or not, he has the power, under the Commander in Chief Clause, to direct military forces as he chooses. In Chief Justice Taney's words in a case arising out of the war with Mexico, "As Commander-in-Chief, he is authorized to direct the movements of the naval and military forces placed by law at his command, and to employ them in the manner he may deem most effectual to harass and conquer and subdue the enemy."[86]

Polk took full advantage of the power recognized by the Taney opinion. Soon after war with Mexico was declared, he asserted "that I hoped my friends in Congress and elsewhere would suffer me to conduct the War with Mexico as I thought proper; and not plan the campaign for me."[87] Throughout the Mexican war he exercised direct control over military strategy and operations. At the outset of the conflict on May 14, 1846, he determined the plan of operations, informing General Winfield Scott "that the first movement should be to march a competent force into the Northern Provinces and seize and hold them." The details of the operation were developed by Polk himself, who reported to the cabinet "My plan . . . to march an army of 2000 men on Santa Fe and near 4000 on Chihuahua . . . leaving Gen'l Scott to occupy the country on the lower Del Norte and in the interior."[88] Two weeks later, it was Polk who devised the plan to send troops to California so that "the U.S. should hold military possession of

---

85 Quoted in *Binkley, supra* note 78, at 30–31.

86 Fleming v. Page, 9 How. 603, 615 (U.S. 1850).

87 1 *Polk, supra* note 59, at 427.

88 1 *Polk, supra* note 59, at 400, 403–4.

California at the time peace was made."[89] The particulars of the expedition were worked out by the president and cabinet and orders to implement them were sent to Colonel Stephen W. Kearny.[90] The plan to land at Vera Cruz—in many ways the key operation of the war—was suggested by Polk and the details of the landing elaborated by him in consultation with military and other officials.[91]

Polk's direct supervision of the military effort demonstrated how right Hamilton had been when he declared that the Commander in Chief Clause vested the president with "the supreme command and direction of the military and naval forces, as first general and admiral of the Confederacy."[92] Polk participated actively in every major decision on military strategy[93] and even devoted time to relatively minor details, such as the small though vexing question of whether mules could be used instead of baggage wagons for Mexican operations. "I find it impossible," he plaintively commented, after a session devoted to the mules-vs.-wagons issue, "to give much attention to the details in conducting the war, and still it is necessary that I should give some attention to them."[94]

There is an obvious risk in having the president take so direct a role in military operations. During the war General Scott complained that he was being placed "in the most perilous of all positions, a fire upon my rear from Washington and the fire in front from the Mexicans."[95] A civilian chief executive, whose background rarely equips him with military competence, may be anything but the best man to direct the details of war strategy. If the danger was more theoretical than real during Polk's direction of the Mexican war, it has not been so in all our other conflicts.

Polk's conduct of the war established more than the power of the president to act as actual commander in chief of the nation's armed forces, however. The Constitution limits the express authority to declare war to the legislative branch. "This," said Abraham Lincoln (then a Whig congressman) in 1848, "our Convention understood to be the most oppressive of all Kingly oppressions; and they resolved to so frame the Constitution that *no one man* should hold the power of bringing this oppression upon us."[96] Yet the presidential power to direct

[89] 1 *Polk, supra* note 59, at 437–38.

[90] 1 *Polk, supra* note 59, at 439, 443–44.

[91] 2 *Polk, supra* note 59, at 104, 195–97.

[92] *The Federalist* No. 69.

[93] *White, supra* note 2, at 53.

[94] 2 *Polk, supra* note 59, at 118–19. *See also* 3 *id.* 158–59.

[95] 1 *Polk, supra* note 59, at 419–20.

[96] Letter from Abraham Lincoln to William H. Herndon, Feb. 15, 1848, in 1 *The Collected Works of Abraham Lincoln* 452 (R.P. Basler ed. 1953).

military movements outside our borders has drastic implications for this congressional authority. As early as August, 1845, Polk sent orders to General Taylor to take military action against Mexico, in certain contingencies, with "discretionary authority to pursue the Mexican army . . . , but not to penetrate any great distance into the interior of the Mexican Territory."[97] In January, 1846, Polk sent American troops into territory then in dispute between Mexico and the United States, which precipitated hostilities.

Though his conduct was criticized on constitutional grounds,[98] after actual hostilities had begun the Congress acceded to his request for a declaration that war existed "by the act of the Republic of Mexico."[99] The House passed the bill declaring war in only two hours, and Senator Benton complained that "in the 19th Century war should not be declared without full discussion and much more consideration."[100] However, the situation presented by Polk's war message left Congress little room for debate. In Lincoln's words, "the news reached Washington of the commencement of hostilities on the Rio Grande, and of the great peril of Gen. Taylor's army. Every body, whig and democrat, was for sending them aid. . . . The Locos . . . brought in a bill with a preamble, saying—*Whereas* war exists by the act of Mexico, therefore we send Gen: Taylor men and money. . . . They could not vote *against* sending help to Gen: Taylor, and therefore they voted *for* both together."[101]

"The battles of Palo Alto and Resaca de la Palma," the Supreme Court informs us, "had been fought before the passage of the Act of Congress of May 13th, 1846, which recognizes 'a state of war as existing. . . .' This act not only provided for the future prosecution of the war, but was itself a vindication and ratification of the Act of the President in accepting the challenge without a previous formal declaration of war by Congress."[102] The result, in constitutional terms, was noted by Lincoln during the war: "Allow the President to invade a neighboring nation, whenever *he* shall deem it necessary to repel an invasion, and you allow him to do so, *whenever he may choose to say* he deems it necessary for such purpose—and you allow him to make war at pleasure."[103] The acuteness of Lincoln's perception has been

---

97 1 *Polk, supra* note 59, at 9.

98 As will be seen (p. 76 below), the House actually voted a resolution that the war had been unconstitutionally begun by the president.

99 9 Stat. 9 (1846); 4 *Richardson, supra* note 4, at 442.

100 1 *Polk, supra* note 59, at 392.

101 Letter from Abraham Lincoln to William H. Herndon, June 22, 1848, *supra* note 96, at 492.

102 Prize Cases, 2 Black 635, 668 (U.S. 1863).

103 Letter from Abraham Lincoln to William H. Herndon, Feb. 15, 1848, *Lincoln, supra* note 96, at 451.

amply demonstrated by the subsequent operation of the war power in American history, not least of all during his own tenure of the highest office.

TRIBUNE OF THE PEOPLE

One of the constant complaints articulated in Polk's diary is about the petty matters with which the president is burdened, particularly those involving appointments to federal office. "The people of the U.S.," he wrote toward the end of his term, "have no idea of the extent to which the President's time, which ought to be devoted to more important matters, is occupied by the voracious and often unprincipled persons who seek office. If a kind Providence permits me length of days and health, I will, after I retire from the Presidential office, write the secret and hitherto unknown history of the workings of the Government in this respect."[104]

Providence was, alas, not willing; Polk died less than four months after leaving office, with his projected volume unwritten. But his annoyance at being troubled with such matters has been echoed by virtually every student of the presidency, as well as by later occupants of the White House. If anything, the burden was even greater a century ago than today, when civil service laws have relieved the president of much of the importunities of office-seekers, which led Polk to exclaim, "will the pressure of office never cease!" [105] Yet we mistake the nature of the presidency if we concentrate solely upon the clamorous throng of aspirants to office and petitioners who made Polk's lot intolerable, or even upon the dreary record of the inanities who succeeded him. The presidency has never meant less than it did during the 1850s, but the power and prestige which it acquired during Jackson's tenure survived even the decline that followed Polk. Just before he retired, Polk expressed his pride at having "filled the highest station on earth." [106] Nothing left undone by the Buchanans and Pierces could diminish its potential, as that had been revealed by Jackson and Polk.

The great presidents of the present century, Franklin Roosevelt said, were "moral leaders, each in his own way and for his own time, who used the Presidency as a pulpit." [107] If the president has thus developed into the leader of the nation, the starting point was the precedent set during Jackson's and Polk's day, and the Jacksonian notion that the

---

[104] 3 *Polk, supra* note 59, at 419.
[105] 1 *Polk, supra* note 59, at 261.
[106] 4 *Polk, supra* note 59, at 177.
[107] Quoted in *Corwin, supra* note 17, at 273.

president is the "agent of the people," as he put it,[108] and that the office is the equal of the other two departments of government was vital in this regard.[109] This conception of the president was shared by Polk. To the claim that Congress alone was the immediate representative of the people, Polk answered that that was even more true of the President: "The President represents . . . the whole people of the United States, as each member of the legislative department represents portions of them."[110]

Jackson and Polk virtually articulated the modern theory of the president as the leader of the nation who relies directly upon the people for his power and support. Jackson unhesitatingly went directly to the people for support for his policies, notably in making his re-election a virtual national referendum ("something like a popular ratification," Nicholas Biddle called it[111]) on his bank policy; he "cast himself upon the support of the *people* against the acts of both houses of *congress*," as an opposing newspaper put it.[112] He was anticipating the famous description in Theodore Roosevelt's autobiography of his conflicts with congressional leaders: "I was forced to abandon the effort to persuade them to come my way, and then I achieved results only by appealing over the heads of the Senate and House leaders to the people, who were the masters of both of us."[113]

When Harvard conferred an honorary Doctor of Laws degree upon President Jackson, ex-President Adams confided to his diary that "as myself an affectionate child of our Alma Mater, I would not be present to witness her disgrace in conferring her highest literary honors upon a barbarian who could not write a sentence of grammar and hardly could spell his own name."[114] To this complaint President Quincy of Harvard responded, "As the people have twice decided that this man knows law enough to be their ruler it is not for Harvard College to maintain that they are mistaken."[115] Barbarian or not, it was the conception of the presidency on which Jackson, and his disciple Polk, acted which looked to the future and showed so clearly what the highest office might become. When the need came a quarter century later for executive power to expand to an extent theretofore thought impossible, it was directly on Jacksonian doctrine that the unprecedented Civil War presidency was grounded.

108 Manuscript of Jackson speech (early in second term), Charles Hamilton, Auction No. 21, Item 307 (1967).

109 See p. 41 and note 17 *supra.*

110 Fourth Annual Message, 6 *Richardson, supra* note 4, at 665.

111 Quoted in *White, supra* note 2, at 23.

112 Quoted in *White, supra* note 2, at 23.

113 *T. Roosevelt, An Autobiography* 342 (1926).

114 8 *Adams, supra* note 19, at 546.

115 Quoted in *James, supra* note 16, at 642.

CHAPTER THREE

Congress and the Executive

CHECKS AND BALANCES

Not long after the people had decided that Andrew Jackson was to be retained in "the highest office in their gift," the president saw fit to address his compatriots on "the policy called for at this interesting period of our history by those charged with the administration of our government." Among other things, he emphasized the key role of the concept of checks and balances: "Those incidents where they have led me to differ with the other coordinate departments of the government impress me the more solemnly with a just sense of the importance of each as checks upon the others in administering our admirable system of government."[1]

Even under a president as strong as Jackson, the outstanding feature of the constitutional structure remained the system of checks and balances. Throughout the pre-Civil War period, the legislative and executive branches continued to serve as restraints upon each other. Powerful though the presidency may have seemed under Jackson (and, to a lesser degree, Polk), it was never able to dominate the Congress to the extent possible under a parliamentary system. Powerful though Congress may have been under weak presidents like Buchanan and Pierce, it could not really aspire to the legislative supremacy of the

---

[1] Jackson, manuscript of speech, undated, but very early in his second term, Charles Hamilton, Auction No. 21, Item 307 (1967).

British Parliament or even that exercised under the Articles of Confederation. And hanging like a Damocles' sword over the legislative and executive departments was the power of judicial review established, in classic terms, over a quarter century earlier in *Marbury* v. *Madison.*[2]

In an 1835 Senate speech, Daniel Webster declared that "the Constitution . . . goes all along upon the idea of dividing the powers of government, so far as practicable, into three great departments. It describes the powers and duties of these departments in an article allotted to each." Webster, however, had no doubt of where the primacy lay: "As first in importance and dignity, it begins with the legislative department."[3] He rejected the conception of executive authority upon which Jackson was then acting and denied that the grant in Article II of the "executive Power" was a wholesale delegation of "whatever might be construed, or supposed, or imagined to be executive power." "What *is* executive power?" he asked. "Did they mean executive power as known in England, or as known in France, or as known in Russia? . . . Now, Sir, I think it perfectly plain and manifest, that, although the framers of the Constitution meant to confer executive power on the President, yet they meant to define and limit that power, and to confer no more than they did thus define and limit."[4] The theory of government upon which the Webster address was based refused to recognize an ascendancy in any of the three branches. Even if, to him, primacy was in the legislature, it was still only a primacy *inter pares*: "Now, Sir, no man doubts that this is a limited legislature."[5] Its essential role was to serve as a check upon executive excesses. Throughout his legislative career, Webster sought to subject presidential power to congressional control.

In part, the Webster posture was a Whig response to occupancy of the White House by Jackson and his Democratic successors, but it is also true that Webster, like the other congressional leaders of his time, was greatly concerned with the legislative role as an essential balance of the governmental system. During all the "history of the contest for liberty," he declared in another Senate speech, "executive power has been regarded as a lion which must be caged."[6] Such caging in the American system was deemed the peculiar province of the legislature. "We are the sworn enemy . . . of Executive . . . usurpation," affirmed John C. Calhoun in the Senate in 1837.[7] Constitutional history in the

2 1 Cranch 137 (U.S. 1803).

3 7 *The Writings and Speeches of Daniel Webster* 187 (1903).

4 *Id.* at 186.

5 *Id.* at 187.

6 *Id.* at 134.

7 *Cong. Globe,* 25th Cong., 1st Sess. 74.

pre-Civil War period, at least so far as Congress was concerned, was largely a record of the legislative attempt to give reality to the Calhoun characterization.

KENDALL V. UNITED STATES

The Congress of a century and a quarter ago was no more exempt than its present-day descendant from the tendency to state its position in relation to the executive in exaggerated terms. In 1837, speaking of the growth of presidential power, Henry Clay proclaimed, "for the last four years our Government could not be said to be a free Government. . . . never before have I felt . . . such a deep and profound regret." Another senator compared the actions of the executive "to that, by which Dionysius the tyrant proposed to relieve the statue of Jupiter. There was a robe of massive gold on the statue, which the tyrant took away, alleging that it was too cold, and substituted a garment of wool."[8] In like manner, it was asserted, had the people been fleeced by the administration.

Underneath the hyperbole, there was a solid constitutional basis for the congressional claim of oversight authority over the executive. In our system, domestic exercises of substantive authority by executive agencies must find their source in the statute book. Our law rejects the notion of inherent or autonomous lawmaking power in the executive—a rejection which received striking articulation not too long ago in the *Steel Seizure* case.[9] It follows that the executive, in the exercise of its delegated powers, acts as the agent of the legislature. If that is true, the Congress must possess authority to exercise continuing control over executive activities. The executive, as the agent of Congress, has a duty to obey the directions of its principal and is accountable to the latter under elementary principles of the law of agency.

Constitutionally speaking, then, it is not true that executive officers and agencies are only agents of the president. An assertion to that effect was made and rejected by the Supreme Court in *Kendall* v. *United States*.[10] The case itself was a political *cause célèbre*, since it arose directly out of an alleged refusal to obey the law by the most controversial member of Jackson's cabinet, Amos Kendall, "honest Iago," as a member of the House termed him at the end of 1838, "the

[8] *Id.* at 67–68.

[9] Youngstown Sheet and Tube Co. v. Sawyer, 343 U.S. 579 (1952).

[10] 12 Pet. 524 (U.S. 1838).

President's *thinking* machine and his *writing* machine—ay, and his *lying* machine!"[11]

Kendall, as postmaster general, had refused to recognize the settlement of certain claims of postal contractors made by his predecessors. Congress passed a law directing the solicitor of the treasury to inquire into the claims and decide what was owing to the claimants, after which the postmaster general was directed to pay the amounts decided by the solicitor. The solicitor allowed the claims, but Kendall still refused to pay. An action of mandamus was brought against Kendall to compel him to make the payments. The Supreme Court affirmed the decision of the Circuit Court issuing the writ. The payments involved were held to be mere ministerial acts, which had been commanded by Congress and "which neither [the postmaster general] nor the President had any authority to deny or control"[12]

The important thing about the *Kendall* case is the refusal of the Supreme Court to accept the claim that executive officers are under the exclusive control and direction of the president and act solely as his agents. To be sure, the high bench conceded, the Constitution vests the executive power in the president, "but it by no means follows, that every officer in every branch of that department is under the exclusive direction of the President. . . . it would be an alarming doctrine, that Congress cannot impose upon any executive officer any duty they may think proper, which is not repugnant to any rights secured and protected by the Constitution."[13]

To contemporaries, the *Kendall* decision was noteworthy primarily as a judicial rebuff to Jackson and his successor. Van Buren himself sharply criticized the decision in his Second Annual Message.[14] He asked Congress to abolish the judicial jurisdiction involved in the case, but Congress ignored his recommendation. The dissenting opinion of Chief Justice Taney was also assailed on political grounds, as an attempt to protect an old associate in the Jackson cabinet. The distorted attacks of Whig newspapers led the Court reporter, Richard Peters, to direct them to the chief justice's attention. Taney, giving voice to a frequently felt view of the press by members of the highest bench, replied: "You were certainly right in declining to notice, in any way, the statements in the newspapers in relation to the opinions delivered . . . in the case of the Postmaster General. The daily press, from the nature of things, can

11 *Cong. Globe* Appendix, 25th Cong., 3d Sess. 386.

12 12 Pet. at 610.

13 *Id.*

14 3 *J.D. Richardson, A Compilation of the Messages and Papers of the Presidents 1789–1897,* at 503–6 (1896).

never be 'the field of fame' for Judges; . . . it is the last place that we should voluntarily select for our discussion."[15]

A century later the political controversy over the *Kendall* case has lost its importance, but the decision remains of significance as a judicial buttress of the constitutional position of Congress vis-à-vis the administration. Executive officers are responsible for the performance of their functions not only to the chief executive, who is the hierarchical head of their department, but also to the legislature, from whence their very being is derived. The authority of such officers finds its source in congressional delegations, and, like all agents, they are subject to the scrutiny and supervision of their principal.

LEGISLATIVE-EXECUTIVE CONFLICTS

"The doctrine of separation of powers," stated Justice Brandeis in a noted passage, "was adopted by the convention of 1787 not to promote efficiency but to preclude the exercise of arbitrary power." The partition of governmental power and the system of checks and balances were not intended to avoid friction. On the contrary, "the purpose was . . . , by means of the inevitable friction incident to the distribution of the governmental powers among three departments, to save the people from autocracy."[16]

The inevitable friction that results from the separation of powers has always been particularly apparent in the relations between Congress and the president. John Adams once said that the legislative and executive branches were natural enemies.[17] Much of pre-Civil War history appeared to confirm this dictum. Under Jackson conflict between the branches mounted to new heights, and it broke out with renewed intensity under Tyler and Polk.[18] Even under weak presidents like Fillmore and Pierce, conflicts with Congress were built into the governmental system.

It was virtually unavoidable that there would be strife between the White House and Capitol Hill under Jackson, for his expansive notions of presidential authority came into direct collision with the congressional view on the proper distribution of governmental power. This struggle culminated in the passage by the Senate, on March 28, 1834, of

[15] Quoted in *S. Tyler, Memoir of Roger Brooke Taney, LL.D.* 307 (1872).

[16] Dissenting, in Myers v. United States, 272 U.S. 52, 293 (1926).

[17] Quoted in *L.D. White, The Jacksonians: A Study in Administrative History, 1829–1861,* at 104 (1954).

[18] *Compare id.*

a resolution censuring the president for ordering the removal of federal deposits from the Bank of the United States. By his action, declared the Senate resolution, "the President . . . has assumed upon himself authority and power not conferred by the constitution and laws, but in derogation of both."[19]

Jackson received the Senate censure with bitterness and indignation. He sent to the upper house an unprecedented Protest[20] "against their . . . daring violation of the constitution in the attempt to encroach upon the constitutional powers of the executive . . . and thereby destroying the checks and balances of the government created by the constitution."[21] Asserting that the Senate resolution "contains an imputation upon my private as well as upon my public character," Jackson asked that his Protest, as "a substitute for that defense which I have not been able to present in the ordinary form," be entered in the Senate journal.[22]

The Jackson Protest led to a sharp Senate debate. Despite the assertion of the president's chief supporter, Senator Thomas Hart Benton, that "our theatrical exhibitions . . . were nothing but a grand farce, amusing some, flattering the hopes of others; but deceiving nobody!" the Senate voted that the president's Protest "be not entered on the Journal."[23] Benton thereupon publicly vowed that he would not rest until Jackson's censure was "expunged" from the journal. He kept his vow on January 16, 1837. By that date the Jacksonians had acquired a majority in the upper chamber and Benton could secure passage of his expunging resolution. Webster objected in vain that "you have no right to mar or mutilate the record of our votes . . . recorded according to the Constitution."[24] Late at night the expunging resolution was voted. By candlelight, the clerk produced the thick journal for 1834 and turned to the censure resolution. Before the packed gallery he drew black lines around the offending words and wrote across them "Expunged by order of the Senate, this 16th day of January, 1837." Jackson was as pleased by the Senate action as by any of the material victories of earlier days. His eyes would light up as he displayed the pen the clerk had used[25] "in *Expunging* . . . the odious sentence which a

[19] *Reg. of Deb.*, 23d Cong., 1st Sess. 1187.

[20] *Richardson, supra* note 14, at 69.

[21] Letter from Andrew Jackson to John D. Coffee, Apr. 6, 1834, in 5 *J.S. Bassett, Correspondence of Andrew Jackson* 260 (1933).

[22] *Richardson, supra* note 14, at 92–93.

[23] *Reg. of Deb.*, 23d Cong., 1st Sess. 1711, 1712.

[24] 8 *Webster, supra* note 3, at 34.

[25] M. James, *The Life of Andrew Jackson* 714 (1938).

few politicians and their odious confederates, the Bank of the United States, caused to be entered up against me."[26]

The "precious *Pen*" may, in Jackson's phrase, have "healed the wound, given by the resolution it was employed to expunge," yet the problem of friction between the legislative and executive branches was scarcely resolved by the old president's tinsel triumph. If anything, the removal of Old Hickory from the Washington scene intensified the congressional tendency to engage in conflicts with the executive. A president like Jackson could work his will in a manner which his successors could scarcely hope to emulate. Polk tells of the comment of a leading senator "that Gen'l Jackson could make appointments over the head and against the will of his Cabinet, but with an oath, he would teach me that I could not."[27]

The legislative-executive conflict became particularly acute under Tyler, who, after being disowned by his own Whig Party, had little or no backing in Congress or in the nation. Jackson could write, from retirement at the Hermitage, after the Senate had rejected a Tyler appointee as U.S. marshal, "I could recommend to Mr. Tyler to do as I did, whenever the Senate rejected a good man, . . . I gave them a hot potatoe, and he will soon bring them to terms, and if not, . . . the vengeance of the people will fall upon them."[28] But Tyler was no Jackson, and, as his term went on, he was less and less able to secure congressional support. During his last two years in office the Senate turned down four of his cabinet nominations, four nominees to the Supreme Court, and a host of lesser nominations. The qualifications of Tyler's nominees, we are told, were not even a secondary consideration in the decisions.[29]

The hectic record of congressional obstreperousness under Tyler has no counterpart during the pre-Civil War period. To a lesser extent, however, the legislature continued to hinder the executive department. Complained Polk to Senator Lewis Cass early in 1846, "the rejection of my prominent nominations by the Senate at the opening of my administration was calculated to weaken my administration before the country, and destroy my power to carry out any of my recommendations of measures before Congress."[30] Though Polk and his successors

[26] Letter from Andrew Jackson to Thomas H. Benton, Jan. 17, 1837, *Bassett, supra* note 21, at 450, 451.

[27] 1 *The Diary of James K. Polk during His Presidency* 187 (M.M. Quaife ed. 1910).

[28] Letter from Andrew Jackson to Major William B. Lewis, Feb. 28, 1842, 6 *Bassett, supra* note 21, at 142.

[29] *White, supra* note 17, at 111.

[30] *Polk, supra* note 27, at 307.

were confronted neither with the major battles that had harrassed Jackson nor with the congressional effort to incapacitate the executive that undermined Tyler, they too, were engaged in a constant struggle for power with Capitol Hill.

APPOINTMENTS

The struggle referred to took place at various levels. First, as noted above, was the control of appointments. Under the Constitution, control is divided between the president and Senate, though the lion's share of the appointing power is vested in the former. His is the affirmative power to propose, the Senate's only the negative one to dispose. The Senate is given the authority to prevent bad appointments but is not given an opportunity to make good ones.[31]

In the pre-Civil War period, the role of the appointing power was, proportionately speaking, far greater than it has since become. During the post-Jacksonian period, the notion of a civil service system to limit the appointing power had scarcely been articulated. In addition, the president was deemed to possess the power to appoint diplomatic agents of any rank, at any place, at his discretion. The authority to appoint, in such cases, ruled Pierce's attorney general in 1855, is derived directly from the law of nations and the Constitution and does not depend upon any affirmative grant by Congress.[32] Then, too, it should be remembered that the Jacksonian practice of rotation greatly increased the number of offices to which appointments might be made.

These factors made the struggle over the appointing power more acute than it has been in more recent times. Even under Jackson, the Senate had refused to follow the earlier practice of almost routine acceptance of presidential appointments. Jackson's broad support had, however, restrained the opposition of the upper house. "Were it not for the fear of the out-of-door popularity of General Jackson," declared Webster, "the Senate would have negatived more than half of his nominations."[33] With Jackson gone, the Senate was unrestrained. Wrote John Quincy Adams, the Senate had had "a paroxysm of servility, and is glad to get back to its more self-complacent attitude of factious dictation to the President."[34] The result was the rash of rejections that met the appointments of a president like Tyler.

---

31 *Compare W. Wilson, Constitutional Government in the United States* 59-60 (1911).

32 7 *Op. Att'y Gen.* 186, 193–94 (1855).

33 17 *Webster, supra* note 3, at 501.

34 8 *Memoirs of John Quincy Adams* 329 (C.F. Adams ed. 1876).

Compounding the problem from the executive point of view was the growth of the principle of senatorial courtesy, which gave senators from the state concerned a virtual veto over all appointments. "Many members of Congress," complained Polk in 1848, "assume that they have the right to make appointments, particularly in their own states, and they often . . . fly into a passion when their wishes are not gratified." [35] Senatorial courtesy has its origins in the beginnings of Washington's first administration,[36] but it was during the period with which we are concerned that the practice really became established as a practical limitation upon the appointing power. The result was to go far, as Jefferson Davis pointed out in 1857, to "strip the Executive of his prerogative of nomination so that in point of fact two members of the Senate would nominate to the Senate in session, the appointments which they might deem it expedient to make."[37]

As time went on, congressmen also came to exert a controlling influence over inferior appointments in their districts. By 1853, a congressman whose choice was not appointed as shoe inspector at an arsenal in his district could protest that "the *practice* has been invariably, under every Democratic Administration of the General Government that appointments immediately local, such as this is, should at least *be approved* by the Member of Congress for the time being."[38]

The result was that while, in form, the constitutional authority of the president over appointments continued unimpaired, in practice, the power was increasingly shared with Congress. While Jackson, and to a lesser extent Polk, were able to maintain executive independence here as elsewhere, presidents like Pierce and Fillmore preferred accommodation to conflict. By 1861, it has been said that the Congress had won substantial control over the appointments made in the executive branch.[39]

FISCAL POWERS

Of the constitutional weapons available to the legislative department in exercising its role as a check upon the executive, none has been of more importance than the power of the purse. That power—the veritable birthright of the Anglo-American legislative assembly—has been the great instrument through which Congress has been able to control

[35] 4 *Polk, supra* note 27, at 29.

[36] See E.S. Corwin, *The President: Office and Powers* 73 (1957).

[37] Quoted in *White, supra* note 17, at 120.

[38] Quoted in *White, supra* note 17, at 120.

[39] *White, supra* note 17, at 124.

virtually every aspect of the governmental machine. Yet, with regard to finance, too, there has been a consistent power struggle between the branches. "From the time of the first enactment to the present," declared an 1868 report of the House Committee on Appropriations, "a continual struggle has been going on by the several executive departments with Congress to relieve their departments from this control of public expenditures by Congress, and as constant endeavors by the legislative department to hold the executive to specific expenditures under specific appropriations."[40]

From Jackson to the Civil War, the two houses struggled continuously to maintain their control over executive expenditures. Just after Jackson's presidency, a member of the House Ways and Means Committee complained of that body's subservience to the executive.[41] Under Jackson's successors, the fiscal balance was redressed. Before 1842, the form of expenditure estimates had been left entirely to the departments. In 1842, Congress imposed upon all departments the duty "to specify, as nearly as may be convenient, the sources from which such estimates are derived, and the calculations upon which they are founded."[42] The requirement thus imposed was strengthened in statutes of 1844 and 1855.[43]

The departments did not readily submit to the restrictive effect of specific estimates and itemized appropriations. Postmaster General Kendall continued to submit lump sum appropriations despite the contrary congressional intent, leaving the sum appropriated at his discretion. "The design was not apparent on the face of the bill—it was disguised under a provision requiring of him specific estimates; and now, in his report, he says his object has been to *substitute* specific accountability instead of specific appropriations."[44] The Congress, nevertheless, continued to press for specific estimates and appropriations. In 1836, John Quincy Adams objected to the Kendall practice in the House of Representatives, arguing "for some time in support of specifying, as the only mode to secure accountability."[45] Despite the claim that "inconvenience and embarrassment can only be prevented, by entrusting the head of that Department with an extent of discretionary power,"[46] the Adams objection prevailed and the motion in favor of the lump sum appropriation was defeated.

[40] *H.R. Rep.* No. 14, 40th Cong., 2d Sess. 2 (Feb. 4, 1868).

[41] 9 *Adams, supra* note 34, at 449.

[42] 5 Stat. 523, 526 (1842).

[43] 5 Stat. 681, 693 (1844); 10 Stat. 643, 670 (1855). *See White, supra* note 17, at 127.

[44] *Adams, supra* note 34, at 515.

[45] *Cong. Globe,* 25th Cong., 2d Sess. 257.

[46] *Id.* at 258.

INVESTIGATORY POWER

Other weapons, too, were developed by the Congress in its continuing conflict with the executive during the pre-Civil War period. Of particular constitutional interest was the development of the investigatory power, which had first been asserted in 1792, when the House of Representatives appointed a select committee to inquire into the disaster that befell General Arthur St. Clair and his army in their expedition against the Indians. From Jackson to Lincoln, the investigatory power was exercised with ever-increasing frequency.

The constitutional sanction behind the congressional power of investigation is the contempt power, under which either house may treat the failure to comply with its process as a contempt and may itself commit or otherwise punish the offender. The contempt power had been recognized as an implied congressional power by *Anderson* v. *Dunn*, [47] but the Supreme Court there had laid down the limitation that imprisonment for contempt of either house must terminate with the adjournment of the chamber concerned. This limitation, it came to be recognized, gravely impaired the effectiveness of the sanction. In 1857 Congress dealt with the problem by a law making it a misdemeanor for a person summoned by authority of either house to refuse to answer or to produce whatever documents were requested.[48] The additional criminal sanction made the power to compel testimony more effective.

Before 1827 congressional investigations were conducted solely by select committees. In that year, a standing committee was first empowered to send for persons and papers.[49] During the pre-Civil War period, investigations were carried on by both standing and select committes, though the preference (unlike that in our own day) was still for the latter type. Mention of some of the important investigations will give an idea of the range of congressional inquiries from the latter part of Jackson's presidency to the end of Buchanan's term. In 1839 a House committee investigated the customhouse defalcations in New York City and uncovered the frauds of the collector, Samuel Swartwout ("the first American to steal a million dollars"[50]), whose misdeeds constituted the great scandal of the Jackson administration. In 1846 an investigation was made by a House committee into a charge that Secretary of State Webster had misappropriated a secret State

---

[47] 6 Wheat. 204 (U.S. 1821).

[48] 11 Stat. 155 (1857). This statute was upheld in *In re* Chapman, 166 U.S. 661 (1897).

[49] *See M.E. Dimock, Congressional Investigating Committees* 58 (1929).

[50] *James, supra* note 25, at 734.

Department fund.[51] In 1850 there was a House inquiry into the political activities of federal officeholders under Polk. Later that year, the Secretary of the Interior was subjected to investigation by a House committee to determine whether he had paid certain claims improperly, and, in 1852, a Senate committee was appointed "to inquire into abuses, bribery, or fraud, in the prosecution of claims before Congress, commissions, or the Departments."[52]

The investigations conducted included inquiries to obtain facts pertinent to the enactment of statutes. The power to authorize such inquiries had been first asserted in the House, over strong opposition, in 1827, in connection with a proposed revision of the tariff laws.[53] In the Senate, the first use of a fact-finding investigation in aid of legislation occurred in 1859, when a select committee was set up to inquire into John Brown's raid at Harper's Ferry and to "report whether and what legislation may, in their opinion, be necessary . . . for the future preservation of the peace of the country, or for the safety of the public property."[54]

Most of the investigations during the pre-Civil War period (including those listed above) were not, however, inquiries in connection with exercise of the legislative function but probes into the working of the executive branch. Such investigations into the operation of federal agencies have always played a major role in the congressional function of executive oversight. "From the earliest times in its history, the Congress has assiduously performed an 'informing function' of this nature."[55]

Perhaps the most controversial congressional effort to investigate the executive during the period under discussion took place at the end of Jackson's second term. In December, 1836, the House set up a select committee "to inquire into the condition of the various executive departments, the ability and integrity with which they have been conducted, . . . and into all causes of complaint, from any quarter, at the manner in which said Departments . . . have fulfilled or failed to accomplish the objects of their creation."[56] The committee was the result of a resolution introduced by Congressman Henry A. Wise, who became its chairman. Wise launched the investigation with what Jack-

---

51 Among those questioned was ex-President Tyler, on the subject of the expenditure of secret funds during his presidency. The committee concluded that there was no proof "to impeach Mr. Webster's integrity, or the purity of his motive in the discharge of the duties of his office," *Cong. Globe,* 29th Cong., 1st Sess. 946.

52 *See Dimock, supra* note 49, at 93-109.

53 *See* Watkins v. United States, 354 U.S. 178, 193 (1957).

54 *See id.*

55 *Id.* at 200.

56 *Reg. of Deb.,* 24th Cong., 2d Sess. 1057.

son called "many severe but vague charges of corruption and abuse in the Executive Departments."[57]

Jackson bitterly opposed the Wise investigation. In a strong letter, he asserted that the committee, "assuming that they [i.e., the president and department heads] have been guilty of the charges alleged, calls upon them to furnish evidence against themselves!"[58] Likening the investigation to a "spanish inquisition" the president wrote that he would repudiate such legislative effort "to invade the just rights of the Executive Departments. . . . I shall repel all such attempts as an invasion of the principles of justice, as well as of the constitution."[59]

It is clear that the House had the constitutional power to authorize a wholesale investigation of the executive such as that contemplated by the Wise committee. It is, at the same time, also clear that the committee's investigation was motivated by political considerations. Thus, Treasury Secretary Woodbury was asked, "Has [*sic*] the President and others established presses . . . to promote the election of Martin Van Buren?"[60] Jackson's opposition effectively frustrated the investigation, and, less than three months after it was established, the committee (over the vigorous dissent of its chairman) voted to discontinue its inquiry. Constitutionally speaking, the Wise minority report was correct in its defense of the congressional power to conduct such a "general" investigation of the executive. The end result, nevertheless, was one of the most successful attempts of a president to resist a congressional inquiry.[61]

EXECUTIVE PRIVILEGE

On February 26, 1842, President Tyler, replying to a House resolution requesting information on the state of negotiations with Britain over the Maine boundary and all correspondence on the subject, wrote: "Desirous always to lay before Congress and the public everything affecting the state of the country to the fullest extent consistent with propriety and prudence, I have to inform the House of Representatives that in my judgment no communication could be made by me at this time on the subject of its resolution without detriment or danger to the public interests."[62] Tyler was asserting a power claimed by presidents

---

57 Letter from Andrew Jackson to Henry A. Wise, Jan. 26, 1837, in *Bassett, supra* note 21, at 453.

58 *Bassett, supra* note 21, at 453.

59 *Bassett, supra* note 21, at 454.

60 Quoted in *Dimock, supra* note 49, at 107.

61 *See* E. J. Eberling, *Congressional Investigations* 142 (1928).

62 4 *Richardson, supra* note 14, at 101.

almost from the founding of the Republic—from Washington's refusal to submit certain correspondence to the House of Representatives relating to the negotiation of the Jay Treaty in 1796 to similar denials in our own day—that of refusal to comply with a congressional demand for information when the president deems production of the information contrary to the public interest.

Tyler was to claim executive privilege again on March 23, 1842, when he refused to comply with a House request for "the names of such of the members (if any) of the Twenty-sixth and Twenty-seventh Congresses who have been applicants for office" and the details relating to their applications.[63] This time the information was refused on the ground that, since the appointing power was vested in the president, the House could have no legitimate concern therein. In a later message, on January 31, 1843, he furnished to the House information relating to an executive investigation of frauds practised on the Cherokee Indians. The same message contained a vigorous defense of the executive power to withhold information from Congress. The nature and practice of the government, Tyler declared, have "sanctioned the principle that there must necessarily be a discretionary authority in reference to the information called for by either House."[64]

Executive privilege as a basis for denying information to Congress was also relied upon by Jackson and Polk. On February 10, 1835, Jackson sent a message to the Senate declining to furnish copies of charges made to him against the conduct of a surveyor general, charges which had led to the man's removal from office. To furnish the information, said Jackson, "would ultimately subject the independent constitutional action of the Executive . . . to the domination and control of the Senate."[65] In 1846, Polk refused to supply the House with "an account of all payments made on President's certificates . . . through the agency of the State Department, for the contingent expenses of foreign intercourse" from 1841 until Webster's resignation as secretary of state in 1843.[66] Polk strongly contested the right of the House to demand information on confidential expenditures involving foreign relations.[67]

We must not make the mistake of overemphasizing the importance of executive privilege in the practical operation of relations between the political branches, however. Against the handful of refusals by Jackson, Tyler, and Polk to furnish information must be placed the plethora of

[63] 4 *Richardson, supra* note 14, at 105.
[64] 4 *Richardson, supra* note 14, at 220.
[65] 3 *Richardson, supra* note 14, at 134.
[66] 4 *Richardson, supra* note 14, at 431.
[67] *See Polk, supra* note 27, at 331-33.

cases in which the requested papers were sent without demur to the house concerned. The general picture from Jackson to Lincoln was one of presidential compliance with congressional requests for information, particularly in the years following Tyler's conflicts with Congress. In 1886, a leading member of the upper chamber, Senator George Franklin Edmunds, was able to state that in the past forty years neither house had "failed on its call to get the information that it has asked for from the public Departments of the Government."[68] After Polk's 1846 refusal, the pre-Civil War practice was one of unfailing assent to such requests. The Edmunds speech contains a list of instances during the 1840s and 1850s in which senatorial requests for papers were complied with without question. They cover "every variety of the functions of government, and yet none of these men, Presidents, Secretaries, Senators, supposed that one was invading the constitutional sacred privacy of the other."[69]

The general pre-Civil War practice may be exemplified by what happened under Polk. Once again, our picture extends beyond what is normally available to the historian in public documents because of the detailed information given in his diary. From it we can see that most congressional requests to see papers were worked out by agreement between Capitol Hill and the White House. Sometimes the legislators concerned were persuaded the disclosure would, indeed, be against the national interest. In July, 1846, the Senate passed a resolution calling for certain papers. Polk called the mover, Senator Reverdy Johnson, to the White House and showed him that the papers contained military plans for the invasion of California, which should not be made public. On Johnson's advice, Polk left the Senate call unanswered.[70]

In other cases, Polk acceded to congressional calls for papers, even against the advice of his cabinet. In one instance, in 1846, the House called for information on the military governments set up in territory conquered from Mexico. Polk decided to "send in all the information called for," despite the strong opposition of Secretary of State Buchanan.[71] Earlier the same year, Polk had sent to Congress the correspondence with Louis McLane, then our minister in London, relating to English military and naval preparations,[72] after having originally decided not to communicate it.[73]

---

68 17 *Cong. Rec.* 2215.

69 *Id.* at 2219. *But see infra*, p. 158.

70 2 *Polk, supra* note 27, at 13–14. *Compare id.* at 366, 369–70, 393.

71 2 *Polk, supra* note 27, at 281.

72 4 *Richardson, supra* note 14, at 422; *Polk, supra* note 27, at 212.

73 *Polk, supra* note 27, at 209.

A particularly difficult case arose in 1848, when the House called for the instructions of John Slidell, who had been engaged, before war with Mexico broke out, as a presidential envoy who was to attempt to negotiate with that country.[74] Polk was most reluctant to communicate the instructions "because I deemed their publication, pending the war with Mexico, and until a Treaty of peace was concluded . . . , prejudicial to the public interests."[75] In accordance with this view, he sent a message declining to comply.[76] On the other hand, he did communicate the instructions confidentially to the Senate, in executive session,[77] and, a few months later, he sent the Slidell instructions to both houses, among the documents included with the transmission of the ratified peace treaty with Mexico: "Upon the conclusion of a definitive Treaty of peace with Mexico, the reasons for withholding them at that time no longer exist."[78]

The general executive willingness to comply with congressional calls for information may also be seen from an incident in 1860. The House had provided for a general investigation to determine whether President Buchanan had, "by money, patronage or other improper means, sought to influence the action of Congress for or against the passage of any bill pertaining to the rights of any State or Territory."[79] Buchanan bitterly protested against the investigation, asserting that "since the time of the star-chamber . . . there has been no such proceeding." Yet, though he characterized the probe as "spreading a drag net . . . to catch any disappointed man willing to malign my character,"[80] he did not seek to interfere with the investigating committee, which examined some eighty witnesses and made a voluminous record, unhampered by any assertion of executive privilege.

WAR OPPOSITION

Writing to his son midway through the Mexican war, Daniel Webster declared, "we may not seek to obstruct the proceedings of a Govt. in carrying on a war, merely because we disapprove the war itself."[81]

[74] *Polk, supra* note 27, at 289.

[75] 3 *Polk, supra* note 27, at 398.

[76] 4 *Richardson, supra* note 14, at 565. *Compare id.* at 602; 4 *Polk, supra* note 27, at 27–28.

[77] 3 *Polk, supra* note 27, at 399.

[78] 4 *Polk, supra* note 27, at 4.

[79] *Cong. Globe,* 36th Cong., 1st Sess. 997

[80] 5 *Richardson, supra* note 14, at 617, 621.

[81] Letter from Daniel Webster to Fletcher Webster, Apr. 24, 1847, Parke-Bernet Galleries, Sale No. 2676, Item 701 (1968).

Even at the time of the Mexican war, however, there were many who did not take the Webster approach in expressing their aversion to their government's war policy. It was Thoreau's opposition to the war and the expansion of slavery that inspired his seminal principle of civil disobedience. In theory, at least, he carried his aversion to the point of advocating obstruction of government itself as a means of protest. "When . . . a whole country is unjustly overrun and conquered by a foreign army, and subjected to military law," he wrote, "I think that it is not too soon for honest men to rebel and revolutionize." All the same, he was too much the theorist to put civil disobedience to more than a token test. A prison may be, as a famous passage from his essay has it, "the only house in a slave State in which a free man can abide with honor."[82] But when he himself sought to carry out his theory, he was satisfied with a symbolic night in Concord jail, leaving in the morning when his poll tax was paid for him by his aunt.

Most opponents of the war did not carry their opposition anywhere near the point advocated by Thoreau. This was especially true of the Whigs on Capitol Hill. For them, the guiding principle was that stated by Webster in the letter quoted. "To the more intelligent portion of the Northern Whigs," says a contemporary observer, "the contest was repulsive. . . . But few forgot their allegiance to this country in the face of the enemy. Congress, repeatedly appealed to by the President, voted men and money without stint to secure the national success and maintain the national honor."[83] Webster himself, like many others who had no sympathy for the war, lost a son to Mexican bullets.

Abraham Lincoln, elected in 1846 as a Whig congressman, was typical of the congressional opposition to the war. Both on the floor of the House and elsewhere, he challenged the constitutionality of war-making by the president.[84] The actual declaration of war had, of course, been voted overwhelmingly by both houses; Polk had, in effect, presented Congress with a demand for a declaration which could not be refused without repudiating the acts of General Zachary Taylor and his men, who had recently been engaged in hostilities. Yet though most members voted for declaration of what John Quincy Adams termed "this most unrighteous war,"[85] that did not mean that the Whig opposition was ready to abandon its opposition to Polk or to the war itself.

[82] Henry David Thoreau, *Unjust Laws,* in *Voices in Court* 485, 490 (W.H. Davenport ed. 1958).

[83] 1 *B.P. Poore, Perley's Reminiscences of Sixty Years in the National Metropolis* 336 (1886).

[84] *See* 1 *The Collected Works of Abraham Lincoln* 432–42, 446–47, 451–52, 472–73, 492 (R.P. Basler ed. 1953).

[85] 12 *Adams, supra* note 34, at 263.

The most spectacular manifestation of the Whig opposition was the passage on January 3, 1848, by a Whig majority, of a House resolution sponsored by Representative George Ashmun affirming that the war with Mexico was "unnecessarily and unconstitutionally begun by the President of the United States."[86] Lincoln, who voted for the resolution, wrote that the House "vote affirms that the war was unnecessarily and unconstitutionally commenced by the President; and I will stake my life that if you had been in my place, you would have voted just as I did."[87]

The Whigs might look on the House vote as "the most recent and authentic expression of the will and opinion of the majority of the people."[88] They may even have been convinced that the Ashmun resolution stated, in Lincoln's words, "the *truth* of the case" and that Polk himself was "deeply conscious of being in the wrong—that he feels the blood of this war, like the blood of Abel, is crying to Heaven against him."[89] Legally speaking, however, the censure had no effect; bitter though the feeling over it might have been, it did not alter the constitutional picture with regard to the war power one whit.

Even those who voted for the resolution did not go so far as to deny the government the financial and other support needed for prosecution of the war. As Lincoln explained his vote in favor, "This vote has nothing to do, in determining my votes on the question of supplies. I have always intended, and still intend, to vote supplies." Opponents of the war had always "made and kept the distinction between . . . vot[ing] supplies, or tak[ing] part in the war . . . [and] approv[ing] the Presidents conduct."[90] Even Senator Thomas Corwin, who made a famous impassioned plea against the war in an 1847 Senate speech—"If I were a Mexican I would tell you, 'Have you not room in your own country to bury your dead men? If you come into mine we will greet you with bloody hands, and welcome you to hospitable graves' "[91] —had earlier accepted the war budget.

CONQUEST AND THE CONSTITUTION

The congressional opponents of the war were particularly critical of the president's policies with regard to Mexican territory occupied by

[86] *Cong. Globe,* 30th Cong., 1st Sess. 95.

[87] *Lincoln, supra* note 84, at 446. On December 22, 1847, he introduced his famous "spot resolutions," requesting the President to inform the House of the "exact spot of soil" where "the blood of our citizens was so shed"; *id.* at 420-22.

[88] 10 *Webster, supra* note 3, at 6.

[89] *Lincoln, supra* note 84, at 432, 439.

[90] *Lincoln, supra* note 84, at 447.

[91] Quoted in *L. Filler, The Crusade against Slavery, 1830–1860,* at 186 (1960).

American troops. The war raised for the first time the constitutional problem of acquisition of territory through conquest. As a practical matter, such acquisition must, in the first place, be brought about by military action carried out in accordance with the orders of the commander in chief. The president as commander in chief, affirmed Chief Justice Taney in a case arising out of the occupation of Tampico, may employ the armed forces in the manner he deems most effectual to defeat the enemy: "He may invade the hostile country, and subject it to the sovereignty and authority of the United States."[92]

But what of government in the Mexican territory occupied by American troops? From the beginning, Polk acted on the view that the president could order "temporary military Governments, . . . established under the authority of our Military and Naval commanders by virtue of the rights of conquest."[93] The presidential power thus exercised by Polk was vigorously challenged by the Whig opposition. "The question is not what power the Government of a Country may exercise over a conquered territory," declared Webster in a well-reasoned attack. "But the question is, what power may the President of the United States of his own authority, exercise over a territory conquered by the arms of the United States. That Congress may make rules for conquered territories . . . there is no doubt; but where is the President found to possess this power"?[94]

The answer to Webster's query was given in *Cross* v. *Harrison,* [95] where the Supreme Court upheld the action of President Polk in ordering the establishment of a military government for the conquered territory of California. In so doing, the high bench said, he was exercising the belligerent rights of a conqueror. Nor according to the Court, could anyone doubt that the orders of the president, and the action of the army and navy commanders in California in conformity with them, were valid, both under the Constitution and the law of nations.

The Whig opposition was especially censorious of presidential orders providing for the collection of duties in the ports of occupied Mexican territory. "We think," reads an apparently unpublished Webster manuscript on the matter, "that orders, edicts, and proclamations, issued by the conquering Government, over a conquered Country, regulating its commerce, external or internal, or levying duties on imports or exports . . . have been always regarded, not as military contributions, *but*

---

[92] Fleming v. Page, 9 How. 603, 615 (U.S. 1850).

[93] 4 *Polk, supra* note 27, at 136.

[94] Letter from Daniel Webster to Editor, Baltimore American, n.d. , Parke-Bernet Galleries, Sale No. 2676, Item 700 (1968).

[95] 16 How. 164 (U.S. 1853).

as acts of Legislation. The power which exercises this authority, is in every Government that power which is competent, in the case, *to exercise legislative authority.*" Webster went on to ask, "Is there any substantial difference, between the Proclamation of George the third, in virtue of his Royal Prerogative, & the Decree of Mr. Polk, issued, as we must continue to think by virtue of an *assumed* Royal Prerogative?"[96]

Polk himself explained the basis for the levying of duties in a special message early in 1849.[97] According to him, the power in question flowed directly from the Commander in Chief Clause. The power to conduct the war included the authority, recognized in international law, to levy contributions on the enemy, in the form of import and export duties. Polk's reasoning was essentially that used by the Supreme Court when it upheld the legality of the duties imposed by the military government of California as "according to the law of arms and the right of conquest."[98]

The peace treaty with Mexico added a further dimension to the constitutional law relating to conquered territory. Though the president, as the Mexican war plainly showed, had the power as commander in chief to occupy and govern enemy territory, he did not have the "authority . . . to enlarge the limits of the United States by subjugating the enemy's country."[99] Territory occupied under military command is occupied only temporarily, to be held until its final disposition is settled by the treaty-making authority.

By the treaty ending the war, there was "added to the U.S. an immense empire, the value of which 20 years hence it would be difficult to calculate."[100] The authority of the nation to acquire new territory by treaty of cession had been established in the Louisiana Purchase. [101] In the years following that first great acquisition, other constitutional questions on the acquisition of territory had been settled. After a treaty to secure the annexation of Texas had been rejected by the Senate, resort was had to another method to acquire the additional territory. A resolution to admit Texas as a state passed both houses (though, in the Senate by only two votes) and the Lone Star State was added as a full member of the Union. Congressional authority to annex Texas was based on the constitutional power to admit new states—a power that could be used as an alternative to the treaty power.

96 *Supra* note 94.

97 4 *Richardson, supra* note 14, at 672.

98 Cross v. Harrison, 16 How. 164, 190 (U.S. 1853).

99 Fleming v. Page, 9 How. 603, 614 (U.S. 1850).

100 3 *Polk, supra* note 27, at 366.

101 The power had been upheld in American Insurance Co. v. Cantor, 1 Pet. 511 (U.S. 1828).

The converse question, that of the cession of territory, was involved in the Webster-Ashburton treaty of 1842, which settled the northeastern boundary between Maine and Canada. That treaty provided, in effect, for the cession of territory which had been claimed since the previous century as a part of Maine. The 1842 treaty demonstrated that the treaty-making power could cede to a foreign power territory within the limits of a state. In the case of the 1842 treaty, the cession was made with the consent of the state concerned. Secretary of State Webster wrote the governor of Maine that he entertained "not the slightest doubt of the just authority of this government to settle this question." As a matter of prudence, however, he thought it best not "to stir in the direction of a compromise without the consent of Maine." [102]

The constitutional picture in this respect was completed with the Treaty of Guadalupe Hidalgo, ending the Mexican war. For the first time, the United States had acquired territory by conquest, and the legal instrument of such acquisition was the peace treaty itself. The authority of the nation thus to acquire territory by conquest was affirmed soon thereafter in *Fleming* v. *Page*. "The United States," said Chief Justice Taney in that case, "may extend its boundaries by conquest . . . , and may demand the cession of territory as the condition of peace." [103]

CONGRESSIONAL DECLINE

If there is one thing that has consistently disturbed students of the American polity, it has been deterioration in the legislative department. The grosser manifestations of congressional decay—the generally low caliber of legislative personnel, the venality and conflicts of interest that permeate Capitol Hill, the common attitude toward congressmen as reflected in popular humor—have been themes in virtually all accounts of Congress in action. Here, as in other areas of American life, the impact of Jacksonian democracy was not entirely beneficial. On the contrary, the quality of popular representation seemed to sink as the full effects of manhood suffrage were felt. [104]

Virtually all observers of the American scene a century and a quarter ago concurred in their estimate of the "slender abilities" [105] of the men

---

[102] Quoted in 2 *C.C. Hyde, International Law* 1400 (1945). Chief Justice Marshall was also of the view that the treaty power extended to cessions of state territory. See *Life and Letters of Joseph Story* 288 (W. Story ed. 1851).

[103] 9 How. 603, 614–15 (U.S. 1850).

[104] *White, supra* note 17, at 25.

[105] 2 *A. de Tocqueville, Democracy in America* 97 (P. Bradley ed. 1954).

who sat in the Capitol. Visiting our legislative chambers in the 1840s, Charles Dickens asked, "Where sat the many legislators of coarse threats; of words and blows such as coal heavers deal upon each other, when they forget their breeding? On every side . . . Dishonest Faction in its most depraved and most unblushing form, stared out from every corner of the crowded hall." [106]

And yet every American schoolboy knows that this was also the age of giants in the national assembly, when men like Clay, Calhoun, Benton, and above all, Webster—no man was ever as great as Webster looked!—trod the legislative stage. Rarely have there been leaders on Capitol Hill to compare in caliber with those who dominated the congressional scene from the 1830s to the early 1850s. "They are striking men to look at, hard to deceive, prompt to act, lions in energy, Crichtons in varied accomplishments, Indians in fire of eye and gesture, Americans in strong and generous impulse; and they as well represent the honour and wisdom of their country at home, as the distinguished gentleman who is now its minister at the British Court sustains its highest character abroad." [107]

The giants like Webster and Calhoun, nevertheless, were only the apex of the congressional iceberg. Below them was a mass of members who fully justified De Tocqueville's description: "On entering the House of Representatives, one is struck by the vulgar demeanor of that great assembly. . . . Its members are almost all obscure individuals." [108] If this was the age of Clay and John Quincy Adams, it was equally the age of "Sausage" Sawyer, House member from Ohio, who earned his sobriquet by happily munching sausages at the speaker's rostrum. [109] It was that worthy who, on May 11, 1846 (the day on which Polk sent his message asking for a declaration of war to Capitol Hill), moved the abolition of West Point as "this wasteful squandering of the public money." Sawyer had to concede that, with war imminent, "a momentous crisis is upon us." But, he went on, with the fervor of the congressional *non sequitur,* "this is not the time to be looking after appropriations for the support of students at a military institution." [110]

Every session had its anecdotes of improper conduct, with the actors all there in the legislative chamber. Comparing the congressional scene after Jackson's election with that before 1829, one observer concludes, "Drunkenness was more common, partisanship more unreasonable,

106 *Charles Dickens, American Notes* Ch. 8 (1842).

107 *Id.*

108 1 *De Tocqueville, supra* note 105, at 211.

109 *See G.G. Van Deusen, The Jacksonian Era, 1828–1848,* at 167 (1959).

110 *Cong. Globe* Appendix, 29th Cong., 1st Sess. 585.

debate more personal, and corruption more widely suspected." [111]
Champagne could be had in the Senate cloakroom, and its cost was
charged against the stationery fund until in the early 1840s President
pro tem. Willie P. Mangum had it shifted to the fuel account. [112]

Contributing to the general picture of legislative deterioration was
the growing frequency of violence and unseemly personal squabbles.
The famous scene in which Charles Sumner was beaten within an inch
of his life on the Senate floor has become a part of the pre-Civil War
historical heritage, yet such physical altercations were by no means
uncommon on Capitol Hill. They ranged from the trading of blows
between members, such as the fist fight between Congressmen George
O. Rathbun and John White in 1844 (broken up by a pistol fired by
another member) [113] to the free-for-all that took place in the House in
1857 in the debate over the Kansas question. [114]

Over all hung the cloud of corruption, scarcely dissipated by the fact
that the widespread suspicions in the matter were rarely supported by
proof. This was the age when lobbyists first appeared and a Sam Ward
could be widely known as "King of the Lobby." [115] By 1859 Jefferson
Davis declared, on the Senate floor, "I hold it to be a curse in
legislation, that such things as lobby men can ever be tolerated about
either of the two Houses of Congress." [116] In 1853 members of
Congress were forbidden by statute to receive compensation for prose-
cuting any claim against the government, and it was made a crime to
attempt to bribe them. [117] In 1857 four members were recommended
for expulsion by a House select committee. [118] A year later, Francis
Wharton asserted that politicians were publicly bought and sold "at the
Washington brokers' board . . . like fancy railroad stock or copper-mine
shares." [119]

The congressional decline made it possible for a strong president like
Jackson (and, to a lesser degree, Polk) to make his mark more effectively; the falling legislative prestige facilitated the growth of the notion
that the president must speak as direct representative of all the people.
More important perhaps was the fact that the deterioration of Congress

[111] *White, supra* note 17, at 25.

[112] *See White, supra* note 17, at 26; *Van Deusen, supra* note 109, at 167.

[113] *See Van Deusen, supra* note 109, at 168.

[114] *See Poore, supra* note 83, at 532-35.

[115] *Cong. Globe,* 35th Cong., 2d Sess. 864.

[116] *See R. Steele, Sam Ward, King of the Lobby* (1965)

[117] 10 Stat. 170 (1853).

[118] *Cong. Globe,* 34th Cong., 3d Sess. 760 *et seq.*

[119] Quoted in *White, supra* note 17, at 27.

made that body scarcely suited to fill the political vacuum left by the low level of most of the post-Jackson presidents. Under presidents like Pierce and Buchanan congressional inadequacy may have saved our system from a Capitol Hill Signory that would have stultified national development as much as did its Venetian original. Instead, the paramount principle remained that of separation of powers between more or less equal departments, with the checks and balances between them continuing to serve as the essential safeguard for the proper functioning of the polity.

CHAPTER FOUR

States' Rights and Slavery

MADISON AND NULLIFICATION

Just before his death in 1836, James Madison dictated to his wife a last message to his countrymen, which, he said, "may be considered as coming from the tomb": "The advice nearest to my heart and deepest in my convictions is that the Union of the States be cherished and perpetuated."[1] Toward the end of his long life, Madison had been a witness to events which case doubt on the continued viability of the federal polity which he had helped so much to create. "Hitherto hasty observers, and unfriendly prophets," he noted in an 1835 letter, "have regarded the Union as too frail to last, and to be split at no distant day."[2] In what may have been his last letter, he himself conceded that "it cannot be denied that there are in the aspect our country presents, Phenomena of an ill omen." The Madisonian misgivings were caused by the conflict between state and federal power that was a principal theme of our early constitutional history, "I have witnessed, also," Madison could write in this last letter, "the vicissitudes, in the apparent tendencies in the Federal and State Governments to encroach each on the authorities of the other."[3] Before Sumter, nation and states appeared

---

[1] 9 *The Writings of James Madison* 610 (G. Hunt ed. 1910).

[2] Letter from James Madison to Daniel Drake, Jan. 12, 1835, *id.* at 547.

[3] Letter from James Madison to ———, Mar. 1836, *id.* at 610, 609.

all too often to confront each other as equals, and all was overshadowed by the danger that centrifugal forces would tear the nation apart.[4]

Toward the end of Madison's life, the basic issues involved in the federal-state problem were crystallized in the nullification controversy with South Carolina during Jackson's second term. Nullification was an attempt to push the doctrine of state sovereignty to one of its logical extremes. "You may cover whole skins of parchment with limitations," John Randolph of Roanoke (one of the intellectual fathers of the nullifiers) had declared, "but power alone can limit power."[5] Federal power could only be restrained by state power independently exercised. Such state power alone, it was asserted, vested in governments endowed with the status of coequal sovereigns, could protect the people against the encroaching nature of federal authority.

State sovereignty was the foundation stone of nullification.[6] Like all extreme states' rights doctrines, it was based on the claim that the states were separate sovereignties whose sovereign rights had not been impaired by adherence to the Union. The foundation of that claim was the assertion that the Constitution was a mere compact among the several states which left them with their sovereignty unimpaired, free to meet federal power with their own authority. Carried to its limits, this approach leads to the assertion that the states need not obey federal laws which they regard as improper. Instead, "a single State may rightfully resist an unconstitutional and tyrannical law of the U.S."[7] As explained by Madison in 1835–1836, under the nullification doctrine "it is asserted, that a single State has a constitutional right to arrest the execution of a law of the U.S. within its limits; that the arrest is to be presumed right and valid, and is to remain in force unless ¾ of the States, in a Convention, shall otherwise decide."[8]

To be sure, the immediate nullification controversy with South Carolina had been settled by President Jackson's resolute action—"nullification is dead," he exulted in a letter to his old comrade in arms John Coffee once the crisis had passed.[9] Yet even Jackson knew that the controversy over state sovereignty had not been ended by South Carolina's repeal of the nullification ordinance. In his heart, he may have felt that "the good sense of the people"[10] would prevent the issue

---

[4] *Compare R.G. McCloskey, The American Supreme Court* 102 (1960).

[5] Quoted in *A.M. Schlesinger, Jr., The Age of Jackson* 34 (1945).

[6] *See A.O. Spain, The Political Theory of John C. Calhoun* 19 (1951).

[7] *Madison, Notes on Nullification, supra* note 1, at 574.

[8] *Madison, supra* note 1, at 573.

[9] Letter from Andrew Jackson to John Coffee, Apr. 9, 1833, 5 *J.S. Bassett, The Correspondence of Andrew Jackson* 56 (1933).

[10] Letter from Andrew Jackson to John Coffee, July 17, 1832, 4 *id.* at 462.

from being resolved by force of arms. "I do not believe," he wrote privately at the height of the dispute, "that the nullifiers will have the madness & folly to attempt to carry their mad schemes into operation,"[11] but he had to acknowledge the extent to which the states' rights philosophy had taken hold even among those who did not openly support the South Carolina stand. "There are more nullifiers here," Jackson wrote from Washington, "than dare openly avow it."[12]

To Madison, spending the last years of his life at Montpelier, the controversy must have been particularly distasteful. Not only did he look upon nullification as a "disguised enemy" to the Union, comparable to "the serpent creeping with his deadly wiles into Paradise,"[13] but, he also saw himself named as one of its intellectual progenitors. The doctrinal seeds of nullification were sown in the Kentucky and Virginia resolutions of 1798 and 1799, which were drafted by Jefferson and Madison, respectively. The Madison-drafted Virginia resolutions expressly affirm that the Constitution is a compact, to which the states are parties; federal powers are limited by "the plain sense and intention" of that compact. And "in case of deliberate, palpable, and dangerous exercise of other powers not granted by the said compact, the states, who are parties thereto, have the right, and are in duty bound, to interpose, for arresting the progress of the evil, and for maintaining, within their respective limits, the authorities, rights, and liberties appertaining to them."[14]

The doctrine thus stated is plainly incompatible with the perpetual, more perfect Union envisaged by the Framers. At the same time, it is fair to say that neither Jefferson nor Madison ever intended to go so far as some of their unguarded language appears to indicate. Their resolutions were prompted by the now-notorious Alien and Sedition Laws of 1798, and their purpose was as much propagandist as was that of the laws they were attacking. Madison himself took pains to indicate that this was the case once he understood the implications of the nullification doctrine. Speaking of "the nullifying party" (in a letter not contained in his published writings), he asserted, "At all events, if an effective Govt., or the Union itself, is to be maintained, a triumph of that party in a scheme fatal to both, must not be permitted."[15] In a

---

[11] Letter from Andrew Jackson to John Coffee, Aug. 18, 1832, Charles Hamilton, Auction No. 14, Item 186 (1966).

[12] Letter from Andrew Jackson to Rev. Hardy M. Cryer, Feb. 20, 1833, 5 *Bassett, supra* note 9, at 19.

[13] *Madison, supra* note 1, at 611.

[14] 4 J. Elliott, *Debates in the Several State Conventions on the Adoption of the Federal Constitution* 528 (1859).

[15] Letter from James Madison to Nicholas P. Trist, Dec. 4, 1832, Parke-Bernet Galleries, Sale No. 2310, Item 86 (1964).

series of letters written during the 1830s, he strongly denied that the resolutions written by him and Jefferson gave any basis for the nullification doctrine. The states, he affirmed, are "mutually and equally bound" to the Constitution, "and certainly there is nothing in the Virginia resolutions of −98, adverse to this principle."[16]

One of the last documents left by Madison was his *Notes on Nullification,* written in 1835–1836, a lengthy essay designed to emphasize "the forbidding aspect of a naked creed." In it, Madison repeated his denial that his Virginia resolutions were intended to support any such extreme doctrine as nullification; he gave a detailed analysis of the resolutions to support his position. About the invalidity of nullification itself he had no doubts: "it follows, from no view of the subject, that a nullification of a law of the U.S. can as is now contended, belong rightfully to a single State. . . . A plainer contradiction in terms, or a more fatal inlet to anarchy, cannot be imagined."[17]

Despite the Madisonian disclaimer, the resolutions drafted by Madison and Jefferson did provide the logical foundation on which the later doctrines of John C. Calhoun and Jefferson Davis grew. In them the extreme states' rights outlook received a constitutional creed which, a generation later, was to become (at least in the South) a gloss upon the basic document believed as authoritative as the original Constitution itself. "Those resolutions . . . ," affirmed John Marshall in 1833, "constitute the creed of every politician, who hopes to rise in Virginia; and to question them . . . is deemed political sacrilege."[18]

CALHOUN AND STATES' RIGHTS

The words used in the Kentucky and Virginia resolutions were given extreme states' rights connotations by John C. Calhoun. To one interested in the development of constitutional doctrine, Calhoun is of particular interest even though today he seems a forbidding figure, both because of the coldness of his character and because he was an apostle of futility. The verdict of history has been so conclusively unfavorable to his doctrines that it may be difficult for the constitutional student even to take them seriously today.

In 1846 Calhoun declared, "If you should ask me the question [what] I would wish engraved on my tombstone, it is *Nullification.*"[19]

---

[16] Letter from James Madison to Nicholas P. Trist, Dec. 23, 1832, *supra* note 1, at 490.

[17] *Madison, supra* note 1, at 573, 575.

[18] Letter from John Marshall to Joseph Story, July 31, 1833, 2 *Life and Letters of Joseph Story* 135–36 (W. Story ed. 1851).

[19] Quoted in *M. L. Coit, John C. Calhoun* 421 (1950).

The crisis was then thirteen years past, but it still held the key to Calhoun's constitutional philosophy. During the 1840s he wrote two volumes[20] greatly expanding upon his famous *Exposition and Protest,* which had furnished the doctrinal basis for the nullification movement in 1828. To the books referred to, he literally gave his last days and almost his last hours.[21] They contain the essence of his political theories and, with his *Exposition,* provide the most complete statement of the doctrine of states' rights that, carried to its logical extreme, was soon to divide the nation.

To its opponents, nullification appeared to be a doctrine of anarchy. Writing in his diary of Calhoun's 1833 Senate speech defending nullification, John Quincy Adams acidly observed, "His learning is shallow, his mind argumentative, and his assumptions of principle destitute of discernment. His insanity begins with his principles from which his deductions are ingeniously drawn."[22] In 1839 he explained the spread of Calhoun's doctrine in terms of the weakness of the human mind: "There is an obliquity of the reasoning faculty, a broken link in the chain of logical deduction, in every mind which can bring itself, or be brought, to the sincere belief of the nullification doctrines."[23]

There was surely more to the Calhoun philosophy than that; human frailty alone can scarcely explain the speed with which it was accepted as constitutional dogma in a large part of the country. Calhoun gave doctrinal voice to a view of the American constitutional system that, from the outset, was sharply opposed to the Federalist philosophy of national supremacy. That philosophy, to exponents of his view, was heresy introduced into the fundamental law. Speaking to a reporter in 1849, Calhoun complained that newspapers, in reporting his speeches, "make me say 'this Nation' instead of 'this Union.' I never use the word Nation. We are not a nation, but a Union, a confederacy of equal and sovereign States. England is a nation, but the United States are not a nation."[24] The general government was thus not a national government; it was a confederated government, a political union to which the confederated states were parties.[25] "It is an acknowledged principle that sovereigns may by compact modify or qualify the exercise of their power, without impairing their sovereignty, of which the confederacy existing at the time furnishes a striking illustration."[26]

20 *J.C. Calhoun, Disquisition on Government* and *A Discourse on the Constitution and Government of the United States* (1854).

21 *See Coit, supra* note 19, at 518.

22 8 *Memoirs of John Quincy Adams* 536 (C.F. Adams ed. 1876).

23 10 *id.* at 168.

24 Quoted in *Coit, supra* note 19, at 461.

25 *See* 1 A. Nevins, *Ordeal of the Union* 155 (1947).

26 1 *The Works of John C. Calhoun* 139 (R.K. Crallé ed. 1857).

In assessing Calhoun's theory, it is important not to confuse nullification with secession; they were distinct doctrines, though both rested on state sovereignty.[27] As it was explained in 1840 by Abel P. Upshur, "The nullifier contends only for the right of a state to prevent the constitution from being violated by the general government.... The seceder insists only that a State is competent to withdraw from the Union whenever it pleases."[28] Nullification was not secession, but rather (to men like Calhoun) a means of conserving the Union in its original character.[29]

By 1850, however, Calhoun saw that his notion of the constitutional system was no longer consistent with reality. In his last great Senate speech—delivered on March 4, 1850, only a few weeks before his death—the Carolinian asserted that the equilibrium intended by the Framers had been all but destroyed. That was true because of the action of the federal government "leading to a radical change in its character, by concentrating all the power of the system in itself." Not only that, but "the Government claims, and practically maintains, the right to decide in the last resort as to the extent of its powers." In addition, the federal government asserts the right to use force to maintain its powers. "Now, I ask, what limitation can possibly be placed upon the powers of a Government claiming and exercising such rights?"[30] The result, he declared, was that "the character of the Government has been changed ... from a Federal Republic, as it originally came from the hands of its framers, and that it has been changed into a great national consolidated Democracy ... as absolute as that of the Autocrat of Russia, and as despotic in its tendency as any absolute Government that ever existed."[31]

How to restore the equilibrium which the growth of national power had thus disturbed? Calhoun's answer was his "concurrent majority" theory, perhaps his most original contribution to political philosophy. Anticipating Lord Acton's famed aphorism, he declared that "government ... has itself a strong tendency to ... abuse of its powers."[32] This tendency can be counteracted only by machinery "to equalize the action of the government, in reference to the various and diversified interests of the community."[33] The way to accomplish this is to

27 *See Spain, supra* note 6, at 205.

28 *A.P. Upshur, A Brief Enquiry into the True Nature and Character of Our Federal Government* 66 (1863).

29 *See Spain, supra* note 6, at 204.

30 *Cong. Globe,* 31st Cong., 1st Sess. 452.

31 *Id.; see C.M. Wiltse, John C. Calhoun: Sectionalist, 1840–1850,* at 460–65 (1951).

32 *Calhoun, supra* note 20, at 7. *See,* similarly, 6 *Calhoun, supra* note 26, at 29.

33 *Calhoun, supra* note 20, at 15.

substitute the "concurrent" for the numerical majority, to ascertain the sense of the community not by merely counting heads but by "considering the community as made up of different and competing interests," and then by taking "the sense of each, through its majority or appropriate organ, and the united sense of all, as the sense of the entire community."[34] As applied to the nation, this would protect the minority from selfish action of the majority: major issues between the sections would be decided only by agreement of a majority of both sections.[35]

The "concurrent majority" theory was first stated in Calhoun's *Disquisition on Government.* A few years later, in his Senate speech of March 4, 1850, however, he admitted that, under the Constitution itself, nothing could be done to redress the balance in favor of the states. Only by an amendment could the power of the states to protect themselves be restored to what it was "before the equilibrium . . . was destroyed by the action of this Government."[36] He had come to see that the extreme states' rights theory was a constitutional cul-de-sac. Unless the nature of the Union itself were changed, it was legally hopeless to argue on the basis of state sovereignty. As Madison put it just after the nullification crisis ended, "the words of the Constitution are explicit" in providing for federal supremacy: "Without a supremacy in those respects it would be like a scabbard in the hand of a soldier without a sword in it."[37]

To Calhoun and his compatriots, nevertheless, the letter of the Constitution was but a small part of the picture. They felt an emotional attachment to their states which could scarcely be affected, much less dispelled, by legal reasoning. When Calhoun spoke of his "dear and honored State" which "has never mistrusted nor forsaken me," he is said to have "hung upon her devotion with all the tenderness . . . with which a lover dwells upon the constancy of his mistress."[38] It was only natural that such devotees should seek to associate with the states the almost mystical attributes connected with the term sovereignty. The states may, in the light of cold fact, have been only provinces whose sovereignty had never been real, but they were still bodies which, with all their limitations, had something of the magic of Athens and Rome, of Venice and Florence. "The word 'State Rights' . . . ," declared John Marshall in 1833, "has a charm against which all reasoning is vain."[39]

---

[34] *Calhoun, supra note 20, at 28.*

[35] *C. Eaton, The Growth of Southern Civilization, 1790–1860,* at 310–11 (1961).

[36] *Cong. Globe,* 31st Cong., 1st Sess. 455.

[37] Letter from James Madison to William Cabell Rives, Mar. 12, 1833, *supra* note 1, at 512.

[38] Quoted in *Coit, supra* note 19, at 421.

[39] Letter from John Marshall to Joseph Story, July 31, 1833, 2 *Story, supra* note 18, at 135.

THE SLAVERY ISSUE

States' rights, pushed to its extreme, contains within itself the seeds of dissolution of the Union. Sovereign consent to a compact must, from the very nature of sovereignty, be consent that can be withdrawn at will: "The terms or conditions of the union were stipulated in the Constitution, and if they were violated, the parties to the compact had a right to withdraw from their engagement."[40] The ultimate right of each adhering sovereign thus comes down to a right of secession. Hence, Madison could characterize the extreme states' rights doctrine as having "the effect of putting powder under the Constitution & Union, and a match in the hand of every party, to blow them up at pleasure."[41]

Two points should be noted about the states' rights doctrine during the period before the Civil War. The first is the fact that employment of the doctrine, from the beginning, depended primarily upon whose ox was being gored. The creed enunciated in the Kentucky and Virginia resolutions was relied upon in New England, when the harsh impact upon the northeast of the embargo and War of 1812 led to the Hartford Convention and assertion by its more extreme members of a right of secession. At that time it was the South, led by Calhoun himself, which vigorously supported federal power. The toast at a noted Richmond dinner then was "the Union of the States. . . . It is treason to secede."[42]

Sectional sentiment was soon to shift, as the South came to feel aggrieved by growing federal authority. By the time of the nullification controversy, it was southern thinkers who came to base their views on the states' rights approach, though most of them did not yet assert it to the extreme of succession. But it is a mistake to assume that this meant that thenceforth there would be a consistent division between the South and the rest of the country on the issue of state versus federal power. On the contrary, the different sections continued to support the constitutional theory that would best serve their immediate interests. This can be seen from the controversy over enforcement of the Fugitive Slave Act. As far as that law was concerned, it was the South which was the advocate of extreme federal power, while northern states opposing the statute relied upon the states' rights philosophy, even going as far as the nullifiers themselves in asserting a state power to frustrate enforcement of federal law.

---

40 *Nevins, supra* note 25.
41 Letter from James Madison to Edward Coles, Aug. 29, 1834, *supra* note 1, at 540.
42 5 *E. Channing, A History of the United States* 405 (1921).

The second point to be noted about states' rights in this period is the pernicious connection between the doctrine and slavery. It may be doubted that states' rights alone would have had the direful consequences that it did had it not become inextricably intertwined with the slavery issue. Slavery was the distorting element that exercised a kind of hydraulic pressure: it made what was previously clear seem doubtful, and before it even settled principles had to shift.[43]

Long before the middle of the century, the fateful connection between the two had become apparent. Calhoun began his March 4, 1850, speech with words of despair: "I have, Senators, believed from the first that the agitation of the subject of slavery would, if not prevented . . . end in disunion." The slavery issue had become the rock upon which the Union itself might break. "Is it, then, not certain," Calhoun went on to ask, "that if something decisive is not now done to arrest it, the South will be forced to choose between abolition and secession?"[44]

If we are to understand the cardinal role which slavery played in pre-Civil War constitutional history, we must not make the mistake of looking at the peculiar institution through the deforming lenses of present-day conceptions. It is all but impossible today to conceive how thoroughly slavery had permeated American law and life before the Civil War. Even a bitter opponent of slavery like John Quincy Adams, in a letter written to a leading abolitionist, could refer casually to slaves as "live stock."[45] In the South, of course, slavery had become part of the economic and social fabric, and it should not be assumed that southern leaders were placed on the moral defensive because of their reliance upon it. On the contrary, from an earlier deprecating attitude which conceded that it was a necessary evil (at least as an abstract proposition), the southern posture shifted, during the 1830s and 1840s, to a vigorous pro-slavery position. By the 1850s the pro-slavery argument had become an increasingly militant element in the southern polemic.

Speaking in the Senate in 1838, Calhoun noted that "the South had been assailed upon the principle that slavery was wicked, and immoral."[46] Its opponents had chosen to fight the institution on moral grounds, and the South felt it necessary to meet such opponents on their own ground. "Many in the South," Calhoun declared in a Senate

[43] Compare Holmes, J., dissenting, in Northern Securities Co. v. United States, 193 U.S. 197, 400 (1904).

[44] *Cong. Globe*, 31st Cong., 1st Sess. 451, 453.

[45] Letter from John Quincy Adams to Gerrit Smith, July 31, 1839, Charles Hamilton, Auction No. 10, Item la (1965).

[46] *Cong. Globe*, 25th Cong., 2d Sess. 74.

speech at the end of 1837, "once believed that it was a moral and political evil. We see it now in its true light and regard it now as the most safe and stable oasis for free institutions in the world."[47] In his *Disquisition on Government* he spelled out his repudiation of the concept of the equality of man; he denied that equality was a necessary basis for a sound polity: "to go further, and make equality . . . essential to liberty, would be to destroy both liberty and progress."[48]

What makes all this more than aberrational support for a lost cause, repudiated alike by logic and ethic, was the takeover by pro-slavery militants of the states' rights doctrine, with all that that meant for constitutional theory and practice. Confined to matters such as the embargo or the tariff, states' rights sentiment could only agitate but scarcely disrupt the steady course of constitutional development. Joined to an issue as emotional as that of the institution upon which the South felt that its very way of life depended, states' rights became a doctrine upon which the Union itself might founder.

THE GAG RULE

The South's justification of slavery was not provoked solely by the attack of the abolitionists;[49] all the features of the pro-slavery argument were already in circulation before the rise of militant abolitionism in the 1830s.[50] Yet the South itself came to feel that "the impertinent interference of Abolitionists . . . provoked us to argument,"[51] and the Garrisonian crusade was, without doubt, the immediate catalyst that led to direct confrontation on the legal issues connected with slavery. William Lloyd Garrison had sounded the emotional tocsin in the first issue of *The Liberator*—"tell a man whose house is on fire, to give a moderate alarm"—and his attack on moderation increasingly set the tone for the whole of the slavery controversy.

A direct result of the agitation for abolition was the sending of innumerable petitions to Congress for the ending of slavery in the District of Columbia, as well as for other antislavery action. The growing volume of petitions[52] provoked southern anger. At the end of

---

47 3 *Calhoun, supra* note 26, at 180.

48 *Calhoun, supra* note 20, at 56.

49 *See R.B. Nye, Fettered Freedom: Civil Liberties and the Slavery Controversy 1830–1860,* at 20 (1963); *W.W. Freehling, Prelude to Civil War: The Nullification Controversy in South Carolina* 357–58 (1966).

50 *Hesseltine, Sections and Politics* 71 (1968).

51 Richmond Enquirer, Oct. 17, 1857, quoted in *Nye, supra* note 49, at 21.

52 According to *Nye, supra* note 49, at 47, there were 412,000 petitions filed in 1837–1838.

1835, a South Carolina member of the House moved that a petition to abolish slavery in the District not be received, saying that "he wished to put an end to these petitions. He could not sit there and see the rights of the Southern people assaulted day after day, by the ignorant fanatics from whom these memorials proceed."[53]

The ultimate result, after several months of debate and committee consideration, was the passage by the House in May, 1836, of the so-called Gag Rule providing that all petitions relating to slavery "shall, without being either printed or referred, be laid upon the table, and that no further action whatever shall be had thereon." Though the gag resolution passed by a large majority, it was bitterly opposed by John Quincy Adams, who declared, when called upon to vote, "I hold the resolution to be a direct violation of the constitution. . . , the rules of this House, and the rights of my constituents."[54] Amid loud cries of "order" from all parts of the hall, Adams thus began his opposition to the congressional attempt to stifle discussion of the slavery issue. In many ways, this was the most noble part of Adams' long career of public service. Year after year, at times all but alone, he fought for repeal of the Gag Rule, despite the threats of censure and expulsion from the House directed at him by slavery supporters.

What makes the Adams crusade of particular interest is the fact that he himself, opponent of slavery though he was, did not agree with the substance of the petitions calling for abolition in the District of Columbia which were sent to him in increasing numbers for submission to the House.[55] In an 1839 letter to Gerrit Smith, the abolitionist, Adams stated "the unqualified declaration of my opinion that the immediate abolition of slavery in the District of Columbia . . . , by act of Congress, is utterly unpracticable and would be eminently unjust." To the claim of his correspondent that God was for immediate abolition, Adams wrote that he was "firmly convinced . . . that the immediate emancipation of Slaves, whether throughout the United States, or in the District of Columbia . . . is *not* the present will of God. I can only lament that our religious impressions upon these points differ so essentially that I see no prospect of their ever harmonizing in this life."[56]

Adams' personal opposition to immediate abolition in the District of Columbia did not diminish; on the contrary, it became "from day to day more firmly fixed in my mind,"[57] but this did not affect his

---

[53] *Reg. of Deb.*, 24th Cong., 1st Sess. 1967.

[54] *Id.* at 4052–53.

[55] *Compare Nye, supra* note 49, at 48.

[56] Letter from John Quincy Adams to Gerrit Smith, July 31, 1839, Charles Hamilton, Auction No. 10, Item la (1965).

[57] *Id.*

readiness to serve as the medium for the transmission of abolition petitions to the House. As the years passed, he presented an ever-increasing flood of petitions—on one occasion he put in as many as 511 at a time.[58] In 1837 Adams explained that "from the time I entered this house down to the present day, I have felt it a duty to present any petition . . . from any citizen . . . ; be the prayer of it that in which I could concur, or that to which I was utterly opposed. It is for the sacredness of the right of petition that I have adopted this course."[59] There was, in the Adams view, a basic distinction between the right to present a petition and have it considered and the substance of the petition itself.[60] "I contend," he urged in the House in 1838, "that the . . . reason for which anyone can rightly reject a petition is the impropriety of granting the prayer it contains."[61] But the petition should be received and considered before being rejected on its merits.

From a constitutional point of view, Adams was correct in his opposition to the Gag Rule as an undue abridgement of the right of petition—"a right . . . not given by parchment, but prior to the constitution; given by the God of Nature, to every man when he created him; it is the right to implore favor, to seek for mercy! a right which the framers of our constitution would have spurned the very idea of abridging or limiting."[62] The First Amendment itself expressly recognizes "the right of the People . . . to petition the Government," but the right is far older than the First Amendment, going back to Magna Carta itself. In 1669, the House of Commons resolved that every Englishman possessed "the inherent right to prepare and present petitions" to it "in case of grievances,"[63] and the Bill of Rights of 1689 expressly confirmed the right of subjects to petition the Crown. In America, too, the right of petition was regarded as a natural right. The 1765 Declaration of Rights and Grievances passed by the Stamp Act Congress asserted "the right of the British subjects . . . to petition the King or either House of parliament."[64]

Supporters of the Gag Rule, however, urged that the Congress had the power to refuse to act on petitions sent to it where the petitions concerned a matter over which Congress itself had no authority, i.e., emancipation in the District of Columbia. Leaving aside the issue of

---

[58] *Channing, supra* note 42, at 167.

[59] *Reg. of Deb.,* 24th Cong., 2d Sess. 1595.

[60] *See Nye, supra* note 49, at 52.

[61] Quoted in *Nye, supra* note 49, at 52.

[62] *Reg. of Deb.,* 24th Cong., 2d Sess. 1674.

[63] *C.G. Robertson, Select Cases and Documents To Illustrate English Constitutional History* 27 (1935 ed.).

[64] *See* 1 B. Schwartz, *The Bill of Rights: A Documentary History* 198 (1971).

congressional power to abolish slavery in the District, one may doubt that the right of petition is secured under a flat rule which absolutely bars in advance any petition on a given subject from consideration. The constitutional right to petition is more than the right to send in supplications; it must, if it is not an empty form, carry with it the right of having those supplications received. As Webster put it in an 1838 letter, "Wherever there is a constitutional right of petition, it seems to me to be quite clear, that it is the duty of those to whom petitions are addressed, to read and consider them; otherwise the whole right of petition is but a vain illusion and a mockery."[65] Absolutely to refuse to receive petitions is to violate the constitutional right of petition itself.[66]

The Gag Rule was readopted in substance in succeeding sessions, over Adams' outspoken opposition, and, in January, 1840, it became a standing rule of the House, providing that anti-slavery petitions "shall not be received by this House, not entertained in any way whatever."[67] At each session, however, the majority against Adams steadily decreased, until, at the end of 1844, when Adams once again moved a resolution to rescind the rule, "the question was then put on the resolution; and it was carried— . . . Blessed, forever blessed, be the name of God!"[68]

As it turned out, the fight over the Gag Rule worked great harm to the slavery cause. As is so often the case, suppression of freedom of expression accomplished precisely the opposite result from that intended by its proponents. Calhoun, in discussing a similar problem in the Senate, declared that southern legislators had to meet the attack of "the fanatics who have flooded this and the other House with their petitions. . . . we must meet the enemy on the frontier, on the question of receiving; we must secure that important pass—it is our Thermopylae."[69] But the cause of slavery could scarcely be saved by enforced silence. The Gag Rule, with its utter prostration of petition[70] — "Beware how you make a martyr to the right of petition!" a southerner warned during one of the House attacks on Adams[71] —served only to link the repression of free expression with the slavery cause and, as such, further to sharpen sectional and ideological divisions.

[65] Letter from Daniel Webster to Mr. Peck, Jan. 11, 1838, 18 *The Writings and Speeches of Daniel Webster* 33 (1903).

[66] *Compare* Henry Clay, *Reg. of Deb.*, 24th Cong., 1st Sess. 779.

[67] Quoted in *Nye, supra* note 49, at 51.

[68] 12 *Adams, supra* note 22, at 116.

[69] *Reg. of Deb.*, 24th Cong., 1st Sess. 774–75.

[70] So characterized in 10 *Adams, supra* note 22, at 527.

[71] Quoted in *Nye, supra* note 49, at 65.

SUPPRESSION OF MAIL

"A young man, named Ralph Waldo Emerson . . . ," confided John Quincy Adams to his diary in 1840, "starts a new doctrine of transcendentalism, . . . and announces the approach of new revelations and prophecies. Garrison and the non-resistant abolitionists, Brownson and the Marat democrats, phrenology and animal magnetism, all come in, furnishing each some plausible rascality as an ingredient for the bubbling cauldron of religion and politics."[72]

The growth of militant abolitionism and the extreme reaction of the South fanned the flames that brought the political cauldron to a boil in the 1830s and 1840s. Abolitionism, based as it was upon a union of politics and morality, had all the fervor of a religious crusade, particularly in the proselytizing zeal of its adherents, but the South was becoming increasingly hostile to any attacks upon its basic institution. The propaganda of the abolitionists was considered a direct threat to the stability of southern society, especially after Nat Turner's insurrection in 1831, which left the South in a state of terror, living, as it now seemed, under the constant threat of slave uprisings.

The founding of Garrison's *Liberator* and the Turner revolt came in the same year (1831), and the coincidence led to repressive measures throughout the South. State after state restricted slave movements and other activities, prohibited the teaching of slaves to read and write, and passed other oppressive legislation. Among these were laws designed to prevent the circulation of incendiary publications. Several statutes went so far as to prescribe the death penalty for violators. In South Carolina, where tempers were still frayed over the nullification controversy, local sentiment was indignant over abolitionist propaganda. In 1835 a citizens' meeting in Charleston passed resolutions demanding the exclusion of incendiary publications from the mail and appointed a committee to inspect the mails as they arrived. On July 30, 1835, having learned that the mail steamer had brought sacks of abolitionist pamphlets, a Charleston mob broke into the post office and burned the offending material. Numerous meetings and resolutions followed throughout the South. They strongly approved the Charleston action, and some of them urged that all mail be censored to screen out abolitionist literature.

In the meantime, the Charleston postmaster wrote the New York postmaster to send no more abolitionist material. The latter laid the matter before Jackson's postmaster general, Amos Kendall, who asked the president for his opinion. Jackson wrote back, with characteristic

---

[72] 10 *Adams, supra* note 22, at 345.

vigor, that "those inflammatory papers be delivered to none but who will demand them as subscribers; and in every instance the Postmaster ought to take the names down, and have them exposed thro the publik journals as subscribers to this wicked plan of exciting the negroes to insurrection and to massacre."[73] In his annual message of December, 1835, Jackson condemned the circulation of "inflammatory appeals addressed to the passions of the slaves." He urged passage of a law to "prohibit, under severe penalties, the circulation in the Southern States, through the mail, of incendiary publications intended to instigate the slaves to insurrection."[74]

The president's proposal was referred to a Senate special committee chaired by Calhoun. It produced a bill making it unlawful for deputy postmasters "to receive and put into the mail, any pamphlet, newspaper, handbill, or other paper . . . touching the subject of slavery, addressed to any person or post office in any State . . . , where, by the law of the said State, . . . their circulation is prohibited."[75] This bill would have virtually assigned to the Post Office the task of giving effect to the laws of the southern states restricting the circulation of incendiary publications; "the object," said Senator Davis of Massachusetts, "is to transfer from the United States the regulation of the mail and of the Post Office, in these matters, to the States."[76] Calhoun was, in effect, seeking to use the state sovereignty doctrine as a shield for slavery.

Calhoun denied that his measure involved any congressional power to exclude material from the mails, since it was only state laws that were to be enforced. The distinction, however, looked more to form than substance: "if I wish," declared a northern senator, "to send a letter, a paper; yes, sir, the declaration of independence itself, through the Post Office, it must first be scrutinized by a clerk, to ascertain whether it violates the laws of Alabama, Carolina, or some other State; and if, in his opinion, the subject of slavery is touched, so as to offend one of these sweeping laws, I am denied the privilege of the mail."[77]

The Calhoun bill was ultimately defeated.[78] In its place, the northern opposition was able to vote a law prohibiting postmasters from preventing any material from reaching its destination.[79] The law did

[73] Letter from Andrew Jackson to Postmaster General Kendall, Aug. 9, 1835, *Bassett, supra* note 9, at 360–61.

[74] 3 *J.D. Richardson, A Compilation of the Messages and Papers of the Presidents 1789–1897,* at 175, 176 (1896).

[75] *Reg. of Deb.,* 24th Cong., 1st Sess. 383–84. *See C.M. Wiltse, John C. Calhoun: Nullifier, 1829–1839,* at 274–77 (1949).

[76] *Reg. of Deb.,* 24th Cong., 1st Sess. 1103.

[77] *Id.* at 1106.

[78] *Id.* at 1737. A similar bill was defeated in the House; *id.* at 3809.

[79] 5 Stat. 80, 87 (1836).

not really affect the situation in the southern states. Decisions on mail delivery were, in practice, left to the local postmasters, in accordance with Postmaster General Kendall's decision when the problem was first raised in 1835. Kendall then wrote that he would not direct post-masters in the matter, asserting that "we owe an obligation to the laws, but we owe a higher one to the communities in which we live."[80]

Throughout the South, postmasters fulfilled their obligations to their local communities by refusing to deliver what they considered aboli-tionist material. In 1857 the refusal of the deputy postmaster of Yazoo City, Mississippi, to deliver a copy of a Cincinnati newspaper on the ground it contained material which would "produce disaffection, dis-order, and rebellion among the colored population" was challenged because of its alleged conflict with the 1836 federal statute prohibiting non-delivery of mailed matter. The case was presented to Caleb Cushing, Pierce's attorney general. As he saw it, the legal issue raised was whether the 1836 law required the deputy postmaster to deliver mail in violation of the laws of his state. Cushing answered the question in the negative: "On the whole, then, it seems clear to me that a deputy postmaster, or other officer of the United States, is not required by law to become, knowingly, the enforced agent or instrument of enemies of the public peace, to disseminate, in their behalf, within the limits of any one of the States of the Union, printed matter, the design and tendency of which are to promote insurrections in such State."[81] The result was to confirm the discretion of the local postmaster, which Kendall and his successors had recognized in their refusal to issue any binding directions in the matter from Washington. In practice, this meant that the mails in the South, during the quarter-century before the Civil War, were effectively closed to anti-slavery materials.

During the 1836 debate on the matter, Webster attacked Calhoun's proposed bill as a violation of the First Amendment. "What was the liberty of the press? he asked. It was the liberty of printing as well as the liberty of publishing, in all the ordinary modes of publication; and was not the circulation of papers through the mails an ordinary mode of publication?"[82] Freedom of the press must include the right to circulate what has been published. It is true that Congress does possess the general authority to determine what may be carried in the mails. But that authority scarcely includes the broadside power to bar from the mail all publications of a certain character. Such a bar has the effect of a prior restraint on communication contrary to the Constitution.[83]

80 Quoted in *L. Filler, The Crusade against Slavery, 1830–1860,* at 98 (1960).

81 8 *Op. Att'y Gen.* 489, 501 (1857).

82 *Reg. of Deb.,* 24th Cong., 1st Sess. 1721.

83 *See* 4 B. Schwartz, *A Commentary on the Constitution of the United States, Rights of the Person* 390 (1968).

While the government need not operate any postal system, while it does, "the use of the mails is almost as much a part of free speech as the right to use our tongues."[84] In addition, we can say today that the suppression of anti-slavery mail violated the constitutional right to receive mail unrestricted by governmental inhibition.[85]

Like the Gag Rule in Congress, southern suppression of abolitionist literature was treated throughout the North as an unconstitutional imposition of a censorship system. Once again, the slavery cause was linked to repression of free expression. As had been true of the fight over the Gag Rule, the dispute over the mails strengthened the abolitionist cause by merging it with the larger cause of civil liberty.[86] Just as important was its effect on the South itself What that section needed most of all in the pre-Civil War period was the free exercise of the critical spirit, particularly toward slavery.[87] Instead, it was becoming increasingly insulated against ideas which questioned the accepted order.

Only a closed society, cut off from the ferment of critical ideas, could hope to set itself against the forces of history by resting upon outgrown constitutional doctrine—to seek at all costs to be keeper of the agrarian conscience in the face of burgeoning industrialism. Now the tie-in between extreme states' rightism and slavery had become crystal clear. In the 1836 debate on his bill to bar incendiary publications from the mail, Calhoun closed by reviving the doctrine of interposition: "If you refuse co-operation with our laws, and conflict should ensue between your and our law, the southern States will never yield to the superiority of yours. We have a remedy in our hands, which, in such event, we shall not fail to apply. We have high authority for asserting that, in such cases, 'State interposition is the rightful remedy.' " [88] Southern laws for the protection of slavery were declared paramount over federal laws regulating the mail, and the banns of wedlock between slavery and state sovereignty were thus formally proclaimed.[89]

THE FUGITIVE SLAVE LAW

Richard Henry Dana, Jr. (known to his contemporaries as a leading lawyer rather than as author of a sea classic), wrote in his diary of the

---

[84] Holmes, J., dissenting, in Milwaukee Publishing Co. v. Burleson, 255 U.S. 407, 437 (1921).

[85] Lamont v. Postmaster General, 381 U.S. 301 (1965).

[86] *Nye, supra* note 49, at 85.

[87] *Compare C. Eaton, The Growth of Southern Civilization, 1790–1860,* at 313 (1961).

[88] *Reg. of Deb.,* 24th Cong., 1st Sess. 1148.

[89] *Compare A.C. McLaughlin, A Constitutional History of the United States* 488 (1935).

decision in the most famous of the fugitive slave cases, that of Anthony Burns in 1854: "Convicted on an *ex parte* record, against the actual evidence, and on his own admission made at the moment of arrest to his alleged master! A tyrannical statute and a weak judge!"[90] The result in the Burns case was virtually compelled by the Fugitive Slave Law[91] —the "tyrannical statute" to which Dana referred—itself the most controversial provision of the Compromise of 1850. The problem of the fugitive slave had been present from the very founding of the republic. The Constitution dealt with the problem by providing that "no person held to Service or Labour in one State, under the Laws thereof, escaping into another, shall, in Consequence of any Law or Regulation therein, be discharged from such Service or Labour, but shall be delivered up on Claim of the Party to whom such Service or Labour may be due."[92]

This constitutional provision was characterized in 1851 by William W. Story as one "which has legalized slavery in our country, and proved the Pandora's box of nearly all our evils."[93] It provided for a positive right on the part of the slaveowner throughout the Union, which no state could control or restrain.[94] The constitutional clause was, however, not self-executing, and, from the beginning, legislation was necessary if it was to be more than a paper provision. In 1793 Congress passed a Fugitive Slave Act, authorizing anyone claiming a fugitive slave to bring him before a federal judge or state magistrate for a certificate authorizing removal to the state from which the fugitive had fled.[95] In operation, the enforcement provisions of the 1793 act did not provide adequate machinery to secure the return of runaways,[96] particularly since state officials and facilities were relied upon for the capture of fugitives. In states where abolitionist sentiment was strong, it proved increasingly difficult to recover escaped slaves.

The enforcement picture was complicated by the enactment in some northern states of "personal liberty laws" designed to protect the rights of alleged fugitives. A law of this type enacted in Pennsylvania in 1826 was challenged in the Supreme Court in *Prigg* v. *Pennsylvania*.[97] A female slave had escaped from her owner in Maryland and crossed into Pennsylvania. The owner sent Prigg to recapture her. Prigg had her

90 *C.F. Adams, Richard Henry Dana* 277 (1891).

91 9 Stat. 462 (1850).

92 Art. IV, § 2.

93 *Story, supra* note 18, at 397.

94 Prigg v. Pennsylvania, 16 Pet. 539, 611 (U.S. 1842).

95 1 Stat. 302 (1793).

96 *See Channing, supra* note 42, at 125–26, 141.

97 16 Pet. 539 (U.S. 1842).

brought as a fugitive slave before a state magistrate, but he refused to hear the case. Prigg thereupon himself returned the woman to Maryland. The case raised a local furor, and Prigg was indicted and found guilty in the Pennsylvania courts of kidnapping, under a state law making it a crime to take away and enslave a Negro. The Supreme Court, in a typically learned opinion by Justice Story, ruled the Pennsylvania statute unconstitutional. The subject of fugitive slaves was held within the exclusive competence of Congress, which alone was vested with the authority to carry out the Fugitive Slave Clause of the Constitution.

At first glance, *Prigg* v. *Pennsylvania* appeared a surrender to the South, for it sustained the federal power to enact fugitive slave laws while, at the same time, striking down state laws furnishing protection for captured Negroes. John Quincy Adams wrote on March 10, 1842, that he had spent the day reading the *Prigg* opinions: "seven judges, every one of them dissenting from the reasoning of all the rest, and every one of them coming to the same conclusion — the transcendent omnipotence of slavery in these United States, riveted by a clause in the Constitution."[98] Justice Story himself saw the *Prigg* decision differently, going so far as to characterize it as "a triumph of freedom"[99] because it not only ruled that the states were without authority to enact legislation on the subject of runaway slaves but also that the states were not required to lend their aid to enforcement of the federal fugitive slave law.

Chief Justice Taney, who dissented, pointed out that the holding that the states were not obliged to aid in enforcement of the Fugitive Slave Act meant the practical nullification of that statute: "Indeed, if the State authorities are absolved from all obligation to protect this right and may stand by and see it violated without an effort to defend it, the Act of Congress of 1793 scarcely deserves the name of a remedy,"[100] for there were simply not enough federal officers available for effective enforcement. The practical effect was just as Taney predicted. The states learned from Story's opinion that they were not obliged to aid in enforcing the Fugitive Slave Law, and a number of northern states enacted laws under which state officers were forbidden to help in any way in carrying the federal statute into effect. The upshot was the virtual "nullification" in the North of the constitutional provision for the return of fugitive slaves.

The South felt increasingly bitter over the ineffectiveness of the

[98] 11 *Adams, supra* note 22, at 336.
[99] *Story, supra* note 18, at 392.
[100] 16 Pet. at 630.

1793 act. As Webster himself conceded in an 1850 speech, "There has not been a case within the knowledge of this generation, in which a man has been taken back from Massachusetts into slavery by process of law, not one." [101] From the southern point of view, the legal remedy for this situation was enactment of an effective federal Fugitive Slave Law to replace the now futile 1793 act. The southerners secured such a statute as part of the price of the Compromise of 1850, that chimera of reconciliation by which men sought for the last time to preserve the Union by the spirit of compromise that created it. [102]

The plain purpose of the Fugitive Slave Law of 1850 was to fill in the enforcement gap created by *Prigg* v. *Pennsylvania.* The congressional intent was expressed early in the Senate debate by Lewis Cass: "The master seeking his slave found his remedy a good one at the time, [103] but now very ineffectual; and this defect is one that imperiously requires a remedy. And this remedy I am willing to provide, fairly and honestly." [104] The new statute set up a complete system of federal enforcement machinery. Commissioners could be appointed by the federal circuit courts to exercise judicial enforcement functions of the type performed by state officials before *Prigg.* In addition, federal marshals and deputies were required directly to enforce the statute, including arresting and detaining fugitives. Federal enforcement of the slaveowner's property right was now provided to a thitherto unprecedented extent. "Sir," declared Webster in the Senate, "the principle of the restitution of runaway slaves is not objectionable, unless the Constitution is objectionable. If the Constitution is right in that respect, the principle is right, and the law providing for carrying it into effect is right." [105] The 1850 Fugitive Slave Law was a direct exercise by Congress of the power recognized by a unanimous Court in the *Prigg* case.

The new law may have been accepted on Capitol Hill as part of the price of the 1850 compromise; increasing numbers of people outside the South did not do so: "It was the Fugitive Slave Act which stuck in Northern throats." [106] Enforcement of the statute, as much as anything, produced the northern revulsion that intensified the growing separation between the sections. Despite *Prigg,* new "personal liberty laws" were enacted in northern states to frustrate enforcement of the

---

[101] 10 *Webster, supra* note 65, at 165.

[102] *Compare* 1 S.E. Morison and H.S. Commager, *The Growth of the American Republic* 606 (1942).

[103] I.e., before Prigg v. Pennsylvania.

[104] *Cong. Globe,* 31st Cong., 1st Sess. 1583.

[105] 10 *Webster, supra* note 65, at 165.

[106] *Morison and Commager, supra* note 102, at 606.

law. [107] The anti-slavery men denied the constitutionality of the 1850 act, as they had earlier denied that of the 1793 statute. They asserted that the Fugitive Slave Clause of Article IV was a prohibition directed against state action, not a grant of power to Congress; [108] it recognized the right of rendition, but did not give Congress power to enforce that right. [109] Their argument was rejected by perhaps the greatest state judge of the period, Chief Justice Shaw of Massachusetts, in *Thomas Sims's* case, [110] decided in 1851. Shaw sustained the 1850 law, holding that the Constitution vested in Congress the authority to make all laws necessary and proper to carry the Fugitive Slave Clause into execution. The Fugitive Slave Law was intended to implement "the power and duty of congress to pass laws to secure and carry into effect a right confirmed by the constitution." [111]

Shaw's reasoning was essentially that followed by the Supreme Court a decade earlier in the *Prigg* case. It virtually precluded further judicial discussion of the matter. [112] Despite recent criticism, [113] the holding that Congress possessed power to enact a fugitive slave statute appears sound. Congressional authority extends to enactment of statutes "necessary and proper" for enforcement of any right protected by the Constitution, including that of the owner in a fugitive slave. The fact that the Fugitive Slave Clause itself is not drafted in terms of a delegation of power to Congress does not change the result. The Necessary and Proper Clause has never been restricted to the letter of the legislative powers specifically enumerated in Article I, section 8. [114] As Chief Justice Shaw put it in an earlier case, the Constitution and the fugitive slave law "were to be obeyed, however disagreeable to our own natural sympathies and views of duty!" [115]

To the legal observer, one provision of the 1850 Fugitive Slave Law is of special interest, for its extreme nature demonstrates the extent to which the slavery issue distorted even key constitutional rights. Under section 6 of the statute, "In no trial or hearing under this act shall the testimony of such alleged fugitive be admitted in evidence." When one bears in mind that the hearings held under the act were, in most cases,

---

107 They are summarized in *D.L. Dumond, Antislavery Origins of the Civil War in the United States* 65 (1939). Such laws were enacted in all the free states except Indiana and Ohio; *Nye, supra* note 49, at 275–76.

108 *See S. Shapiro, Richard Henry Dana, Jr.* 63 (1961).

109 *See D. Donald, Charles Sumner and the Coming of the Civil War* 232 (1960).

110 7 Cush. 285 (Mass. 1851).

111 *Id.* at 300.

112 *See L.W. Levy, The Law of the Commonwealth and Chief Justice Shaw* 98 (1957).

113 See *id.* at 99.

114 *See B. Schwartz, Constitutional Law: A Textbook* 62–63 (1972).

115 Quoted in *Levy, supra* note 112, at 81.

before commissioners (not judges), he can see that the whole purpose of the law was to provide for prompt and summary return of alleged fugitives, without real regard to the question of whether persons seized were, in fact, the runaway slaves claimed in the affidavits submitted by asserted owners. The personal liberty of seized Negroes was to be determined solely on the basis of affidavit evidence. The point was made graphically by an abolitionist in 1855: "The simple truth is, at this moment, that if an affidavit comes from Georgia that A.B. has escaped from service there, and somebody can be found to testify that I am A.B., and an irresponsible *Commissioner* . . . chooses to say, for the fee of ten dollars, that he believes his testimony, I must go to Georgia . . . and there is no remedy for me whatever in the laws of my country." [116] What Dana termed the "infamous" and "odious" [117] nature of the 1850 statute in this respect was not altered by the right of the fugitive to a trial in the state from which he had fled. In practice, that right was more theoretical than real; there are no cases reported where the returned fugitive was given the jury trial to which he was presumptively entitled in the state to which he was returned.

Today, the indefensible nature of this *ex parte* procedure appears beyond question. Certainly it violates virtually all the safeguards contained in the Bill of Rights, particularly that to jury trial. To the law of pre-Civil War days, however, it was only begging the question to ask whether the Constitution did not require procedural protection for personal liberty. As senators candidly put it during the 1850 debate, the law then was clear "in putting horses and negroes together as property." Indeed, Negroes were not constitutionally as well off, since there is no "clause in the Constitution . . . which provides for the restitution of fugitive horses by this Government." [118]

To those who rejected the notion that a slave was not a person, the Fugitive Slave Law was a patent violation of the Bill of Rights. Their attitude was well summarized by Charles Sumner: "This is the Fugitive Slave Bill—a bill which despoils the party claimed as a slave—whether he be in reality a slave or a freeman—of the sacred right of Trial by Jury, and commits the question of Human Freedom—the highest question known by law—to the unaided judgment of a single magistrate, on *ex parte* evidence." [119] When the law was passed, Emerson wrote in his journal, "This filthy enactment was made in the nineteenth century, by people who could read and write. I will not obey it, by

---

[116] John G. Palfrey, quoted in *Filler, supra* note 80, at 162.

[117] *Shapiro, supra* note 108, at 57.

[118] *Cong. Globe,* 31st Cong., 1st Sess. 1618.

[119] 2 *C. Sumner, Orations and Speeches, 1845–1850,* at 400 (1850).

God!" [120] Emerson was scarcely alone in his resolve. Throughout the North, men worked to frustrate the effectiveness of the statute. "In a very large section of the free states," said Charles Francis Adams on the eve of the Civil War, "the [Fugitive Slave Law] is inoperative, and always will be; and the reason is that its harshness . . . runs counter to the sympathies of the people." [121]

Efforts to enforce the law raised, more sharply than the Mexican war had done, the problem of the conflict between law and morality and the question of civil disobedience in the face of a law deemed unjust. Opponents, like William H. Seward and Salmon P. Chase, asserted their duty to a "higher law," which made it necessary for them to do whatever they could to render the statute nugatory. [122] On the floor of Congress, Horace Mann declared in 1852 that "this doctrine—which is one of the off-shoots of slavery—that there is no higher law than the law of the State, is palpable and practical atheism," [123] and William Lloyd Garrison that same year, in the presence of a large congregation, produced and burned copies of the Fugitive Slave Law and the Constitution, exclaiming, "So perish all compromises with tyranny! And let all the people say, Amen." [124]

The problem of the unjust law is a most difficult one from a moral point of view. From a purely legal standpoint, however, there can be no problem. A statute, legally speaking, must be treated as laying down a binding norm — at least until it is ruled unconstitutional. Such, at least, was the attitude taken by the federal government with regard to enforcement of the Fugitive Slave Law. Even as weak a president as Pierce did his best to see that the statute was "unhesitatingly carried into effect." [125] "If you can justify," wrote Pierce with uncharacteristic vigor, "refusal to execute the requirements of the law of 1850—you can justify the enticement of slaves—If you can justify enticement you can justify running them off. . . . It all rests upon the doctrine of a 'higher law' to be obeyed in the conduct of governmental affairs. It is alike unsound and dangerous." [126]

Federal efforts to enforce the law led directly to the case of *Ableman v. Booth,* already mentioned. [127] It arose out of the seizure of a fugitive

[120] Quoted in *Morison and Commager, supra* note 102, at 606.

[121] *Cong. Globe* Appendix, 36th Cong., 2d Sess. 125.

[122] For the most complete contemporary analysis of the "higher law" theory, *see* W. Hosmer, *The Higher Law* (1852).

[123] *Cong. Globe* Appendix, 32nd Cong., 1st Sess. 1075.

[124] Quoted in *Filler, supra* note 80, at 216.

[125] 5 *Richardson, supra* note 74, at 202.

[126] Letter from Franklin Pierce to William Butterfield, Dec. 1, 1859, Parke-Bernet Galleries, Sale No. 2310, Item 109 (1964).

[127] 21 How. 506 (U.S. 1859); p. 28 *supra.*

slave in Racine under the 1850 statute. Sherman M. Booth, a militant abolitionist editor, rode through the streets like Paul Revere crying, "Freemen! To the rescue! Slave-catchers are in our midst! Be at the courthouse at two o'clock!" [128] At the appointed hour, the fugitive was forcibly released and spirited away. Booth was found guilty in a federal court of violating the Fugitive Slave Law by having aided and abetted the escape of a fugitive in custody. He was fined and imprisoned but ordered released on habeas corpus by the highest court of Wisconsin, on the ground that the federal statute was unconstitutional.

The Fugitive Slave Law, as was pointed out earlier in this chapter, made for an inverted repetition of the nullification controversy. This time it was the South which urged an extreme assertion of federal power and a northern state which relied on state power to frustrate a federal law. Wisconsin proceeded on the view that the Fugitive Slave Law was invalid and that a state could determine this for itself regardless of any contrary decision by the nation's highest bench. After the Supreme Court reversal in *Ableman* v. *Booth,* the Wisconsin legislature adopted resolutions denouncing the decision as "in direct conflict" with the Constitution. Relying on the doctrine that the states were separate sovereignties, the resolutions asserted "that a *positive defiance* of those sovereignties of all unauthorized acts done under color of that instrument is the rightful remedy." [129]

Constitutionally speaking, Wisconsin's counterpart of nullification was as unwarranted as the doctrine previously asserted by Calhoun. At the time, however, the stand did its part in fostering the widespread disregard of law that was itself a prelude to the ultimate defiance posed by Sumter. To more and more people in the North, it was becoming plain that the law supporting slavery was unworthy of obedience. In the South, the same attitude of defiance was becoming even more dominant. Uncompromising sentiment in both sections was making it increasingly impossible for the basic issue to be resolved within the constitutional framework, even when backed by the authority and prestige of the nation's highest bench.

---

128 *See Filler, supra* note 80, at 236.
129 Quoted in S. *Tyler, Memoir of Roger Brooke Taney, LL.D.* 397–98 (1872).

CHAPTER FIVE

The Dred Scott *Case*

"THE UNJUST JUDGE"

In August, 1865, an anonymous pamphlet was published in New York entitled *The Unjust Judge—A Memorial of Roger Brooke Taney, Late Chief Justice of the United States.* In it, Taney, dead less than a year, was excoriated "with hatred so malignant that it seems obscene."[1] Its vilification culminated in the assertion that "as a jurist, or more strictly speaking as a Judge,... he was, next to Pontius Pilate, perhaps the worst that ever occupied the seat of judgment among men."[2]

Without a doubt, this attack on Taney at the end of his career and the cloud that has since hung over his judicial reputation were a result of the decision in the *Dred Scott* case.[3] Before that decision, the prestige of the Supreme Court had never been greater. Taney was universally acclaimed worthy of his predecessor, destined to rank almost with Marshall himself in the judicial pantheon. After the *Dred Scott* decision all was changed. "The name of Taney," declared Charles Sumner early in 1865, "is to be hooted down the page of history.... The Senator says that he for twenty-five years administered justice. He administered justice, at last, wickedly, and degraded the Judiciary of the country and degraded the age."[4]

To so many of his contemporaries, *Dred Scott* made Taney the very prototype of "the unjust judge." After conceding that the deceased

---

[1] W. Lewis, *Without Fear or Favor: A Biography of Chief Justice Roger Brooke Taney* 470 (1965).

[2] Quoted in *id.* at 471.

[3] Dred Scott v. Sandford, 19 How. 393 (U.S. 1857).

[4] *Cong. Globe*, 38th Cong., 2d Sess. 1013.

chief justice may have had "good qualities and . . . ability," Gideon Welles wrote in his diary, "But the course pursued in the Dred Scott case . . . forfeited respect for him as a man or a judge."[5] For more than a century the case has stood as a monument of judicial indiscretion: as Justice Jackson acidly commented: "One such precedent is enough!"[6]

Yet if we take the *Dred Scott* case on its own terms, as a decision of the highest court, we shall find that it has not deserved the contumely directed against it. To characterize it as the case in which "judicial baseness reached its lowest point"[7] and to charge that the Taney Court was acting as "the tool of unjust power"[8] was extreme, but we also know how great an error it was for the Supreme Court to assume that it could resolve the basic controversy over slavery. A question which resulted in a civil war was hardly a proper one for the judicial forum.

The *Dred Scott* case was not so much a judicial crime as a judicial blunder, a blunder which resulted from the Taney Court's failure to follow the doctrine of judicial self-restraint that (as has been pointed out) was one of Taney's great contributions to our constitutional law. In it the Court fell victim to its own success as a governmental institution. The power and prestige which had been built up under Marshall and continued under Taney had led men to expect too much of judicial power. The justices themselves too readily accepted the notion that judicial power could succeed where political power had failed. From this point of view, Taney may be characterized not as an "unjust judge" but as an "unwise judge." His essential mistake was to imagine that a flaming political issue could be quenched by calling it a "legal" question and deciding it judicially.[9]

SLAVERY IN THE TERRITORIES

To understand the issues in the *Dred Scott* case, it is necessary to have some knowledge of what had by the 1850s become the thorniest aspect of the slavery controversy—the question of slavery in the territories. "Everybody knew that this issue of the Negro in the Territories was the central question before the country."[10] From the founding of the republic, the question had been dealt with by the Congress. When the

[5] Quoted in *C.B. Swisher, Roger B. Taney* 578 (1935).

[6] *R.H. Jackson, The Struggle for Judicial Supremacy* 327 (1949).

[7] Charles Sumner, *Cong. Globe*, 38th Cong., 2d Sess. 1012.

[8] *Id.*

[9] *R.G. McCloskey, The American Supreme Court* 96 (1960).

[10] 1 *A. Nevins, The Emergence of Lincoln* 90 (1950).

Constitution went into effect, the United States possessed vast territories which had been ceded by Virginia and various other states. The Confederation Congress had provided for the government of the territory northwest of the Ohio River by the famous Northwest Ordinance of 1787, which flatly prohibited slavery in the territory governed by it.

One of the earliest measures enacted by the first Congress that convened under the Constitution was a law providing that the Northwest Ordinance should "continue to have full effect."[11] In 1790, Congress passed an act accepting a deed of cession by North Carolina of the territory that later became the State of Tennessee. That statute declared that no regulations were to be made in the territory which "tend to emancipate slaves."[12] These early assertions of congressional power to govern slavery in the territories were reinforced in scores of later statutes, some of which contained the express prohibition of the Northwest Ordinance.

Then, in 1820, came the Missouri Compromise, by which, it was hoped, the question of slavery in the territories had finally been settled. It prohibited slavery in the remainder of the territory included in the Louisiana Purchase north of a prescribed line—36° 30' of north latitude.[13] As it turned out, this provision did not really resolve the issue of the extension of slavery. All it did was establish a temporary armistice in the growing conflict between the pro- and anti-slavery forces. In this sense, John Quincy Adams was correct when he wrote in his diary at the time "that the present question is a mere preamble—a title-page to a great tragic volume."[14]

The question of slavery in the territories arose again at the end of the Mexican war, when large areas were acquired. Conflict over the extension of slavery into the new regions grew in intensity in the decade that followed and towered over other political issues; the crisis that sounded in Jefferson's ears "like a fire bell in the night"[15] in 1819 had become a primary cause of sectional animosity.

The slavery issue was brought to the fore by the so-called Wilmot Proviso. In the summer of 1846, President Polk asked for an appropriation to enable him to negotiate a cession of Mexican territory. On August 8, he wrote in his diary, "I learned that after an excited debate in the House a bill passed that body, but with a mischievous & foolish amendment to the effect that no territory which might be acquired by treaty from Mexico should ever be a slave-holding country. What

[11] 1 Stat. 50 (1789).
[12] 1 Stat. 106 (1790).
[13] 3 Stat. 545 (1820).
[14] 4 *Memoirs of John Quincy Adams* 502 (C.F. Adams ed. 1876).
[15] Quoted in *M.L. Coit, John C. Calhoun* 146 (1950).

connection slavery had with making peace with Mexico it is difficult to conceive."[16]

If the president, eager to vindicate his Mexican policy by expansion of the Union, could not see the intimate relationship between adding "to the U.S. an immense empire"[17] and the question of whether the new territories would be slave or free, others in the political arena did. The war on the battlefield was minor compared to the one that now arose. The Wilmot Proviso itself never did become part of Polk's appropriation bill, but the issue it raised overshadowed all others. "The United States," Emerson foresaw in 1846, "will conquer Mexico, but it will be as the man who swallows the arsenic which brings him down in turn. Mexico will poison us."[18] The struggle over slavery in the new territories soon showed how valid this prophecy was.

CONSTITUTIONAL THEORIES

The controversy catalyzed by the Wilmot Proviso brought to the fore sharply opposed constitutional theories on the issue of slavery in the territories. The anti-slavery men relied upon the express congressional power to "make all needful Rules and Regulations respecting the Territory . . . belonging to the United States," and urged that it included the authority to deal with slavery in the territories. Such authority had been exercised by the national legislature from the beginning, and its constitutionality had not been questioned. From the Wilmot Proviso debates a new version of this theory emerged: Congress had the moral duty to prohibit slavery wherever its jurisdiction extended; freedom must be national, slavery only sectional.[19] This version, soon to be adopted by the Free Soil and Republican parties, also rested upon the constitutional power of Congress to regulate slavery in the territories.

The southerners put forward an opposing constitutional theory denying that Congress had any legitimate authority to exclude slavery from the territories. This rejection of congressional power represented a shift in the southern position. At the time of the Missouri Compromise, John Quincy Adams could say that only some "zealots . . . on the slave side" argued "that Congress have not power by the Constitution to prohibit slavery . . . in any territory."[20] Responsible southern leaders

---

[16] 2 *The Diary of James K. Polk during His Presidency* 75 (M.M. Quaife ed. 1910).

[17] 3 *id.* at 366.

[18] Quoted in *G.G. Van Deusen, The Jacksonian Era: 1828 to 1848*, at 245 (1959).

[19] *Compare D.L. Dumond, Antislavery Origins of the Civil War in the United States* 76–77 (1939).

[20] *Adams, supra* note 14, at 530.

did not take any such extreme position. When President Monroe put the question to his cabinet in March, 1820, "it was unanimously agreed that Congress have the power to prohibit slavery in the Territories."[21] Among those who strongly argued in support of that authority was Secretary of War Calhoun.

However, southerners came to believe that the Union itself depended upon an equal division between slave and free states. "Sir," Calhoun declared to the Senate in 1847, "the day that the balance between the two sections of the country—the slaveholding States and the nonslaveholding States—is destroyed, is a day that will not be far removed from political revolution, anarchy, civil war, and wide-spread disaster."[22] The controversy over the Wilmot Proviso made it plain that the delicate free-slave equilibrium would soon be upset. Calhoun sought to preserve the balance by having the Missouri Compromise line extended to the Pacific. His efforts proved futile: all proposals to extend the Missouri line were voted down.

The rejection of the Compromise approach led Calhoun to reexamine his constitutional position. Now he saw that the westward march of the nation meant the inevitable end of equality for the slave states. Senate protection had to be replaced by some other instrument to defend slaveholding interests. That need was met by a change in constitutional theory. The only hope now, declared Calhoun in an 1847 speech, lay in the basic document itself: "The constitution . . . is a rock. . . . Let us be done with compromises. Let us go back and stand upon the Constitution."[23]

It is usually said that Chief Justice Taney, in his *Dred Scott* opinion, was simply elevating to the constitutional plane the new Calhoun theory on slavery in the territories. This view, as we shall see, is an oversimplification. While Calhoun, like Taney in *Dred Scott,* denied the constitutional power of Congress to prohibit slavery in the territories, the Carolinian's approach was far more extreme in its rejection of federal power than that later adopted by the Supreme Court. The Calhoun theory was based upon the doctrine of state sovereignty pushed almost to absurdity. The territories, he argued, were "the common property of the States of this Union. They are called 'the territories of the United States.' And what are the 'United States' but the States united? Sir, these territories are the property of the States united; held jointly for their common use."[24] The federal government, as the agent of the sovereign states, held the territories in trust for their

---

21 5 *Adams, supra* note 14, at 5.
22 4 *The Works of John C. Calhoun* 343 (R.K. Crallé ed. 1854).
23 *Id.* at 347.
24 *Id.* at 344–45.

common benefit; consequently it could not prevent a citizen of any one state from carrying with him into the territories property the legal status of which was recognized by his home state.[25]

In February, 1847, Calhoun introduced resolutions before the Senate stating the essentials of his new position: the territories were the joint property of the states; Congress, as the states' agent, could not make any discriminations between states depriving any one of them of its equal right in any territory; a law depriving citizens of any state of the right to emigrate into any territory with their property would violate the Constitution and the rights of the states.[26] These resolutions, adopted by many southern legislatures, became the virtual platform of the South. Under the Constitution, wrote Jefferson Davis, there was an "obligation of the U.S. Govt. to recognize property in slaves, as denominated in the compact, . . . to enforce the rights of its citizens to equal enjoyment of the territorial property which had been acquired and held as a common possession."[27]

This constitutional issue gave rise to most of the increasingly bitter political dialogue of the decade after the Mexican war. To the South particularly, defense of the Calhoun theory was seen as a matter of life and death. Only by denying congressional authority to prohibit slavery in the territories could the South prevent itself from being swamped by a vast new free-soil area that would reduce the slave states to an ever smaller minority. If the balance of power were altered, the very ability of the South to defend itself would be at an end. "The surrender of life," Calhoun warned in a famous 1847 speech, "is nothing to sinking down into acknowledged inferiority."[28]

NEED FOR JUDICIAL RESOLUTION

Although the primary error of the Supreme Court in the *Dred Scott* case was its assumption that the issue of slavery in the territories could be resolved judicially, it is a mistake to picture the justices as blithely rushing into the political arena, officiously seeking to save the nation. Perhaps Taney and his colleagues should never have tried to settle the slavery issue, particularly since the case before them could have been disposed of without consideration of the slavery question; yet it is fair to say that their action was a response to a widespread popular desire to have the issue decided by the highest court.

[25] *A.O. Spain, The Political Theory of John C. Calhoun* 24 (1951).

[26] *Calhoun, supra* note 22, at 348.

[27] Jefferson Davis, Notes for W.T.W. (n.d.), Charles Hamilton, Auction No. 31, Item 83 (1968).

[28] *Calhoun, supra* note 22, at 348.

The opposing constitutional theories on congressional power could scarcely be resolved through normal political processes. Upon the issue joined by those theories, Congress itself was largely helpless:[29] "no Bill to establish a Territorial Government could be passed through the Ho. Repts. without having the Wilmot Proviso attached to it as a condition ... with this provision the Bill would probably be rejected by the Senate, ... and ... the people of California would be left without a Government."[30] Settlers in the Far West had to do without government because Congress could not decide whether or not they should have slaves.[31]

In this situation, it was not unnatural to turn to the tribunal vested with the primary function of resolving disputed constitutional issues. The impasse between the northern and southern views led a Senate select committee to propose the so-called Clayton Compromise. Under it, Congress was to provide for governments in California and New Mexico, and "they should be restrained by Congress from Legislating on the subject of slavery, leaving that question, if it should arise, to be decided by the judiciary."[32] In this way, the right to introduce or prohibit slavery was to rest "on the Constitution, as the same should be expounded by the judges, with a right to appeal to the Supreme Court."[33]

With the support of Calhoun,[34] the Clayton attempt to have Congress "avoid the decision of this distracting question, leaving it to be settled by the silent operation of the Constitution itself"[35] passed the Senate, but it was defeated in the House. In his last Annual Message, Polk restated the essence of the Clayton proposal, "to leave the subject to the decision of the Judiciary,"[36] as a possible solution: "If the whole subject be submitted to the judiciary, all parts of the Union should cheerfully acquiesce in the final decision of the tribunal created by the Constitution for the settlement of all questions which may arise under the Constitution."[37]

Buchanan used strikingly similar language in his Inaugural Address, referring to the then-pending *Dred Scott* case,[38] and called down upon

---

[29] W. Mendelson, in *S.I. Kutler, The Dred Scott Decision: Law or Politics* 153 (1967).

[30] 4 *Polk, supra* note 16, at 297-98.

[31] *Compare S. E. Morison, The Oxford History of the American People* 567 (1965).

[32] 4 *Polk, supra* note 16, at 20.

[33] *Cong. Globe*, 30th Cong., 1st Sess. 950.

[34] *Id.* at 1002; 4 *Polk, supra* note 16, at 21.

[35] *Cong. Globe*, 30th Cong., 1st Sess. 950.

[36] 4 *Polk, supra* note 16, at 207.

[37] 4 *J.D. Richardson, A Compilation of the Messages and Papers of the Presidents 1789–1897*, at 642 (1896).

[38] 5 *id.* at 431.

himself the vitriolic abuse of the anti-slavery press. By then, opponents of slavery feared an adverse decision, but almost a decade earlier the movement to have the Supreme Court resolve the issue was supported by political leaders on both sides. It was widely recognized, Jefferson Davis wrote later, that "it was necessary to settle finally the asserted right of the Southern people to migrate with their slaves to the territories and there to have for that property the protection which was given to other property of citizens by the U.S. Govt."[39]

The Compromise of 1850 itself was essentially based upon the need to have the key constitutional question settled judicially. On that point, Senator Davis could agree with Senator E. J. Phelps of Vermont: "The Constitution has provided its remedy . . . —that tribunal which sits in the chamber below us, Mr. President. . . . we are entitled to a decision of the Supreme Court."[40] The Compromise established territorial governments for Utah and New Mexico and provided that "the legislative power of the Territory shall extend to all rightful subjects of legislation consistent with the Constitution of the United States."[41] Provision was made for judicial settlement of the constitutional question by special provisons liberalizing federal court jurisdiction in slavery litigation. In "all cases involving title to slaves," appeals to the Supreme Court were to be allowed without regard to the jurisdictional amount normally required for such appeals.[42]

It has been questioned whether the framers of the Compromise really intended to turn over the constitutional issue to the highest tribunal.[43] During the debates, however, Henry Clay (the prime author of the 1850 measure) did indicate that such was his intent. What, he asked the Senate, could be "more satisfactory to both sides" than to have Congress keep its hands off the issue "and to leave the question of slavery or no slavery to be decided by the only competent authority that can definitely settle it forever, the authority of the Supreme Court."[44] And the judicial review provisions of the Compromise are a virtual copy of the parts of the Clayton Compromise which proposed leaving the slavery question to the highest court.[45]

The Kansas-Nebraska Act of 1854 followed the Compromise approach, containing, like the 1850 measure, provisions indicating

---

[39] Jefferson Davis, Notes for W.T.W. (n.d.), Charles Hamilton, Auction No. 31, Item 83 (1968).

[40] *Cong. Globe* Appendix, 31st Cong., 1st Sess. 95. *See also id.* at 154.

[41] 9 Stat. 446, 449; *id.* at 453, 454 (1850).

[42] 9 Stat. 446, 450; *id.* at 453, 456 (1850).

[43] *A.C. McLaughlin, Constitutional History of the United States* 534 (1935).

[44] *Cong. Globe,* 31st Cong. 1st Sess. 1155.

[45] *See Kutler, supra* note 29, at 156.

congressional intent not to deal with slavery in the territory (this time in terms of Stephen A. Douglas' theory of popular sovereignty) and authorizing liberalized appeals to the Supreme Court in slavery cases. The purpose was to leave "the question where . . . it should be left—to the ultimate decision of the courts. It is purely a judicial question." [46] Douglas himself affirmed in 1856 that "I stated [in the Kansas-Nebraska debate] I would not discuss this legal question, for by the bill we referred it to the Courts."[47]

This widespread sentiment is plainly relevant to the charge that the Court's decision in the *Dred Scott* case amounted to mere judicial usurpation. It acted in response to congressional invitation[48] and did no more than yield to the prevalent public demand for judicial pronouncement on the matter. Even Lincoln, severe critic of the decision though he later showed himself, welcomed Supreme Court action in 1856. Noting the Democratic view that restrictions of slavery in the territories would be unconstitutional, he declared that he was not bound by such political construction of the Constitution: "The Supreme Court of the United States is the tribunal to decide such questions, and we will submit to its decisions."[49]

FACTS AND ISSUES

Dred Scott was originally called Sam and was so listed in the inventory of his first owner's estate. The name made so famous by the Supreme Court decision was acquired in Illinois or the Wisconsin Territory, where Sam was taken by his new owner, Dr. Emerson, an army surgeon. The case itself, of course, made the short, stubby Negro "the hero of the day, if not of the age. He has thrown Anthony Burns, Bully Bowlegs, Uncle Tom and Fred Douglass into . . . oblivion."[50]

The detailed history of the case need not concern us here. In 1846 Scott brought suit in a Missouri court for his freedom against Mrs. Emerson, who had acquired title to him on her husband's death. Scott's counsel argued that his service for Dr. Emerson in Illinois and in territory from which slavery had been excluded by the Missouri Com-

---

[46] *Cong. Globe* Appendix, 33rd Cong., 1st Sess. 232. *See also Cong. Globe*, 35th Cong., 2d Sess. 1258.

[47] *Cong. Globe* Appendix, 34th Cong., 1st Sess. 797.

[48] To be sure, *Dred Scott* itself did not reach the Supreme Court by the procedural route provided in the 1850 Compromise or the Kansas-Nebraska Act, yet it did dispose of the substantive issue contemplated by those laws; *Kutler, supra* note 29, at 160.

[49] 2 *The Collected Works of Abraham Lincoln* 355 (R.P. Basler ed. 1953). *But see* 4 *id.* at 67.

[50] Washington Union, quoted in *Lewis, supra* note 1, at 420.

promise made him a free man. The jury returned a verdict in Scott's favor, but the Missouri Supreme Court reversed on the ground that Missouri law governed, and under it Scott was still a slave. His attorneys next maneuvered the case into the federal courts. Mrs. Emerson had remarried, and Scott found himself the purported property of her brother, John Sanford, of New York. Scott, claiming Missouri citizenship, could now sue in a federal court on the ground of diversity of citizenship. In 1853 an action was instituted in the United States Circuit Court for Missouri. Scott, as a citizen of Missouri, brought an action for damages, alleging that Sanford,[51] a citizen of New York, had assaulted him. Defendant filed a plea in abatement, alleging that plaintiff was not a citizen of Missouri "because he is a Negro of African descent; his ancestors . . . were brought into this country and sold as negro slaves." The court sustained a demurrer to this plea, and defendant then pleaded that Scott was his slave and that, therefore, no assault could have occurred. After a jury verdict, judgment was given for defendant on the ground that Scott was still Sanford's property. A writ of error was taken by Scott to the Supreme Court.

Until the high bench appeal, the *Dred Scott* case was like many others heard in the courts on behalf of slaves, scarcely noted except by the participants. But from the beginning it was really "enclosed in a tumultuous privacy of storm,"[52] for inherent in it was "the much vexed [question] whether the removal by the master of his slave to Illinois or Wisconsin marks an absolute emancipation."[53] And that, in turn, involved consideration of the effect of the provisions prohibiting slavery found in the Illinois Constitution and the Missouri Compromise. Necessarily included in that issue was the question of power over slavery in the territories.

When Dred Scott first instituted his suit, debate over the crucial constitutional issue had been relatively low-keyed. Between that time and the date of the Supreme Court decision, however, it intensifed, and just before the case was appealed to the highest court the whole question was brought to the boiling point by the Kansas-Nebraska Act and its repeal of the Missouri Compromise. The potential of the case for resolution of the issue of congressional power over slavery in the territories was now widely grasped. "This is a question of more importance, perhaps," Scott's attorney could say in his Supreme Court argument, "than any which was ever submitted to this court; and the

[51] Defendant's name was misspelled in the official report, so it is as Dred Scott v. Sandford that the case is still known.

[52] The quote is from Emerson's "The Snow-Storm."

[53] Letter from Roswell Field to Montgomery Blair, Dec. 24, 1855, quoted in *J.J. Marke, Vignettes of Legal History* 85 (1965).

decision of the court is looked for with a degree of interest by the country which seldom attends its proceedings. It is, indeed, the great question of our day."[54]

But there was more in the case than this: defendant's plea in abatement had posed the question of whether even a free Negro could be a citizen. In some ways, that question was more fundamental than that of congressional authority over slavery. Legislative power to eliminate slavery would be empty form if those freed could not attain citizenship. If even the free Negro would have to remain "like some dishonoured stranger"[55] in the community, the northern majority who hoped that slavery would gradually disappear throughout the country was doomed to disappointment. Extralegal means would be needed to end the degraded status of the enslaved race. What had come to the Supreme Court as a question of law now became a matter of morality.

MANEUVERINGS TOWARD DECISION

When the Supreme Court first considered the *Dred Scott* case in conference in April, 1856, eight justices were evenly divided on whether the issue of Scott's citizenship was properly before them. The ninth, Justice Nelson, tended toward the affirmative, but moved that the case be reargued on whether the Court should take notice of the citizenship issue, which the lower court had decided in Scott's favor and which had not, therefore, been included in Scott's writ of error to the highest bench. Nelson's motion carried and the case was reargued on December 15, 1856—a delay which postponed any decision until after the 1856 presidential election.

At their first conference, the justices also doubted the propriety of deciding the issue of congressional power over slavery in the territories. The day after the conference Justice Curtis wrote his uncle, "The court will not decide the question of the Missouri Compromise line—a majority of the judges being of the opinion that it is not necessary to do so."[56] After the second argument, a majority of the justices, in conference on February 14, 1857, were of the opinion that the case should be decided without consideration of the two crucial issues. Five now felt that the issue of citizenship was not properly before them, and seven took the position that they need not consider the Missouri Compromise because Scott's status was a matter for Missouri law and

[54] Quoted in *V.C. Hopkins, Dred Scott's Case* 38 (1967).
[55] Aristotle, *Politics* bk. 3, at 5.
[56] 1 *Memoir of Benjamin Robbins Curtis, LL.D.* 179 (1879).

had already been determined against him by that state's highest court. Justice Nelson was selected to write an opinion disposing of the case in this manner.

Had the Nelson opinion (limiting itself to Scott's status under Missouri law after his return to that state) prevailed as the opinion of the Court, the *Dred Scott* case would scarcely be known today except to the curious student of high bench miscellany. Pressures were, however, building up which soon led the justices to abandon their original intent. Soon after his election to the presidency, James Buchanan wrote to Justice Grier that "the great object of my administration will be, if possible to destroy the dangerous slavery agitation and thus restore peace to our distracted country."[57] The pending decision of the Supreme Court gave him hope that a major part of the problem could be solved at a single stroke.[58] On February 3, the president-elect wrote to Justice Catron, a close friend, asking him whether the case would be decided before March 4, the date of the inauguration. Catron replied that "it rests entirely with the Chief Justice to move in the matter" and that he had said nothing about it. Then, on February 10, Catron wrote Buchanan that the case would be decided four days later but that no opinion would be announced before the end of the month. The decision would not help Buchanan in his Inaugural Address, he said, since the question of congressional power over the territories would probably not be touched on in it.[59]

In the meantime, the justices had been shaken in their initial resolve to decide the case without considering the issues of citizenship or slavery in the territories. It was apparent that the two justices who refused to agree to the narrow decision voted at the February 14 conference — McLean and Curtis — would file separate dissents which would cover both Negro citizenship and congressional authority to enact the Missouri Compromise. The southern members of the Court were concerned about the propaganda effect of the McLean and Curtis dissents, demonstrating as they would the constitutionality of the Missouri Compromise. They proposed to answer the dissenters with an opinion of the Court written by the chief justice, which would deal with all the points presented in the case and effectively rebut the McLean and Curtis opinions. A motion to that effect by Justice Wayne was agreed to by a majority of the justices.[60]

Recent writers, particularly Allen Nevins,[61] have questioned the

57 Quoted in *Swisher, supra* note 5, at 493.

58 *P.S. Klein, President James Buchanan* 269 (1962).

59 The Catron letters are summarized in *Swisher, supra* note 5, at 496.

60 *See Hopkins, supra* note 54, at 55–56.

61 *Nevins, supra* note 10, at 112; 2 *id.* at 473.

assumption that the persistence of the dissenters forced the broad majority decision. It is true that we do not have sufficient evidence of what went on behind the scenes to be dogmatic, yet what we do know seems to support the traditional view. In a letter of February 19, Justice Catron stated flatly to President-Elect Buchanan that "a majority of my brethren will be forced up to this point [i.e., to rule on the constitutional issues of citizenship and slavery in the territories] by two dissentients."[62] A February 23 letter of Justice Grier to Buchanan also makes the same point: "it appeared that our brothers who dissented from the majority, especially Justice McLean, were determined to come out with a long and labored dissent, including their opinions and arguments on both the troublesome points, although not necessary to a decision of the case . . . . Those who hold a different opinion from Messrs. McLean and Curtis on the power of Congress and the validity of the Compromise Act feel compelled to express their opinions on the subject."[63] To this Nevins replies that "hastily written letters usually give but a partial view of the truth,"[64] but he himself relies on an 1879 letter of Justice Campbell to sustain the view that the majority was not induced to act by the McLean-Curtis resolve.[65] Surely the contemporary Catron-Grier letters are more likely to be accurate than a letter written by another justice over twenty years later. (It should be stressed that there was no reason for Catron and Grier to distort the truth in their letters to Buchanan.)

In addition, the logic of the case confirms the evidence of the Catron-Grier letters. The majority could readily have disposed of the case without dealing with the issues of citizenship and slavery in the territories. The same was not true of the dissenters. Since they denied that Scott's status was a matter to be determined solely by Missouri's highest court, they had to deal with the remaining constitutional issues. In these circumstances, it is hard to agree that "the letters of Catron and Grier can be explained simply as a distortion of the painful controversy then raging"[66] in the Court. If anything, the circumstantial evidence tends to bear out the accuracy of the Catron-Grier letters.

Justice Catron's February 19 letter to Buchanan was intended primarily to inform the president-elect of the Court's plan to have the chief justice write a broad majority opinion in answer to the McLean and Curtis dissents. Catron urged Buchanan to write to Grier (a fellow

---

62 *Hopkins, supra* note 54, at 56.

63 Grier's letter is contained in 3 *C. Warren, The Supreme Court in United States History,* 17–19 (1924).

64 *Nevins, supra* note 10, at 112.

65 2 *Nevins, supra* note 10, at 473.

66 2 *Nevins, supra* note 10, at 476.

Pennsylvanian), who hesitated to join the new majority, telling him "how necessary it is—and how good the opportunity is to settle the agitation by an affirmative decision of the Supreme Court." [67] Buchanan did write to Grier, who showed the letter to Taney and Wayne and then wrote Buchanan that he fully concurred with the need for decision on "this troublesome question." He was afraid that the case would be decided on sectional lines; so "that it should not appear that the line of latitude should mark the line of division in the Court," he would concur with Taney. Both justices wrote Buchanan that the Court's decision would not be announced till just after the inauguration because of the chief justice's poor health. [68]

By present-day standards, the correspondence between Buchanan and two members of the Court was improper. Even more so was Buchanan's pressure on Grier, at the invitation of another justice, to join the majority. To say, as the Supreme Court historian does,[69] that it was not infrequent at the time for justices to tell a friend or relative the probable outcome of a pending case scarcely excuses Buchanan and the justices concerned. Buchanan was not just a friend; he was the new president and was hoping to use the information and his influence over Grier for political purposes. Even given the more permissive standards of an earlier day, the propriety of their conduct cannot be defended. Yet this is not to say, as was widely charged at the time, that the *Dred Scott* decision itself was the result of a conspiracy between Buchanan and the southern members of the Court. Though Lincoln asserted, in his famous "House Divided" speech, that the decision was the product of an understanding between "Stephen, Franklin, Roger, and James" in which "all worked upon a common *plan* . . . drawn up before the first lick was struck,"[70] all we now know about the case indicates that it did not happen that way. [71]

DECISION

On March 6, 1857, the nine justices filed into their basement courtroom, led by the now-feeble chief justice, exhausted by age and illness —a mere shadow, save in intellect, of the man who first presided over the high bench two decades earlier. Taney began the reading of the opinions in a voice so weak that, during much of the two hours during

67 *Hopkins, supra* note 54, at 56.

68 *Hopkins, supra* note 54, at 56.

69 *Warren, supra* note 63, at 17.

70 *Lincoln, supra* note 49, at 466.

71 *But see Morison, supra* note 31, at 593.

which he spoke, it sank almost to a whisper. Each of the majority justices read his own opinion, and Justices McLean and Curtis read lengthy dissents.[72] The reading of the opinions took two days.

"No wonder," declaimed Horace Greeley's *New York Tribune,* just after the decision was announced, "that the Chief Justice should have sunk his voice to a whisper . . . knowing that he was engaged in a pitiful attempt to impose upon the public."[73] To Greeley and other abolitionist editors, the decision was a patent triumph for slavery—a view which was accepted by the South as well. On the day that Justice Wayne's motion was adopted, he is said to have told a senator that he had "gained a triumph for the Southern section of the country by persuading the Chief Justice that the Court could put an end to all further agitation of the subject of slavery in the Territories."[74]

It is, however, erroneous to assume that the Taney opinion made the Calhoun position the law of the land, even though only temporarily and in less extreme form. Taney's opinion was not based upon Calhoun's states-rights theories; it was, on the contrary, strongly nationalistic, or more precisely federalistic, in character.[75] He followed Marshall in tracing the power of Congress to govern territories to its power to acquire them: "The power to acquire necessarily carries with it the power to preserve and apply to the purposes for which it was acquired."[76] Thus Congress had discretionary authority to determine how territories should be governed and to lay down laws to control their inhabitants. Taney did refer to Congress as "trustee," but it was as trustee of the "whole people of the Union" and of all its powers. [77] This differed not only in degree but also in kind from the Calhoun notion of the federal government as trustee for the states so far as the territories were concerned.

At any rate, it is clear that the effort to settle the troublesome constitutional issues once and for all failed dismally. In his concurring opinion, Justice Wayne stated that the issues involved had become so controversial "that the peace and harmony of the country required the settlement of them by judicial decision."[78] Seldom has wishful thinking been so spectacularly wrong.[79] Whatever *Dred Scott* brought about,

---

[72] The actual order of reading was somewhat different, since the dissenters read their opinions first on March 7, followed by Justices Daniel, Grier, Campbell, and Wayne.

[73] Quoted in *Warren, supra* note 63, at 27.

[74] Quoted in *Lewis, supra* note 1, at 392.

[75] *See* Corwin, in *Kutler, supra* note 29, at 131.

[76] 19 How. at 448.

[77] *Id.*

[78] *Id.* at 455.

[79] *Lewis, supra* note 1, at 420–21.

it was anything but peace and harmony—either for the Court or for the country.

Taney's opinion for the Court contained three main points: (1) Negroes, even those who were free, were not and could not become citizens of the United States within the meaning of the Constitution; (2) Scott had not become a free man by virtue of residence in a territory from which slavery had been excluded by the Missouri Compromise because the Compromise provision excluding slavery was itself beyond the constitutional power of Congress; (3) Scott was not free by reason of his stay in Illinois because the law of Missouri alone governed his status once he returned to that state.

Only on the third point (which was the sole ground upon which the majority had originally agreed to decide[80]) was the Taney opinion relatively uncontroversial.[81] The seven majority justices concurred on this point, and the Court's opinion was but a reaffirmation of the law laid down in earlier decisions.[82] What burst with such dramatic impact upon the nation was the fact that the highest Court in the land had denied both the right of Negroes to be citizens and the power of Congress to interfere with slaveholding in the territories. Acquiescence in these rulings was fatal to the Republicans and the advocates of popular sovereignty alike. It frustrated the hopes of those who sought to confine slavery to an area that would become an ever-smaller portion of an expanding nation. It meant instead that slavery was a national institution; there was now no legal way in which it could be excluded from any territory.

CONGRESSIONAL POWER

The higher court of history has, without a doubt, concurred with Justice Curtis in his dissent from the Taney conclusions on citizenship and slavery in the territories. Even recent writers who have attempted to mitigate the extreme vilifications of Taney have expressed the greatest deference toward the masterful nature of the Curtis opinion, hesitating to differ with the dissenter's presentation of the law on the matter. Has the historical verdict in favor of the Curtis dissent been justified? If the Taney opinion was not as erroneous in its principal rulings as critics have contended, the lesson of *Dred Scott* for the

---

80 Justice Nelson alone stuck to such ground; he filed as a separate concurrence the opinion written by him as the original opinion of the Court.

81 According to the monumental study on the law of slavery, 5 *H.H. Catterall, Judicial Cases concerning American Slavery and the Negro* 121 (1968), the decision on the third point was "unquestionably correct."

82 Notably Strader v. Graham, 10 How. 82 (U.S. 1850).

student of constitutional history becomes even more suggestive, for it indicates that the storm in which the case embroiled the high bench had little to do with the legal merits of the decision.

To the contemporary observer, the most important part of the opinion of the Court was its holding that the Missouri Compromise was unconstitutional. Five justices[83] concurred with Taney in this holding. This aspect of the opinion was also most strongly censured by critics. Speaking on the Court's view "on the question of the power of the Constitution to carry slavery" into the territories, a leading northern senator declared "beyond all question, to any fair and unprejudiced mind, that the decision has nothing to stand upon except assumption, and bad logic from the assumptions made."[84] The Taney holding was deceptively simple. It began by recognizing congressional authority to acquire new territory and to determine what rules and regulations to make for any territory.[85] Such authority was, however, subject to the limitations imposed by the Constitution upon governmental power, including those designed to safeguard private property rights. In particular, property rights are protected by the Due Process Clause of the Fifth Amendment: "And an Act of Congress which deprives a citizen of the United States of his liberty or property, merely because he came himself or brought his property into a particular Territory of the United States, and who had committed no offence against the laws, could hardly be dignified with the name of due process of law." [86] Hence the Missouri Compromise prohibition against the holding of property in slaves is unconstitutional and void.

Two aspects of the reasoning just summarized are of special significance. In the first place, Taney depends upon the assumption that congressional power over slavery in the territories is limited by the Constitution itself. This basic holding was sharply censured by former Senator Thomas H. Benton, who, though near death from cancer, published a lengthy attack on the decision soon after it was handed down: "The Court sets out with a fundamental mistake, which pervades its entire opinion, and is the parent of its portentous error. That mistake is the assumption, that the Constitution extends to Territories as well as to States."[87]

[83] Justices Wayne, Grier, Daniel, Campbell, and Catron.

[84] *Cong. Globe*, 35th Cong., 1st Sess. 617.

[85] Though it did so in what we should now consider a peculiar way—recognizing it as an implied power rather than one expressly provided in Article IV, section 3, giving Congress power to make rules and regulations for the territories.

[86] 19 How. at 450.

[87] *T.H. Benton, Historical and Legal Examination of That Part of the Decision of the Supreme Court of the United States in the Dred Scott Case Which Declares the Unconstitutionality of the Missouri Compromise Act* 11–12 (1857).

Though the law on the matter may not have been settled over a century ago, today we can see that Taney was correct in his approach to the question of the applicability of constitutional limitations in the territories. The alternative is to hold that Congress may, "when it enters a Territory . . . , put off its character, and assume discretionary or despotic powers which the Constitution has denied to it."[88] Americans migrating to a territory would, if that were true, be mere colonists, dependent upon the will of the federal government.

Later decisions of the Supreme Court confirm the Taney reasoning. The landmark *Insular Cases*,[89] decided at the turn of the last century, held that a fundamental provision such as the Due Process Clause is definitely binding in all American territory, including conquered territory subject to military government.[90] More recently, Justice Black has used language recalling that of Taney himself; according to Black, whenever our government acts, it can only act, regardless of locale, "in accordance with all the limitations imposed by the Constitution."[91]

Having held the Congress bound by the requirements of due process in legislating for the territories, Taney next proceeded to hold that the prohibition of slavery violated due process. Here we come to the second significant aspect of his holding on congressional power. In his ruling that the Missouri Compromise was unconstitutional, Taney was, for the first time in Supreme Court jurisprudence, holding that the Due Process Clause has a substantive as well as a procedural aspect. It was as a violation of substantive due process that the congressional prohibition of slavery was stricken down; what Taney was saying was that a law which deprives a citizen of his property in slaves simply because he brings such property into a territory is arbitrary and unreasonable and hence violative of due process.

Although *Dred Scott* was the first case in which the Supreme Court used the Due Process Clause as a substantive restriction upon governmental power, the Taney approach was not something made up out of legal whole cloth. On the contrary, the development of substantive due process was one of the outstanding judicial achievements of the last century. It began in several state courts during the 1830s and 1840s and culminated in *Wynehamer* v. *People*,[92] decided by the highest court of New York in the period between the first and second arguments in

88 Taney, C.J., 19 How. at 449.

89 De Lima v. Bidwell, 182 U.S. 1 (1901); Dooley v. United States, 182 U.S. 222 (1901); Downes v. Bidwell, 182 U.S. 244 (1901).

90 *See* 2 B. Schwartz, *A Commentary on the Constitution of the United States: The Powers of Government* 299 (1963).

91 Reid v. Covert, 354 U.S. 1, 6 (1957).

92 13 N.Y. 378 (1856).

Dred Scott.[93] That decision (recognized as epoch-making almost as soon as it was rendered) may well have been the immediate source of Taney's opinion on due process.[94]

Nor was the notion that congressional prohibition of slavery violated due process original with Taney. In the debates preceding the Missouri Compromise, several members of Congress expressed the view that prohibiting slavery in Missouri would violate the Due Process Clause. [95] In 1841 a member of the Supreme Court declared, with regard to slaves, "Being property . . . , the owners are protected from any violations of the rights of property by Congress, under the fifth amendment."[96] Plainly, this was getting very close to Taney's approach in the *Dred Scott* opinion.

Even more relevant to the Taney treatment of due process as a substantive restraint was the fact that Justice Curtis himself in 1852, while on circuit, had stricken down a state liquor law on substantive due process grounds.[97] Particularly suggestive is the fact that Curtis discussed his approach in this case with Taney, who approved the reasoning employed.[98] Taney had only to change the word "liquor" in the Curtis opinion to "slave" and he had the substance of the reasoning by which he invalidated the Missouri Compromise.[99] In view of this, it is surprising that the Curtis dissent in *Dred Scott* emphasized the novel nature of the Taney approach on due process.

Today the Taney application of substantive due process may be considered unduly simplistic, if not naive. The mere fact that a law destroys property rights, we now know, does not necessarily mean that it violates due process. Governmental power does, in appropriate circumstances, include the power to prohibit as well as the power to regulate.[100] It should, however, be borne in mind that Taney was speaking at the very infancy of the doctrine of substantive due process. If his approach was relatively unsophisticated, the same was true of the other early opinions that developed it. In the era after the Civil War the

[93] *See* 3 B. Schwartz, *A Commentary on the Constitution of the United States: The Rights of Property* 31 (1965).

[94] *See* Corwin, in *Kutler, supra* note 29, at 134.

[95] *See*, e.g., *Annals of Cong.*, 16th Cong., 1st Sess. 1262, 1521.

[96] Baldwin, J., in Groves v. Slaughter, 15 Pet. 449, 515 (U.S. 1841). In view of this statement, it is curious that Nevins refers to the fact that Justice Baldwin was no longer on the Court by the time of Dred Scott as contributing to the bitterness of the Free Soilers. *Nevins, supra* note 10, at 92.

[97] Greene v. Briggs, 1 Curtis 311 (C.C.R.I. 1852). *See also* Greene v. James, 2 Curtis 187 (C.C.R.I. 1854). The Curtis approach here was not exactly that of substantive due process, but it went far in that direction.

[98] *Curtis, supra* note 56, at 173.

[99] *See Hopkins, supra* note 54, at 137.

[100] *See* 1 *Schwartz, supra* note 90, at 222–29.

Taney approach became established in the law. Toward the end of the century, substantive due process was to be used as *the* fundamental restriction upon governmental action interfering with property rights. The discrediting of the *Dred Scott* decision did not really affect the seminal nature of the concept invoked by Taney. Though the particular property interest which he sought to protect was soon to become anachronistic, the doctrine he articulated opened a new chapter in our constitutional law.[101]

NEGRO CITIZENSHIP

In 1834 the status of the free colored population in Pennsylvania was elaborately set forth in a pamphlet published by a member of the bar of that state. It arrived at the conclusion that the free Negro was neither a citizen of the United States nor a citizen of Pennsylvania. A copy of the pamphlet was sent to Chief Justice Marshall, and he sent the author a letter expressly endorsing his conclusion on Negro citizenship.[102] That Marshall, not long before his death, came to the same conclusion as Taney with regard to Negro citizenship is a fact that (so far as the present writer could determine) has been unknown to previous commentators. It is surely relevant, in considering the legal correctness of the Taney ruling on citizenship, to bear in mind that the same result was reached (albeit extra-judicially) by the greatest judge in our history. At the least, it indicates that the Taney ruling was not as contrary to law as most of its critics have contended.

At the time, however, Taney's holding on the citizenship issue was concurred in expressly only by Justices Wayne and Daniel; the other majority justices did not deal with the issue in their opinions. This led George Ticknor Curtis (a younger brother of the *Dred Scott* dissenter) to assert that, since only three justices were on the Taney side of the citizenship issue, the Taney opinion on the matter could not be considered binding: "As *three* is not a majority of *nine*, the case of Dred Scott does not furnish a judicial precedent or judicial decision on this question."[103] Two points should be borne in mind. An opinion delivered just after *Dred Scott* by a member of the Supreme Judicial Court of Maine stated that the citizenship holding in the Taney opinion "cannot be questioned. It was announced by him as 'the opinion of the court;' and I do not perceive why the other members of the court

101 *Compare Kutler, supra* note 29, at xix.

102 *Cong. Globe*, 42nd Cong., 1st Sess. 576.

103 *G.T. Curtis, The Just Supremacy of Congress over the Territories* (1859), in *Kutler, supra* note 29, at 103.

should not be regarded as concurring in it, except upon those points which they have expressly disclaimed."[104]   Recent commentators like Allan Nevins who have restated the George Ticknor Curtis assertion rely solely upon the opinions pronounced by the majority justices.[105]   They ignore the technical rule that the decision of the Court is expressed in the Court's mandate. "The mandate to the circuit court could not have issued, except by order of a majority of the court. This mandate directed the case 'to be dismissed for want of jurisdiction, for the reason that the plaintiff in error is not a citizen of Missouri, in the sense in which that word is used in the Constitution.' This was equivalent to an express denial that he was a citizen of the United States. And the ground of the decision was, that he belonged to a class of persons none of whom are citizens."[106]   Even more important is the fact that the country was not at all concerned with the technical distinction between decision and *obiter*. To almost everyone at the time, the Taney opinion was synonymous with the decision of the Court. When Taney ruled on the citizenship issue, people assumed, with *Harper's Weekly*, "that the Court has decided that free negroes are not citizens of the United States."[107]

The denial of Negro citizenship is the aspect of *Dred Scott* that is most anomalous today. It seems completely out of line with constitutional conceptions to doom the members of a particular race to live in permanent limbo, forever barred from the dignity of citizenship. We must, however, be careful not to look at the problem presented to the Taney Court through the distorting lenses of conceptions postdating the Fourteenth Amendment. Before the Civil War the question of Negro citizenship was by no means settled clearly. What authority there was tended to support Taney rather than Curtis on the matter. Several attorneys general (including Taney himself in 1832 [108]) and a number of state courts had concluded that free Negroes were not citizens. [109] Their decisions were based upon the many disabilities from which Negroes suffered, which made it plain that they did not enjoy the full rights of citizens.

It is true that there were state decisions cited by the Curtis dissent holding that free Negroes were citizens. But those decisions use the

---

104 Opinions of the Justices, 44 Maine 505, 591 (1857), per Davis, J.

105 *See Nevins, supra* note 10, at 92.

106 Supra note 104.

107 *Kutler, supra* note 29, at 49.

108 1 *Op. Att'y Gen.* 506 (1821); 7 *Op. Att'y Gen.* 746, 753 (1856). See also an unpublished 1832 Taney opinion to such effect quoted in *Swisher, supra* note 5, at 154.

109 E.g., Amy v. Smith, 1 Littell 326 (Ky. 1822); Crandell v. State, 10 Conn. 339 (Conn. 1834); Hobbs v. Fogg, 6 Watts 553 (Pa. 1837).

notion of citizenship itself in a manner which now seems most peculiar. Thus *State* v. *Manuel* [110] —the case most relied on in the Curtis dissent— involved a North Carolina law providing that, where a free Negro had been convicted of a misdemeanor and could not pay the fine, his services could be sold for up to five years to the highest bidder. This statute (which applied only to Negroes, not whites) was upheld by the state court, which stated in its opinion that what "citizenship" the Negro had was of a most restricted sort—on a lower level, as it were, than that possessed by other citizens. Taney could easily have used the *Manuel* case to support his basic thesis of inequality in the treatment of the races.

Curtis also used *State* v. *Newsom*, [111] a later North Carolina case, to support the *Manuel* citation, but *Newsom* sustained a law making it a crime for "any free Negro" to carry a gun or knife. Here again we have a disability which seems inconsistent with the rights of citizenship. The law was attacked on the ground that free Negroes, as citizens, were entitled to the same rights as other citizens. The court stated that *Manuel* was a "controlling influence." Yet, in upholding the law, it went on to say, "the free people of color cannot be considered as citizens, in the largest sense of the term, or if they are, they occupy such a position in society, as justifies the Legislature in adopting a course of policy in its acts peculiar to them." [112]

The truth seems to be that implied in the *Newsom* case: Negro citizenship was a legal euphemism. The current of judicial decision was relegating the free Negro to a subordinate status, regardless of whether he was clothed with the formal title of citizen. Actually, a third class of free residents in this country was being created in the law: there were now citizens, free Negroes, and aliens. [113] In this sense, the *Dred Scott* decision was, despite the Curtis dissent, only confirming the pre-Civil War trend of court decisions on the subject.

Yet, if the Taney conclusion on citizenship had stronger support in the law than most commentators have recognized, it must still be conceded that the decision was little short of disastrous. It meant that, without constitutional amendment, the Negro was consigned to a permanent second-class status which could not be changed even if all the slaves were ultimately freed. More fundamentally, it gave the lie to the very basis of the American heritage: the notion of equality was the

---

110 4 Devereaux and Battle 144 (N.C. 1838).

111 5 Iredell 203 (N.C. 1840).

112 *Id*. at 206–7.

113 *See Hopkins, supra* note 54, at 99. *Compare* 4 *Op. Att'y Gen*. 147 (1843), which states something like the view just stated.

central theme of the Declaration of Independence itself, "the electric cord in that Declaration that links the hearts of patriotic and liberty-loving men together."[114] The ruling would have aborted the effort to give effect to the "progressive improvement in the condition of all men" [115] that had been a dominant force since the founding of the republic.

CODA

On June 12, 1857, Stephen A. Douglas, himself the chief political victim of the *Dred Scott* decision, addressed a grand jury at Springfield, vigorously defending the Supreme Court and rejecting the charge that the justices had gone out of their way to decide the crucial constitutional issues. According to Douglas, if the Court had relied on a technicality to avoid the main issues, the outcry against it would have been even worse: "If the case had been disposed of in that way, who can doubt . . . the character of the denunciations which would have been hurled upon the devoted heads of those illustrious judges, with much more plausibility and show of fairness than they are now denounced for having decided the case . . . upon its merits?"[116] The Court might, as Douglas claimed, have disappointed many, but it could scarcely have tarnished its reputation to the extent that the actual decision did. As a general proposition, it may be said that the Supreme Court as an institution has never been harmed by abstention from political issues. On the contrary, most of the controversies in which it has been embroiled have been caused by failure to follow the doctrine of judicial self-restraint.

Regardless of legal logic, the opponents of slavery could not accept the Court's decision as final, particularly the Republican Party, whose very *raison d'être* was undercut by it. This explains (though it may not justify) the vituperation which Republican orators directed against both the decision and the Court. Lincoln's repeated claim that there was a master conspiratorial plan which sought to use the Supreme Court to make the country "an entire slave nation"[117] by a decision "ere long . . . declaring that the Constitution . . . does not permit a *state* to exclude slavery"[118] must be laid to a lack of understanding of consti-

---

114 *Lincoln, supra* note 49, at 500.

115 *Lincoln, supra* note 49, at 407.

116 *Remarks of the Hon. Stephen A. Douglas on Kansas, Utah, and the Dred Scott Decision* 6 (1857).

117 *Lincoln, supra* note 49, at 453.

118 *Lincoln, supra* note 49, at 467.

tutional doctrine. *Dred Scott* could be based upon the Fifth Amendment, for it dealt with congressional authority; before the Fourteenth Amendment, there was no organic provision upon which the Court could base a comparable limitation upon state power.[119]

After the Civil War, Jefferson Davis prepared some notes for Major W. T. Walthall, who was helping him prepare his well-known history of the Confederacy, "on the assigned causes for the invasion of the South." In these notes he made the curious assertion that "the unjust and offensive denial of an equal right to occupy the territories with any species of property recognized by the laws of their states was one of the causes which provoked the Southern people to withdraw from an association in which the terms of the partnership were disregarded." [120] Davis was confused in his recollection of what had happened. It was not until 1862, well after the southern states had seceded, that Congress passed a law expressly prohibiting slavery in the territories[121] (thus legislatively denying the right in slave property in the territories which *Dred Scott* had recognized). Davis' recollection does, however, demonstrate the crucial importance of *Dred Scott* in the events leading to the Civil War. In his notes for Walthall, he stated flatly that "the territorial question . . . is another . . . pretext for the war waged against the Southern states."[122]

The *Dred Scott* decision was thus a major factor in precipitating the political polarization of the nation. It was actually the catalyst for the civil conflict that soon followed. With it collapsed the practical possibility of resolving by political and legal means the issues which divided the nation. Thenceforth, extremists dominated the scene. Bloodshed alone could settle the issue of slavery and of the very nature of the Union, which that issue had placed in the balance.

[119] Barron v. Mayor of Baltimore, 7 Pet. 243 (U.S. 1833). *See also* 3 *Lincoln, supra* note 49, at 100–101, where Lincoln assumed that the Fifth Amendment was applicable to the states. In support of the Lincoln view, see *H. V. Jaffa, Crisis of the House Divided* 280–93 (1959).

[120] Jefferson Davis, Notes for W.T.W., Charles Hamilton, Auction No. 31, Item 83 (1968). This apparently unpublished manuscript is not dated, but appears, from its condition and context, to have been written shortly after the Civil War.

[121] 12 Stat. 432 (1862).

[122] *Supra* note 120.

CHAPTER SIX

Constitutional Crucible

SECESSION AND UNION

In his 1839 letter to Gerrit Smith, John Quincy Adams predicted that the slavery conflict would ultimately lead to both secession and civil war. "I believe that long before [emancipation] . . . the slave holding representation would Secede in a mass, and that the States represented by them would secede from the Union. I know that among the abolitionists there are some leading and able men, who consider this a desirable event. I myself believe that it would naturally and infallibly lead to the total abolition of Slavery but it would be through the ultimate operation of a War, more terrible than the thirty years war . . . and I shrink from it with horror."[1]

The conflict which Adams so graphically foresaw raised the overriding issue of the nature of the Union itself. That issue had been at the core of most of the pre-Civil War constitutional controversy. "That the Slave holders of the South." Adams went on in his letter to Smith, "should flatter themselves that by seceding from this Union they could establish their peculiar institutions in perpetuity, is in my judgment one of those absurd self-delusions which would be surprising if they did not compose the first chapter in the history of human nature." Yet, he

---

[1] Letter from John Quincy Adams to Gerrit Smith, July 31, 1839, Charles Hamilton, Auction No. 10, Item 1a (1965).

accurately guessed, "the Slaveholders do so flatter themselves, and will act accordingly."[2]

This "delusion" was a natural consequence of the southern conception of the Constitution. Secession was but the logical culmination of the doctrine of states' rights and state sovereignty which dominated thinking below the Mason-Dixon Line. That doctrine was so ingrained in the southern mind that it enabled the movers of secession to (in Lincoln's phrase) "sugar-coat" their rebellion "by an insidious debauching of the public mind. They invented an ingenious sophism, which, if conceded, was followed by perfectly logical steps, through all the incidents, to the complete destruction of the Union. The sophism itself is, that any state of the Union may, *consistently* with the national Constitution, and therefore *lawfully*, and *peacefully*, withdraw from the Union, without the consent of the Union, or of any other state."[3] The truth is that secession and union are constitutionally incompatible. If the Civil War accomplished anything in the constitutional sphere, it was to reject categorically "the position that secession is *consistent* with the Constitution—is *lawful* and peaceful."[4] That position was relegated to the realm of constitutional heresy along with the Calhoun doctrine of the states as separate sovereignties upon which it was based.

From a southern point of view, the Civil War may be looked at as an attempt to overrule the nationalistic conception of the Constitution which had prevailed since Marshall became chief justice. Virginian though he was, Marshall's dominant aim was to establish a strong nation, with the powers needed to govern a continent. The decisions of Marshall and his colleagues constructed federal supremacy upon so strong a base that it has never since been subjected to successful *legal* attack. The adherents of state sovereignty could hope to prevail only by resorting to methods outside the judicial arena. To render the Constitution workable, it had to incorporate "a coercive principle"—the question being, as one of the Framers put it, whether it should be "a coercion of law, or a coercion of arms."[5] With national supremacy so firmly established by the coercion of law, its opponents deemed themselves relegated to the coercion of arms if their view of the nature of the nation was to prevail.

Thus regarded, the Civil War was the test of fire for the national system created in 1787. "In the body of our Constitution," Chief

---

[2] *Id.*

[3] 4 *The Collected Works of Abraham Lincoln* 432–33 (R.P. Basler ed. 1953).

[4] *Id.* at 435.

[5] Oliver Ellsworth, in 3 M. Farrand, *The Records of the Federal Convention of 1787*, at 241 (1911).

Justice Warren has stated, "the Founding Fathers insured that the Government would have the power necessary to govern."[6] The defeat of the South placed the imprimatur of arms upon both the intent of the Framers and the Marshall interpretation of federal power. The conduct of the war itself furnished ample proof of the soundness of the Marshall conception. "The Federal Government," Winston Churchill tells us, "gaining power steadily at the expense of the states, rapidly won unquestioned control over all the forces of the Union. The Southern 'Sovereign States,' on the other hand, were unable even under the stress of war to abandon the principle of decentralisation for which they had been contending."[7] The kind of government southerners wanted was not the type that could win a lengthy war; states' rights was a hopeless base for total conflict.

The war not only confirmed but accelerated the trend toward strong national government that has been the underlying theme of our constitutional development. "The South," says a leading southerner, "with whatever justification, tried in '61 to break the Union. She succeeded only in strengthening what she fought against."[8] Out of the conflict arose a stronger national government—no longer merely *primus inter pares*. Until the war the advocates of state sovereignty could, despite the uniform case law in opposition to the view, continue to assert the temporary contractual nature of the Union. The defeat of the South meant the final repudiation of such an assertion. In the law itself this repudiation was marked by *Texas* v. *White*,[9] decided by the Supreme Court shortly after the war ended.

In *Texas* v. *White*, the State of Texas brought an original action to enjoin the payment of certain United States bonds owned by the state before the war and negotiated by the Confederate state government to the defendants. The key issue presented was whether Texas was then a state of the Union and, as such, capable of bringing suit. Defendants contended that she was not—that, having seceded and not yet being represented in the Congress, she was still out of the Union. According to Chief Justice Chase's opinion, the ordinance of secession by Texas was a legal nullity. Texas consequently always remained a state within the purview of the Constitution: "When, therefore, Texas became one of the United States, she entered into an indissoluble relation. . . . The act which consummated her admission into the Union was something more than a compact; it was the incorporation of a new member into

---

6 Chief Justice Warren, in *The Great Rights* 89 (E. Cahn ed. 1963).

7 4 *W.S. Churchill, A History of the English Speaking Peoples* 176 (1958).

8 *J.M. Dabbs, The Southern Heritage* 116 (1958).

9 7 Wall. 700 (U.S. 1869).

the political body. And it was final. . . . There was no place for reconsideration, or revocation."[10]

It is all too easy to dismiss the case as only the judicial ratification of the real decision on the validity of secession made at Appomattox courthouse. To be sure, if the actual outcome of the conflict had been different, the Supreme Court decision could never have been made, but that is true because the constitutional nature of the Union would have been completely altered by military power. As a purely legal decision, under the Constitution as it is written, *Texas* v. *White* is sound. It is "self-evident that the Union could scarcely have had a valuable existence had it been judicially determined that powers of sovereignty were exclusively in the States":[11] the very language of the Constitution refutes the notion that the states have a sovereign right to secede at will. The Articles of Confederation declare the Union's character to be "perpetual." Says Chief Justice Chase, "when these Articles were found to be inadequate to the exigencies of the country, the Constitution was ordained 'to form a more perfect Union.' It is difficult to convey the idea of indissoluble unity more clearly than by these words. What can be indissoluble if a perpetual Union, made more perfect, is not?"[12]

The Constitution is thus a bond of national unity, not a mere league which may be dissolved at the pleasure of any party.[13] "The Constitution of the United States," said a member of the highest court in 1871, "established a government, and not a league, compact or partnership. . . . The doctrine so long contended for, that the Federal Union was a mere compact of States, and that the States, if they chose, might annul or disregard the acts of the National legislature, or might secede from the Union at their pleasure, and that the General Government had no power to coerce them into submission to the Constitution, should be regarded as definitely and forever overthrown."[14]

PRIZE CASES

The one decision of consequence rendered by the Supreme Court during the Civil War was that in the 1863 *Prize Cases*.[15] It arose out of one of the emergency measures taken by President Lincoln just after

---

[10] *Id.* at 726.

[11] *T.M. Cooley, Constitutional History of the United States* 49 (1889).

[12] 7 Wall. at 725.

[13] *Cooley, supra* note 11.

[14] Bradley, J., concurring, in Legal Tender Cases, 12 Wall. 457, 554–55 (U.S. 1871).

[15] 2 Black 635 (U.S. 1862). For a good discussion, *see* D. Silver, *Lincoln's Supreme Court* ch. 9 (1956).

the fall of Fort Sumter, his proclamation in April, 1861, of a blockade of southern ports. Four ships had been captured by Union naval vessels enforcing the blockade and had been brought into ports to be libeled as prizes. Their owners contended that they had not been lawfully seized because a blockade was a belligerent act which could not be proclaimed in the absence of a state of war declared by the Congress.

The formal proclamation of a blockade at the outset of the Civil War has been criticized as a tactical error.[16] In international law, a blockade implies a state of belligerency. In its neutrality proclamation of May, 1861, Great Britain took note of such belligerency, and the British foreign secretary was able to state, in reply to the claim that the proclamation was "precipitate," "It was, on the contrary, your own Government which, in assuming the belligerent right of blockade, recognized the Southern States as belligerents."[17] Legally speaking, the proclamation of a blockade, with its recognition of belligerency, constitutes an act of war. To the Supreme Court, indeed, it was Lincoln's blockade proclamation that constituted the beginning of the Civil War.[18] But could the president thus begin a war without violating the claimed "inexorable rule" that the country could be involved in war legally only by declaration of the Congress?

The Court in the *Prize Cases* avoided a direct answer to this question by stating that the president did not, by his blockade proclamation or any other act, initiate the conflict. In his argument on behalf of the Government, William M. Evarts urged that "war is, emphatically, a question of actualities."[19] Whenever a situation assumes the proportions and pursues the methods of war, he said, the peace is driven out, and the president may assert the warlike strength of the nation. Evarts' approach was essentially that followed by the Court. The actuality of the situation confronting the president after Sumter was one of war: "However long may have been its previous conception, it nevertheless sprung forth from the parent brain, a Minerva in the full panoply of *war*." The president did not initiate such war, but he was bound to accept the challenge "in the shape it presented itself, without waiting for Congress to baptize it with a name; and no name given to it by him or them could change the fact."[20]

A commentary on the *Prize Cases* asserts that that case was as important as a case can be in shaping the contours of presidential power

[16] *See C. Sandburg, Abraham Lincoln* 275 (1966).

[17] 7 *J.B. Moore, A Digest of International Law* 190 (1906).

[18] The Protector, 12 Wall. 700, 702 (U.S. 1872).

[19] Prize Cases, 17 L. Ed. 459, 465. The Evarts argument is not given in the official report of the case.

[20] 2 Black at 669.

for future occasions when presidents would wage war without congressional authorization.[21] The decision itself holds only that the president could deal with the situation presented after Sumter as a war and employ what belligerent measures he deemed necessary without waiting for Congress to declare war.[22] It would be absurd for the president to be required, simply because the Congress had not declared its existence, "to affect a technical ignorance of the existence of a war, which all the world acknowledges to be the greatest civil war known in the history of the human race, and thus cripple the arms of the Government and paralyze its power by subtle definitions and ingenious sophisms."[23]

It is when we look beyond the bare holding to the language of the Court and its import that we can understand the wide implications of the *Prize Cases*. War, said the opinion of Justice Grier, is "that state in which a nation prosecutes its right by force."[24] Under such a definition, the president can in fact (if not in the technical contemplation of the Constitution) initiate a war. The *Prize Cases* constitute a rejection of the doctrine that only Congress can stamp a hostile situation with the character of war and thereby authorize the legal consequences which ensue from a state of war.[25]

Rejection of the rule that only Congress can initiate a war has been of tremendous practical significance. If the president can initiate belligerent measures to cope with civil rebellion, why may he not do so to deal with hostile invasion? In such a case also he would be empowered to meet the challenge as war without waiting for Congress to act. It would be no less a war for the fact that it was begun not by formal declaration but by unilateral act.[26] Must the president take belligerent measures only after the first blow has been struck? Such a limitation on his powers could mean national annihilation in an age in which a nation has the absolute power to destroy an enemy. A constitution which did not permit the commander in chief to order belligerent acts whenever necessary to defend his country's interests would be little more than a suicide pact.[27]

The key passage of the *Prize Cases* opinion asserts that whether the president "has met with such armed hostile resistance, and a civil war of such alarming proportions as will compel him to accord to them the

---

[21] C. Rossiter, *The Supreme Court and the Commander-in-Chief* 75 (1951).

[22] Williams v. Bruffy, 96 U.S. 176, 189 (1878).

[23] Prize Cases, 2 Black at 669–70.

[24] *Id.* at 666.

[25] This was the view of the dissent in *id.* at 690.

[26] *Id.* at 668.

[27] *Compare* Jackson, J., dissenting, in Terminiello v. Chicago, 337 U.S. 1, 37 (1949).

character of belligerents, is a question to be decided *by him*."[28] A state
of war may exist without a declaration,[29] and the president's action in
ordering an act of war is itself a clear indication that such a state does
exist. In the words of the *Prize Cases* opinion, "The proclamation of
blockade is itself official and conclusive evidence to the Court that a
state of war existed which demanded and authorized a recourse to such
a measure."[30]

The difficulty, of course, is that noted by Lincoln himself in his
Mexican war statement quoted in Chapter II above. If we give the
president the power to order the commission of belligerent acts whenever he deems necessary, we invest him with the power to make war
without legal check. His authority is to act to defend the interests of
the United States, but history shows that this is no real restraint, since
even aggressive action can be framed in ostensibly defensive terms.

MERRYMAN AND MILITARY POWER

"Determining the proper role to be assigned to the military in a
democratic society," declared Chief Justice Warren in his 1962 James
Madison lecture, "has been a troublesome problem for every nation
that has aspired to a free political life."[31] The claims of military power
were first asserted in extreme form in the American constitutional
system during the Civil War. It cannot be said that a proper balance
between military power and law was achieved during that conflict. On
the contrary, in the midst of civil strife most of all, as Burke pointed
out in his *Reflections on the French Revolution* "laws are commanded
to hold their tongues amongst arms; and tribunals fall to the ground
with the peace they are no longer able to uphold."

At the outset the extreme claims of both war and law were presented. The former was personified by President Lincoln, the latter by
Chief Justice Taney. To deal with the life-and-death crisis which faced
the government after Sumter, Lincoln assumed unprecedented powers.
On his own authority he suspended the writ of habeas corpus and
ordered wholesale arrests without warrants, detentions without trials,
and imprisonments without judicial convictions. Newspapers were

28 2 Black at 670.
29 Jackson, J., concurring, in Youngstown Sheet & Tube Co. v. Sawyer, 343 U.S. 579, 642
(1952).
30 2 Black at 670.
31 *Supra* note 6, at 90.

seized and their publication suppressed;[32] persons were arrested and held incommunicado by military officers acting under presidential authority. As Taney put it, the military had "thrust aside the judicial authorities and officers to whom the constitution has confided the power and duty of interpreting and administering the laws, and substituted a military government in its place, to be administered and executed by military officers."[33]

The passage quoted is from an opinion Taney delivered in May, 1861, in the celebrated *Merryman* case.[34] On April 27 Lincoln authorized the commanding general of the army to suspend the right of habeas corpus along any military line between Philadelphia and Washington. A month later Taney, sitting in the federal Circuit Court in Baltimore, was petitioned for habeas corpus by John Merryman, who had been arrested by the army and confined in Fort McHenry for his secessionist activities, particularly his participation in the attack upon the Sixth Massachusetts Militia while it was en route to Washington and the destruction of railroad bridges to prevent the passage of troops. Sitting in chambers, Taney granted a writ of habeas corpus directed to the general commanding the fort. On the return date, an aide-de-camp (in full military uniform and wearing, appropriately, a sword and bright red sash) appeared in the courtroom and declined obedience to the writ on the ground that it had been suspended by the commanding general pursuant to the April 27 order of the president. Taney issued a writ of attachment for contempt against the general, but the marshal seeking to serve it was refused entry to the fort. Taney then delivered his *Merryman* opinion, in which he sharply condemned as illegal the suspension of habeas corpus by the president and the arrest, without warrant and hearing, of a civilian by military order, but his attempt to uphold the letter of the law against military claims of emergency was fruitless. As he himself plaintively put it, "I have exercised all the power which the constitution and laws confer upon me, but that power has been resisted by a force too strong for me to overcome."[35]

Taney filed his opinion with the clerk of the Circuit Court, with the direction that a copy be sent to the president: "It will then remain for that high officer, in fulfilment of his constitutional obligation, to 'take care that the laws be faithfully executed,' to determine what measures he will take to cause the civil process of the United States to be respected and enforced."[36] We do not know what Lincoln did with his

[32] R.S. Harper, *Lincoln and the Press* 109 (1951).
[33] *Ex parte* Merryman, 17 F. Cas. 144, 153 (D. Md. 1861).
[34] 17 F. Cas. 144 (D. Md. 1861).
[35] *Id.* at 153.
[36] *Id.*

copy of the Taney opinion (or whether he ever received it), but we do know that he went right on exercising the power that Taney had branded unconstitutional. In addition to other limited suspensions, such as that in the *Merryman* case, he issued an order on September 24, 1862, suspending the writ throughout the country for all persons confined by military authority.[37] Despite the refusal of the military to obey Taney's writ, however, Merryman was released from military custody shortly afterwards, and a subsequent indictment against him was never prosecuted.[38]

A century later, looking back at the conflict, we can see that neither the Lincoln nor the Taney philosophy alone is adequate. What is needed at such times is a reconciliation of the extreme demands of war and law, not exclusion of the one or the other. It was with keen perception that Justice Jackson wrote, shortly before his death, "Had Mr. Lincoln scrupulously observed the Taney policy, I do not know whether we would have had any liberty, and had the Chief Justice adopted Mr. Lincoln's philosophy as the philosophy of the law, I again do not know whether we would have had any liberty."[39]

When all is said and done, however, there remains something admirable in Taney's action in the *Merryman* case: "There is no sublimer picture in our history than this of the aged Chief Justice—the fires of Civil War kindling around him . . . —serene and unafraid, . . . interposing the shield of law in the defense of the liberty of the citizen. Chief-Justice Coke when the question was put to him by the King as to what he would do in a case where the King believed his prerogative concerned, made the answer which has become immortal, 'When the case happens, I shall do that which shall be fit for a judge to do.' Chief Justice Taney when presented with a case of presidential prerogative did that which was fit for a judge to do."[40]

SUSPENSION OF HABEAS CORPUS

The *Merryman* case raised in dramatic form the constitutional issue of the suspension of habeas corpus. The Constitution expressly recognizes that the writ may be suspended where emergency requires it, but where in the government is the power of suspension lodged? The refusal of the military authorities to obey the *Merryman* writ raised the question of

37 5 *Lincoln, supra* note 3 at 436–37.

38 *See J.G. Randall, Constitutional Problems under Lincoln* 161 (rev. ed. 1951); *D. Sprague, Freedom under Lincoln* 43–44 (1965).

39 *R.H. Jackson, The Supreme Court in the American System of Government* 76 (1955).

40 Mikell, in 4 *Great American Lawyers* 188–89 (W.D. Lewis ed. 1908).

whether the president had such power. Taney's answer was an unqualified negative. The claim, said he, was one that he had listened to "with some surprise, for I had supposed it to be one of those points of constitutional law upon which there was no difference of opinion, and that it was admitted on all hands, that the privilege of the writ could not be suspended, except by act of congress."[41]

His conclusion was based in large part upon the fact that the Habeas Corpus Clause is found in Article I; "this article is devoted to the legislative department of the United States, and has not the slightest reference to the executive department."[42] Article II, from which presidential power is derived, contains nothing on habeas corpus or its suspension. According to Taney, "if the high power over the liberty of the citizen now claimed, was intended to be conferred on the president, it would undoubtedly be found in plain words in this article, but there is not a word in it that can furnish the slightest ground to justify the exercise of the power."[43]

Some five months after Lincoln's September 24, 1862, general suspension order, the Congress enacted an 1863 statute which expressly authorized the president to suspend the privilege of the writ of habeas corpus, in any part of the United States, "during the present rebellion . . . whenever, in his judgment, the public safety may require it."[44] This was the statute involved in the celebrated *Milligan* case,[45] which will be discussed in the next chapter. The *Milligan* case assumes the validity of the 1863 act both as a ratification of prior executive suspensions and as a delegation to the president of prospective power to suspend the writ.

No one has ever doubted that, at the least, the Habeas Corpus Clause of Article I, section 9, empowered the legislative department to suspend the writ when the public safety required it. The only possible question concerns the delegation to the president in the 1863 act. Delegation of the power to suspend in particular instances appears to be essential if the authority of suspension is to prove effective: the Framers could scarcely have intended that Congress itself was to decide, in every case, while the danger was running its course, whether the writ should issue.[46] On the contrary, the legislature has the power to suspend generally or in

---

[41] 17 F. Cas. at 148. Taney's assumption was general at the time; *see Ex parte* Bollman, 4 Cranch 75, 101 (U.S. 1807); 3 *J. Story, Commentaries on the Constitution of the United States* 209 (1833).

[42] *Id.*

[43] *Id.* at 149.

[44] 12 Stat. 755 (1863).

[45] *Ex parte* Milligan, 4 Wall. 2 (U.S. 1866), p. 170 *infra.*

[46] *Compare Lincoln, supra* note 3, at 431.

particular cases, or it may (as it did in 1863) commit the matter to the judgment of the president. [47] The act of 1863, viewed both as ratification and delegation, settled the immediate legal question of Lincoln's power to suspend the writ, but the broader issue raised in the *Merryman* case remained in question. From the Civil War to the present, however, the consensus of learned opinion has been that Taney was right and Lincoln was wrong.[48]

RAISING OF ARMED FORCES

Under the Constitution the authority to raise and support the armed forces is expressly vested only in the legislative department.[49] The president, as commander in chief, may direct how the military establishment is to be employed and may also call the militia and reserves into service, but it is the Congress which must supply him with actual forces to command. What happens, however, if the country is confronted with a war emergency without a military establishment adequate to meet it? In such a case, may the president act on his own authority to secure the necessary troops and other personnel?

These questions were no longer hypothetical after Sumter. The circumstances in which the government then found itself have been characterized as unprecedented.[50] Congress was not in session, and immediate executive action to preserve the Union was called for. The armed forces in the spring of 1861 numbered only some sixteen thousand men, a pitifully inadequate number to deal with the emergency. Acting under a statute of 1795,[51] President Lincoln issued a proclamation on April 15, 1861, calling seventy-five thousand of the militia into federal service, but the militia system alone could not furnish the personnel needed. On May 3, without statutory authority, Lincoln issued a call for over forty-two thousand volunteers, to serve for three years unless sooner discharged, and ordered an increase in the regular army and navy.[52]

In calling out the militia, Lincoln was clearly acting within the

[47] *See* McCall v. McDowell, 15 F. Cas. 1235 (C.C. Cal. 1867); *In re* Oliver, 17 Wis. 681, 686 (1864).

[48] *See Ex parte* Benedict, 3 F. Cas. 159 (C.C.N.Y. 1862); McCall v. McDowell, 15 F. Cas. 1235 (C.C. Cal. 1867); Griffin v. Wilcox,, 21 Ind. 370 (1863); Jones v. Seward, 40 Barbour 563 (N.Y. 1863); *In re* Kemp, 16 Wis. 359 (1863). *But see Ex parte* Field, 9 F. Cas. 1 (C.C. Vt. 1862). For a recent opinion, *see* E.S. Corwin, *The President: Office and Powers* 146 (4th ed. 1957).

[49] Art. I, § 8.

[50] W.A. Dunning, *Essays on the Civil War and Reconstruction* 14 (1910).

[51] 1 Stat. 424 (1795).

[52] *Lincoln, supra* note 3, at 331, 353.

powers given to him by the Constitution and laws.[53] Of more doubtful legality was his action in increasing the personnel of the armed forces without congressional authorization. He himself recognized this and, in reporting to Congress on July 4, 1861, stated that "these measures, whether strictly legal or not, were ventured upon, under what appeared to be a popular demand and a public necessity; trusting, then as now, that Congress would readily ratify them."[54]

Congress did speedily ratify the president's action increasing the armed forces.[55] On August 6, 1861, it passed a law providing that all of his acts respecting the army and navy and the calling out of the militia or volunteers taken after March 4 "are hereby approved and in all respects legalized and made valid . . . as if they had been issued and done under the previous express authority and direction of the Congress."[56] The ratification, the Supreme Court held, gave full legal effect to Lincoln's action, just as though it had been authorized in advance by statute.[57] Since, as Lincoln put it in his July 4 message, "nothing has been done beyond the constitutional competency of Congress,"[58] the congressional ratification made it possible to bypass the issue of the power of the president to act solely on his own authority as he did. It is unlikely that the issue will arise again. The techniques of present-day warfare make it most improbable that the nation would be able to survive a major conflict in future by establishing the necessary forces after war has begun. The letter of the Constitution may not support the immediate action taken by Lincoln, yet if, in a future emergency, a president feels compelled to act as Lincoln did, is it at all likely that Congress will not ratify his action? In actual practice, one must recognize a power in the president to raise an army to meet a war emergency, with either the prospective or retroactive approval of the Congress.[59]

CONSCRIPTION

The congressional power to raise and maintain armed forces was first used to conscript men in 1863, when the first federal con-

[53] Though, it should be noted, President Buchanan had been of the view that he did not have such power.

[54] *Lincoln, supra* note 3, at 429.

[55] 12 Stat. 326 (1861).

[56] *Id.*

[57] United States v. Hosmer, 9 Wall. 432, 434 (U.S. 1870).

[58] *Lincoln, supra* note 3, at 429.

[59] *Compare G. Schubert, The Presidency in the Courts* 179 (1957).

scription law was enacted.[60] Its legality was never tested directly in the federal courts,[61] but it is known that Chief Justice Taney prepared a draft opinion in which he pronounced the Conscription Act unconstitutional, an encroachment by the federal government upon the power of the states to maintain their own militia.[62] It is difficult to see any legal basis for Taney's opinion, in view of the categorical grant to Congress of the power to raise armies. Lincoln, like Taney, also wrote an unpublished opinion on the draft law. The Lincoln paper was a strong defense of the constitutionality of conscription: "Whether a power can be implied, when it is not expressed, has often been the subject of controversy; but this is the first case in which the degree of effrontery has been ventured upon, of denying a power which is plainly and distinctly written down in the constitution." [63] The power is given fully, without condition; "it is a power to raise and support armies . . . without an 'if.' "[64]

The Lincoln opinion on the matter—reminiscent of Marshall in the masterful simplicity of its logic—was far superior to the feeble Taney draft. Yet (as already indicated) the question was not authoritatively settled during the Civil War because the legality of the Conscription Act of 1863, as well as that of a successor statute of 1864,[65] was not decided directly by a federal court.[66] During World War I the Supreme Court upheld federal conscription in terms which constituted an unqualified affirmation of the congressional authority to procure manpower for the armed forces and to subject to military service both the willing and the unwilling.[67] More recently, the Court has said that "the constitutionality of the conscription of manpower for military service is beyond question."[68] This time it was Lincoln who was right and Taney wrong.

---

[60] 12 Stat. 731 (1863).

[61] *But see* Tarble's case, 13 Wall. 397, 408 (U.S. 1872), where the power to conscript men was declared by way of *obiter* to be in the federal government.

[62] *See C.B. Swisher, Roger B. Taney,* 570–71 (1935).

[63] 6 *Lincoln, supra* note 3, at 446.

[64] 6 *Lincoln, supra* note 3, at 446.

[65] 13 Stat. 6 (1864).

[66] During the Civil War period, the conscription statute was upheld in several state decisions. Drueker v. Salomon, 21 Wis. 621 (1867) is the best known of these decisions. *See also* Allen v. Colby, 47 N.H. 544 (1867); Kneedler v. Lane, 45 Pa. 238 (1863); *In re* Griner, 16 Wis. 423 (1863). For a more recent discussion of one of these cases, see United States v. Richmond, 274 F. Supp. 43, 66–68 (C.D. Cal. 1967).

[67] Selective Draft Law cases, 245 U.S. 366 (1918).

[68] Lichter v. United States, 334 U.S. 742, 756 (1948).

CONGRESSIONAL RATIFICATION

"I think," declared Lincoln in an 1863 letter, "the constitution invests its commander-in-chief, with the law of war, in time of war."[69] If he meant by this that the basic document vests the president as commander in chief with the entire war power possessed by the nation, his view is contrary to both the text of the Constitution and the jurisprudence on the subject. In Justice Jackson's words, "the Constitution did not contemplate that the title Commander in Chief *of the Army and Navy* will constitute him also Commander in Chief of the country, its industries and its inhabitants. He has no monopoly of 'war powers.' "[70] Any presidential action to increase the military establishment must be supported by some congressional authorization, whether prospective or, as we have seen, retroactive. In other cases, too, presidential action taken under the war power may be invalid if it has not been sanctioned by the legislative department.

The legal effect of subsequent ratification of presidential action such as Lincoln's was outlined in the *Prize Cases*.[71] There the Court stated: "it is plain that if the President had in any manner assumed powers which it was necessary should have the authority or sanction of Congress, that on the well known principle of law, '*omnis ratihabitio retrotrahitur et mandato equiparatur,*' this ratification has operated to perfectly cure the defect."[72] In other words, while there was no legal defect to the president's blockade order, if such had existed, the ratification statute would have sufficed to cure it.[73] This holding has been confirmed repeatedly, both in cases arising under the war power and elsewhere.[74] In effect, then, Congress may retrospectively delegate to the president power to do anything which, in Lincoln's phrase, is not "beyond the constitutional competency of Congress."

A word should be said about the significance of this interpretation for the war power. The congressional power of ratification has meant that few cases have reached the courts involving the validity of exercises of presidential power alone. In practice, where the highest officer has deemed immediate emergency action essential, he has taken such ac-

---

[69] 6 *Lincoln, supra* note 3, at 408.

[70] Concurring in Youngstown Sheet & Tube Co. v. Sawyer, 343 U.S. 579, 643 (1952).

[71] *See* n. 15 *supra*.

[72] "Every ratification dates back and is equivalent to a prior authority," 2 Black at 671.

[73] *Compare Randall, supra* note 38, at 56.

[74] *See* cases cited in Hirabayashi v. United States, 320 U.S. 81, 91 (1943). *See also* Ludecke v. Watkins, 335 U.S. 160, 173 (1948); Fleming v. Mohawk Wrecking co., 331 U.S. 111, 118 (1948).

tion—"whether strictly legal or not," in Lincoln's words. The result has been that, since Congress has almost invariably ratified the president's acts, the judges have been confronted with the issue of the war power of the Congress and the president acting together.[75] In such cases, the presidential action is supported by the total war power delegated by the Constitution.[76] If the action is held invalid under these circumstances, it means that it is beyond the power of the federal government as an undivided whole.

LINCOLN AND CIVIL LIBERTIES

"In the interval between April 12 and July 4, 1861," says Dunning, "a new principle thus appeared in the constitutional system of the United States, namely, that of a temporary dictatorship. All the powers of government were virtually concentrated in a single department, and that the department whose energies were directed by the will of a single man."[77] According to Lincoln's critics, this situation did not really change even after Congress met, at the president's call, on July 4, 1861. Wendell Phillips continued to denounce Lincoln's government as a "fearful peril to democratic institutions,"[78] and a law professor at Harvard characterized Lincoln as a government in himself—"an absolute, . . . uncontrollable government; a perfect military despotism."[79]

In Lincoln's expansive view of presidential power in wartime even constitutional doctrine might have to give way if it conflicted with the national necessity. "By general law," he asserted, at the height of what must still be considered our greatest national emergency, "life *and* limb must be protected, yet often a limb must be amputated to save a life; but a life is never wisely given to save a limb."[80] In assessing this philosophy, we should recognize the difficult choices which confronted him when strong measures seemed the only alternative to disintegration and defeat. In a famous statement he posed the "grave question whether any government, not *too* strong for the liberties of its people, can be strong *enough* to maintain its own existence, in great emergencies."[81] If the war were lost, government, country, and Constitution

---

[75] Hirabayashi v. United States, 320 U.S. 81, 91 (1943).

[76] *Compare* Jackson, J., concurring, in Youngstown Sheet & Tube Co. v. Sawyer, 343 U.S. 579, 636 (1952).

[77] *Dunning, supra* note 50, at 20–21.

[78] Quoted in *Randall, supra* note 38, at 1.

[79] Quoted in *Randall, supra* note 38, at 2.

[80] *Lincoln, supra* note 3, at 281.

[81] 7 *Lincoln, supra* note 3, at 100.

itself would all fall together: "I felt that measures, otherwise unconstitutional, might become lawful, by becoming indispensable to the preservation of the constitution, through the preservation of the nation."[82]

Throughout his presidency Lincoln expressed his distaste for the extra-constitutional measures which he had taken. At the very outset of the conflict he told General Winfield Scott "how disagreeable it is to me to do a thing arbitrarily."[83] This theme he developed in both public and private utterances. When he was informed of military arrests of civilians in the District of Columbia, he wrote, "Unless the *necessity* for these arbitrary arrests is *manifest* and *urgent*, I prefer they should cease,"[84] and to Benjamin Butler, at the height of that officer's conflict with the "restored" Pierpoint government of Virginia, he declared, "Nothing justifies the suspending of the civil by the military authority, but military necessity."[85] In a letter to General Scott concerning the session of the Maryland legislature scheduled for April 26, 1861, he conceded that it "not improbably, will take action to arm the people of that State against the United States." Therefore, the question arose of whether it would not be justifiable for Scott to arrest or disperse the legislators. Lincoln answered the question with a categorical "I think it would *not* be justifiable; nor, efficient for the desired object." The legislators "have a clearly legal right to assemble," and all that the government could do was "adopt the most prompt, and efficient means to counteract their action."[86] Perhaps the best statement of Lincoln's inner conflict is found in an 1862 letter: "I am a patient man—always willing to forgive on the Christian terms of repentance; and also to give ample *time* for repentance. Still I must save this government if possible."[87] If measures of dubious constitutionality were necessary to accomplish that end, that was a card that had to be played to prevent losing the game.[88]

Lincoln's approach to the war power rests on the theory that the Constitution in time of war is not to be regarded in exactly the same manner as it is in time of peace. "Certain proceedings," he stated in an 1863 letter, "are constitutional when in cases of rebellion or Invasion, the public Safety requires them, which would not be constitutional

[82] 7 *Lincoln, supra* note 3, at 281.

[83] *Lincoln, supra* note 3, at 394.

[84] *Lincoln, supra* note 3, at 372.

[85] 7 *Lincoln, supra* note 3, at 488. On Lincoln's reluctance, as compared with his subordinates, *see Sprague, supra* note 38, at 157, 299.

[86] *Lincoln, supra* note 3, at 344.

[87] 5 *Lincoln, supra* note 3, at 343.

[88] Paraphrasing 5 *Lincoln, supra* note 3, at 343.

when, in absence of rebellion or invasion, the public Safety does not require them—in other words . . . the constitution is not in its application in all respects the same, in cases of Rebellion or invasion involving the public Safety, as it is in times of profound peace and public security."[89]

Such an approach does not mean that the Constitution and the guaranteed rights of individuals may be overridden in wartime at the pleasure of the executive, but it may justify actions which could not be permitted in more normal times. From this point of view, many of Lincoln's emergency measures can be reconciled with the proper working of our constitutional law. If there is difficulty in justifying any of his actions under the Constitution, it is those which infringed upon civil liberties. He himself sought to justify his "supposed unconstitutional action such as the making of military arrests"[90] in a noted 1863 letter to Erastus Corning. The arrests of which his critics complained, he said, were preventive, rather than vindictive. Such preventive detentions could scarcely be accomplished by the traditional processes of the ordinary law. "Nothing is better known to history than that courts of justice are utterly incompetent to try such cases." Far from conceding that he had abused the power to make military arrests, the time would come, he asserted, "when I shall be blamed for having made too few arrests rather than too many."[91] In a celebrated passage in the letter he compared the mildness of military detention with the penalties imposed upon those in the armed forces: "Must I shoot a simple-minded soldier boy who deserts, while I must not touch a hair of a wily agitator who induces him to desert? . . . in such a case to silence the agitator, and save the boy, is not only constitutional, but, withal, a great mercy." [92] He rejected the "claim that men may, if they choose, embarrass those whose duty it is, to combat a giant rebellion, and then be dealt with in turn, only as if there was no rebellion."[93] Nor would he accept the view that military arrests were "constitutional [only] in localities where rebellion actually exists." He asserted that such arrests "are constitutional *wherever* the public safety does require them—as well in places to which they may prevent the rebellion extending as in those where it may be already prevailing."[94]

As will be seen in the next chapter, the view thus rejected by Lincoln was precisely that accepted by the Supreme Court in 1866 in the

89 6 *Lincoln, supra* note 3, at 267.
90 6 *Lincoln, supra* note 3, at 261.
91 6 *Lincoln, supra* note 3, at 264, 265.
92 6 *Lincoln, supra* note 3, at 266–67.
93 6 *Lincoln, supra* note 3, at 303.
94 6 *Lincoln, supra* note 3, at 265–66.

Milligan case.[95] From that case down to the present day, the law has held that the validity of military arrests depends on where they take place. It is now settled that military jurisdiction in this country may not be exercised over civilians except in "the locality of actual war" where "the courts are [not] open and in the proper and unobstructed exercise of their jurisdiction,"[96] and even in time of war, the Constitution does not permit military jurisdiction over civilians on the mere *ipse dixit* of the executive. As Justice Black puts it, "The exigencies which have required military rule on the battlefront are not present in areas where no conflict exists. Military trial of civilians 'in the field' is an extraordinary jurisdiction and it should not be expanded at the expense of the Bill of Rights."[97] If constitutional guarantees are to give way at all, it must be not to military fiat but to military necessity.[98]

Among the most controversial Civil War measures were those dealing with the press. Lincoln adopted a milder attitude toward the press than did many of his subordinates, especially those connected with the military. In an 1863 letter to General J. M. Schofield in Missouri, he directed, "you will only . . . suppress . . . newspapers when they may be working *palpable* injury to the Military . . . ; and in no other case will you interfere with the expression of opinion in any form."[99] The military attitude toward the press, on the other hand, is well shown in a letter of General Sherman dealing with "certain mischievous and treasonable newspapers": "Let the Commanding officer . . . put in a public stocks any vendors of obscene [100] or libelous sheets. And give a good horsewhipping to any editor who would dare advise our soldiers to avoid their honorable contracts of enlistment. Confiscate his press." [101]

There is no doubt that Lincoln did try to restrain the military. When General Schofield ordered the arrest of the editor of the Missouri *Democrat* for publishing an official letter of the president, Lincoln wrote expressing his "regret to learn of the arrest." Though he thought there was "an apparent impropriety in the publication," Lincoln concluded it was something "which I am entirely willing to overlook." [102] And when the Chicago *Times* was suspended by order of General A. M. Burnside for "disloyal and incendiary sentiments," Lincoln promptly

95 *Ex parte* Milligan, 4 Wall. 2 (U.S. 1866).

96 *Id.* at 127.

97 Reid v. Covert, 354 U.S. 1, 35 (1957).

98 *Compare* Murphy, J., in Duncan v. Kahanamoku, 327 U.S. 304, 328 (1946).

99 6 *Lincoln, supra* note 3, at 492.

100 *Compare* the statement of Tacitus that, in the time of Augustus, it became obscene to criticize the emperor.

101 W.T. Sherman to General Thomas, Aug. 5, 1864, Parke-Bernet Galleries, Sale No. 2676, Item 626 (1968).

102 *Lincoln, supra* note 3, at 326. *See Harper, supra* note 32, at 145.

revoked the order. [103] Yet he himself ordered the arrest of the editors and publishers of the New York *World* for printing a bogus presidential proclamation calling for four hundred thousand men and setting a day of fasting, humiliation, and prayer. [104] Various "obnoxious" newspapers were suspended or suppressed at different times without protest from the president. Such suppression has no justification in our law and can scarcely be excused by the claim of military necessity. [105]

Even more immoderate were military interferences in religious affairs. It was one thing for Lincoln to approve the takeover of a church "if the military have military need of the church building." [106] It was something else again for a church to be taken possession of because of a "traitorous resolution adopted by the Trustees." [107] Other actions went even further. In 1863 the secretary of war ordered "all houses of worship belonging to the Methodist Episcopal Church in which a loyal minister, who had been appointed by a loyal Bishop of said church, does not now officiate" to be placed at the disposal of the Methodist chaplain of the army.[108]

Certain things should, however, be said, if not in justification, at least in explanation. First, the line of demarcation between military and civil authority was more blurred a century ago than it has since become. When Lincoln, in the letter quoted, declared that "the constitution invests its commander-in-chief, with the law of war, in time of war," he was uttering what today would be considered constitutional heresy, but to the jurist of his time, the constitutional separation between military and civil power was by no means well delineated. With the law thus unsettled, it is not surprising that the Constitution was at times "stretched" at the expense of individual rights. Most of the arbitrary measures in individual cases were acts of subordinates, not of the president himself. Thus, in the notorious *Vallandigham* case, it was General Burnside who acted in an arbitrary manner. In justifying the

---

103 6 *Lincoln, supra* note 3, at 338, 364.

104 7 *Lincoln, supra* note 3, at 347–48. For a full account, *see Harper, supra* note 32, at 289–303.

105 *See also* 3 *Diary of Gideon Welles* 432 (H. Beale ed. 1960) ("if Judge Lowry and others continued to interfere and interrupt the draft he [Lincoln] would send them after Vallandigham").

106 7 *Lincoln, supra* note 3, at 323, 339.

107 *Id.* at 427–28. *Compare* Kotohira Jinsha v. McGrath, 90 F. Supp. 892 (D. Hawaii 1950) (governmental seizure of Shinto shrine in Hawaii after Pearl Harbor violative of First Amendment).

108 6 *Lincoln, supra* note 3, at 33–34; 7 *id.* at 178–80. *See id.* at 85–86 (pastor prevented from preaching for Rebel sympathies as indicated by, among other things, baptizing a baby with the name of a Confederate general). *Compare Cong. Globe,* 41st Cong., 2d Sess. 3675: "you put a poor preacher in jail in Buffalo during the war because he read that Sermon on the Mount; because the Sermon on the Mount was not 'loyal' during the war!"

arrest of Vallandigham, he asserted that incendiary speeches "create dissensions and discord which, just now, amounts to treason," and indicated further that the distributors of demoralizing speeches should be "hung if found guilty." [109]

Such was not Lincoln's view. As Gideon Welles's diary notes, "Good men . . . find it difficult to defend these acts. They are Burnside's, unprompted . . . by any member of the Administration." He added, "the President . . . regrets what has been done." [110] Over and over, Lincoln had to caution and rebuke military commanders who went to extremes in overriding basic rights. He was surprised and distressed when he first learned of the facts in such celebrated cases as *Vallandigham*, [111] and, when he found out about the takeover of a church, he wrote the general concerned, "the U.S. Government must not . . . undertake to run the churches." [112]

The important thing to remember, however, is that Lincoln's elastic conception of the Constitution did not cause the American people to lose their liberties. Dunning's characterization, a generation after the event, of Lincoln as a temporary dictator was wide of the mark insofar as the president's personal temperament was concerned. His dislike of arbitrary rule, his reasonableness in practice, his willingness to make political compromises, his attempts to check military excess—all are inconsistent with the dictatorial posture. Furthermore, no dictator would have tolerated the often venomous attacks of much of the Democratic press or permitted his own power to be put to the electoral test in the middle of the conflict. The measures Lincoln took were much milder than those urged by extremists in his party and in the country as a whole. The Reconstruction experience gives some indication of what would have happened during the war itself had his restraining hand not been present. Most of the nation was ready to go far beyond the president in suppressing disloyalty. Even so respected a journal as the *Atlantic Monthly* could delete from its pages a description by Nathaniel Hawthorne of an interview with the president because it "lacks *reverence*." [113]

---

109 Quoted in *J.J. Marke, Vignettes of Legal History* 122 (1965).

110 1 *Welles, supra* note 105, at 321.

111 6 *Lincoln, supra* note 3, at 237.

112 7 *Lincoln, supra* note 3, at 85, 178–79, 223. Lincoln also disclaimed "any thought of interfering as to who shall or shall not preach in any church" in the case of the pastor referred to in note 108 *supra; id.* at 86.

113 *Hawthorne, Chiefly about War Matters, Atlantic Monthly* 43, 47 (July, 1962).

COMMANDER IN CHIEF

When Lincoln's assassins were captured, they were tried and convicted by a military tribunal authorized by President Johnson, on the theory that the crime involved was the murder of the commander in chief while he was in command of the armed forces in wartime. The specifications drawn up by the judge advocate general never mentioned "Abraham Lincoln, President of the United States" without adding "and Commander-in-Chief of the Army and Navy thereof." [114]   In 1868, habeas corpus was sought by one of the convicted defendants serving a sentence of imprisonment. The petition was rejected by the district court, which held that the crime of murdering the president in time of war was properly triable by a military commission. [115]

It may be doubted whether present-day courts would sanction the subjection of presidential assassins to military justice. It again illustrates the emphasis placed during the Civil War upon the president's constitutional position as commander in chief. If Polk demonstrated for the first time the potential inherent in the commander in chief clause, Lincoln demonstrated from the beginning his undisputed leadership in this respect. When he first took office in 1861, there was doubt about his abilities. Wrote Salmon P. Chase at the end of 1860, "It is uncertain how the administration will be organized—who will have influence with the President and his advisers." [116]   Men like Chase and Seward hoped to dominate the government—each had "a passion to be thought a master spirit in the Administration." [117]   But they had overlooked both the true personality of the president and the constitutional realities of their position. As soon as he took office, Lincoln demonstrated his intention to be master of the executive branch. "It was," says Gideon Welles (in a manuscript not included in his famous diary), "a primary object with Mr. Seward and those in his immediate interest to secure for him the first place in Mr. Lincoln's cabinet, . . . but the President . . . was immovable in his determination." [118]

Lincoln used his paramount position to interfere directly in military matters to an extent that even Polk had not found necessary. His basic

---

[114] *See Rossiter, supra* note 21, at 110.

[115] *Ex parte* Mudd, 17 F. Cas. 954 (S.D. Fla. 1868).

[116] Letter from S.P. Chase to Homer G. Plantz, Nov. 21, 1860, Charles Hamilton, Auction No. 10, Item 136 (1965).

[117] 1 *Welles, supra* note 105, at 79.

[118] Gideon Welles, undated autograph manuscript, Charles Hamilton, Auction No. 14, Item 257 (1966).

approach was that, however inexpert he might be in military matters, the Constitution had made him commander in chief and that it was his duty to exercise the role of over-all chief of the military effort. As he put it in a letter to General Joseph Hooker, then commanding the Army of the Potomac, "please inform me, so that I, incompetent as I may be, can try [to] assist in the formation of some plan for the Army." [119]

There has been a sharp difference of opinion among historians with regard to Lincoln's control over military decisions. Some look upon his constant interferences in military matters as a virtual plague to the Union Army, [120] while others believe that his grasp of strategy did more than "any general to win the war for the Union." [121] A general in this century has written a book, *The Military Genius of Abraham Lincoln*, which concludes that "Lincoln was solely responsible for the strategy of the North and proved himself a very capable strategist." [122] What is beyond dispute is that he did act as a virtual generalissimo of the Union armies, never hesitating, where he saw fit, to overrule the decisions made by commanders in the field. At the very outset, just before Bull Run, he refused to give Generals Scott and McDowell more time to prepare for battle. When McDowell asked for additional time to drill and discipline his troops, Lincoln made his famous reply, "You are green, it is true, but they are green also."[123]

After Bull Run, Lincoln was so dissatisfied with the dilatory tactics of his generals that, on January 12, 1862, according to one of his confidants, "He told me he was thinking of taking the field himself, and suggested several plans of operation." [124] On January 27 Lincoln showed that his remark was not entirely hyperbole when he issued President's General War Order No. 1. It ordered that February 22, 1862, "be the day for a general movement of the Land and Naval forces of the United States against the insurgent forces." The Army of the Potomac and the five other major military commands were named as the forces to "be ready for a movement on that day." Department heads, commanding generals, and subordinates "will severally be held to their strict and full responsibilities, for the prompt execution of this order." [125] Four days later Lincoln sent General McClellan his Presi-

---

119 6 *Lincoln, supra* note 3, at 201.

120 *See J.G. Randall* and *D. Donald, The Civil War and Reconstruction* 209 (2d ed. 1961).

121 *Id.* at 210.

122 *C.R. Ballard, The Military Genius of Abraham Lincoln* 2 (1926). *See also T.H. Williams, Lincoln and His Generals* 7–8 (1952).

123 *See Williams, supra* note 122, at 21.

124 *Sandburg, supra* note 16, at 276.

125 5 *Lincoln, supra* note 3, at 111–12.

dent's Special War Order No. 1. It ordered the Army of the Potomac to move by February 22 "for the immediate object of seizing and occupying . . . Manassas Junction." [126] A few days later, he wrote McClellan urging his own plan for a land attack on Richmond. [127] Similar interventions occurred throughout the conflict, though they became less frequent after Lincoln found a general whom he could trust to act as commander of the northern armies. After Grant was appointed to command the Union forces in 1864, Lincoln interposed in the conduct of military operations only at rare intervals. [128]

EMANCIPATION PROCLAMATION

It was as commander in chief that Lincoln took that action which gave rise to the greatest contemporary controversy: the Emancipation Proclamation. It is difficult for us today to realize the controversial nature of Lincoln's historical action. Even Lord Acton, apostle of liberty though he was later to become, wrote soon after Sumter, "It is as impossible to sympathise on religious grounds with the categorical prohibition of slavery as, on political grounds, with the opinions of the abolitionists."[129]

Lincoln himself was far from an extreme abolitionist. Regardless of his personal conviction of the immorality of slavery—that "institution . . . founded on . . . injustice," he had called it as early as 1837 [130] —he was a relative moderate when it came to practical measures to eliminate the evil. He conceded that the federal government lacked power to interfere with the institution in the states, and, in his First Inaugural Address, he expressly disclaimed any intention to infringe upon it. [131] On August 22, 1862, he wrote Horace Greeley that his paramount object was to save the Union, not to save or destroy slavery: "If I could save the Union without freeing *any* slave, I would do it, and if I could do it by freeing *all* the slaves, I would do it, and if I could save it by freeing some and leaving others alone I would also do that." [132] As late as December, 1862 (more than two months after he had issued his Preliminary Emancipation Proclamation), he proposed a constitutional amendment providing for gradual compensated abolition

126 5 *Lincoln, supra* note 3, at 115.
127 5 *Lincoln, supra* note 3, at 118–19.
128 *See Williams, supra* note 122, at 336.
129 *J.E. Acton, Essays on Freedom and Power* 246 (1948).
130 1 *Lincoln, supra* note 3, at 75.
131 *Lincoln, supra* note 3, at 250–51.
132 5 *Lincoln, supra* note 3, at 388.

as the proper solution. [133] By the end of 1862, however, Charles Sumner wrote, "the Presdt. is firm. He says that he would not stop the Procltn. if he could, & he could not if he would." [134] On the first day of 1863, the definitive step was taken. By his proclamation, issued without express constitutional or statutory authority, Lincoln ordered and declared "that all persons held as slaves" within the states then in rebellion "are, and henceforward shall be free." [135]

The proclamation immediately became the object of lively constitutional controversy. It was attacked on legal grounds both as beyond the scope of federal authority and as a usurpation of executive power. The proclamation declared that it was issued "by virtue of the power in me vested as Commander-in-Chief of the Army and Navy . . . and as a fit and necessary war measure," [136] and Lincoln himself later conceded that "the . . . proclamation has no constitutional or legal justification, except as a military measure." [137] As Sumner put it earlier, emancipation "is to be presented strictly as a measure of military necessity, and the argument is to be thus supported rather than on grounds of philanthropy." [138]

The president's powers as a military commander include belligerent rights derived from the usages of war as well as the authority to govern occupied territory. He may, as the *Prize Cases* squarely recognized, proclaim a blockade of an enemy's coast or (as was first done in the Mexican war) set up military governments in conquered areas. The decreeing of emancipation may be considered an analogous exercise of this war power. A military occupier, the Supreme Court affirmed in a case growing out of the military government established in conquered New Orleans, "may do anything necessary to strengthen itself and weaken the enemy." [139] The power to free the enemy's slaves, like the power to take over his other property, is included within the power of military occupation.

From another point of view, the power to emancipate may be said to flow from the military power to requisition property, a power expressly recognized by the Supreme Court during the Civil War: [140] "The most that can be said, if so much, is, that slaves are property. Is there — has there ever been—any question that by the law of war, property, both

133 5 *Lincoln, supra* note 3, at 529–37.
134 Quoted in *J.M. McPherson, The Struggle for Equality* 120 (1964).
135 6 *Lincoln, supra* note 3, at 28.
136 6 *Lincoln, supra* note 3, at 29.
137 6 *Lincoln, supra* note 3, at 428.
138 Quoted in *McPherson, supra* note 134, at 90–91.
139 New Orleans v. The Steamship Co., 20 Wall. 387, 394 (U.S. 1874).
140 United States v. Russell, 13 Wall. 623 (U.S. 1871).

of enemies and friends, may be taken when needed? And is it not needed whenever taking it, helps us, or hurts the enemy?" [141] As Richard Henry Dana, Jr., expressed it in an 1865 address, "that an army may free the slaves of an enemy is a settled right of law." [142]

Dana feared, however, that the Emancipation Proclamation "is to be a *dead failure*. . . . It is, Slavery where we can emancipate, and freedom where we cannot." [143] Lincoln himself recognized this danger: "I do not want to issue a document that the whole world will see must necessarily be inoperative, like the Pope's bull against the comet!" Events soon showed that the proclamation was anything but that. Slavery was "the root of the rebellion or at least its *sine qua non*." [144] To win the war, the northern armies had to deprive the Confederacy of the slave labor which supported it. Where the Union forces penetrated, slavery went out of existence. More than that, the war proved the validity of Sumner's 1861 prophecy: "Slavery is our Catiline. . . . It is often said that war will make an end of Slavery. This is probable. But it is surer still that the overthrow of slavery will make an end of the war." [145]

Legally speaking, Lincoln's proclamation was effective only as a war measure. "If any man," said Dana, "fears or hopes that the proclamation did as a matter of law by its own force, alter the legal status of one slave . . . he builds his fears or hopes on sand. It is a military act and not a decree of a legislator." [146] That decree came with the ratification on January 31, 1865, of the Thirteenth Amendment—that "King's cure" for the evil of slavery, Lincoln aptly termed it. [147] It consigned the question of the legality of the proclamation to the realm of academic controversy.

CONGRESS AND WAR POWERS

"Pray, Sir," asked Senator Charles Sumner in a noted 1862 debate, "where in the Constitution is any limitation of the War Powers? Let Senators who would limit them mention a single section, line, or phrase, which even hints at any limitation." Sumner's expansive interpretation was scarcely challenged. A sharp difference of opinion did

[141] 6 *Lincoln, supra* note 3, at 408.
[142] Quoted in *Randall, supra* note 38, at 383.
[143] 2 *C.F. Adams, Richard Henry Dana* 263 (1891).
[144] 5 *Lincoln, supra* note 3, at 420, 423.
[145] 6 *The Works of Charles Sumner* 12 (1874).
[146] Quoted in *Randall, supra* note 38, at 383.
[147] 8 *Lincoln, supra* note 3, at 254.

arise, however, on the location of the war power in the governmental structure. "There are Senators," Sumner said, "who claim these vast War Powers for the President, and deny them to Congress." [148] Foremost among them was Lincoln's close confidant Orville H. Browning, who claimed that the war power, by its very nature, was wholly executive, not legislative, in character: "It is not true that Congress may assume and exercise all the active war powers. . . . The Constitution invests it with no such prerogative." [149] Sumner took a contrary view: "Read the text of the Constitution, and you will find its powers vast as all the requirements of war. . . . I claim for Congress all that belongs to any Government in the exercise of the Rights of War."[150]

Judicial authority lends support to the Sumner, rather than the Browning, approach. [151] According to the Supreme Court, "the power to declare war involves the power to prosecute it by all means and in any manner." [152] In actual practice, nevertheless, it was the Browning view that prevailed during the Civil War. That conflict demonstrates dramatically that, whatever may be the theoretical distribution of war powers, the department directing the force of the nation will, in fact, secure the primacy in a war emergency. If the operation of the war power has too often been a field of contention between the two political branches, few familiar with its history will deny that the principal advantages in such struggles have been with the president. His alone has been the constitutional command of the armed forces, which of itself overrides any theoretically coordinate authority that the legislature possesses.

The presidential primacy that existed during the Civil War was distasteful to congressional leaders. To them, the Union cause might well founder "as penalty for having a *timid & ignorant* President, all the more injurious because *honest.*" [153] It was up to the legislative department to assert for itself the overriding power to supervise the war which they claimed was inherent in congressional power. To them, the president "is only the instrument of Congress. . . . Congress is the arbiter and regulator of the War Powers." [154] The difficulty was how to make the congressional position more than a matter of constitutional theory. The true situation was stated, with his customary acuity, by John Marshall. The president, he declared in a noted House debate, "holds and directs the force of the nation. Of consequence, any act to be

148 7 *Sumner, supra* note 145, at 131, 138.
149 *Cong. Globe,* 37th Cong., 2d Sess. 2919.
150 7 *Sumner, supra* note 145, at 138.
151 *See Randall, supra* note 38, at 42.
152 Miller v. United States, 11 Wall. 268, 305 (U.S. 1871).
153 Wendell Phillips, quoted in *McPherson, supra* note 134, at 110.
154 7 *Sumner, supra* note 145, at 139.

performed by the force of the nation is to be performed through him." [155] The result is to limit Congress to the role of overseer, with power in the executive and the legislature serving as a check—the president as motor and the Congress as brake. All the same, during such a total conflict it was power that waxed and control that waned. In practice the bulk of the actions taken by Lincoln and his generals was beyond the reach of congressional scrutiny, much less direction by the legislative department, despite the establishment of the Joint Committee on the Conduct of the War, which sought to oversee the war effort.

The work of this committee illustrates both the potential present in the congressional watchdog power and its inherent limitations. An 1861 enabling resolution empowered it "to inquire into the conduct of the present war." [156] The committee construed this language most broadly. It "concluded that they would best perform their duty by endeavoring to obtain such information in respect to the conduct of the war as would best enable them to advise what mistakes had been made in the past, and the proper course to be pursued in the future." [157] It deemed itself vested with a virtual roving commission to make inquiry wherever it chose—to assume the role of "mischievous busybody," [158] with authority to pry into the war's innermost affairs, to run the eye up and down all military accounts, sniff into every corner, peep behind military curtains, and open every cupboard, no matter how private.

Though none of its members had military experience, the committee did not hesitate to play a direct part in command decisions. [159] It may be said in its defense that it was only following Lincoln's example, but there is a vast difference between presidential and congressional direction of military strategy and operations. History attests to the futility of headless administration, in which executive as well as legislative responsibility is concentrated in the legislative department. This is particularly true of legislative direction of military affairs in wartime. The present-day observer must agree with the contemporary conclusion of Gideon Welles: "This method of supervising military operations is of more than questionable utility. . . . They are partisan and made up of persons not very competent to form correct and intelligent opinions of Army or Navy operations." [160]

---

[155] Marshall's speech is reported in 5 Wheat. app. 3, 26.

[156] *Cong. Globe,* 37th Cong., 2d Sess. 30–32.

[157] *The Conduct of the War, Report of the Congressional Committee on the Operations of the Army of the Potomac* 3 (1853).

[158] 2 *Welles, supra* note 105, at 226.

[159] *See Williams, The Committee on the Conduct of the War,* 3 *Military Aff.* 139, 144–45 (1939); *Pierson, The Committee on the Conduct of the Civil War,* 23 *Am. Hist. Rev.* 550, 566 (1918).

[160] 1 *Welles, supra* note 112, at 262.

Though the committee did do unexceptionable work in many areas, at its worst it perpetrated serious abuses. Gideon Welles may have gone too far when he asserted that "mean and contemptible partisanship colors all their acts," [161] but some of its more extreme investigations lend substance to the charge, notably its destruction of the career of General Charles P. Stone without informing him of the charges against him or giving him any opportunity to crossexamine witnesses. [162] Not long ago, the common view was that voiced by Harry S. Truman: "the 'Joint Committee of Congress to Inquire into the Management of the Civil War' . . . proved to be a handicap to President Lincoln." [163] More recent studies have shown that there was more cooperation between the committee and the president than had been supposed. [164] In addition, the actual impact of such a committee should not be overstated. After all, it could not really impair presidential control, for the areas it could look into constituted but a small part of the total military picture. The maxim that knowledge is power has its most dramatic governmental application in the relationship between the legislative and executive branches. While the committee could try to assert a voice in the direction of the armies, it could not compete with Lincoln in his role of commander in chief. Furthermore, the very authority of such a body to acquire specific information is limited by the presidential prerogative (which all presidents have claimed) of withholding information even from Congress. While Lincoln was usually willing to furnish what was requested, he invoked the doctrine of executive privilege when he felt it appropriate. Thus, as early as July 27, 1861, he rejected a House request for information as "incompatible with the public interest at this time." [165] Like other presidents, he acted on the assumption that it was his responsibility to determine what information should be withheld.

Toward the end of the war, a serious constitutional conflict between the legislative and executive branches did develop. The potential for conflict was shown by the congressional reaction to Lincoln's pocket veto of the 1864 Wade-Davis bill, a legislative scheme of reconstruction. In response, Senator Wade and Representative Davis issued their famous manifesto, which set forth an extreme view of congressional supremacy. The president, they asserted, "must understand . . . that the authority of Congress is paramount. . . . he must confine himself to his executive

161 2 *Welles, supra* note 112, at 226.

162 *See H.L. Trefousse, The Radical Republicans: Lincoln's Vanguard for Racial Justice* 188 (1969).

163 *W. Hillman, Mr. President* 94 (1952).

164 *See Trefouse, supra* note 162, at 182 *et seq.*

165 *Lincoln, supra* note 3, at 462. *See also* another case cited in *Randall, supra* note 38, at 165, n. 48.

duties—to obey and execute." [166] Here was a ministerial conception of presidential power which no chief executive (and certainly not Lincoln) could accept. For the moment, however, the conflict was overshadowed by the need to win the war. Once the struggle with the South was resolved, it would emerge as the central constitutional theme. Presidential primacy would give way, under a president who proved unable to prevent a post-war reversion to congressional predominance.

[166] *H.W. Davis, Speeches and Addresses* 425 (1867).

CHAPTER SEVEN

Reconstruction and the Constitution

RECONSTRUCTION AND REVISION

In 1849 John C. Calhoun evoked what must have seemed to his supporters an apocalyptic vision of the consequences of forcible emancipation. If emancipation ever should be effected, he asserted, "it will be through the agency of the Federal Government, controlled by the dominant power of the Northern States." Emancipation itself would come "under the color of an amendment of the Constitution," forced through by the North. It "would lead to consequences unparalleled in history." The North would not stop at emancipation of the slaves: "Another step would be taken—to raise them to a political and social equality with their former owners, by giving them the right of voting and holding public offices under the Federal Government." The ex-slaves would become "the fast political associates of the North," cementing the political union by acting and voting with them. "The blacks, and the profligate whites that might unite with them, would become the principal recipients of federal offices and patronage, and would, in consequence, be raised above the whites of the South in the political and social scale."[1]

The Carolinian's forecast bears a striking resemblance to what used to be the accepted view of the constitutional history of the postbellum South. If, in the end, it did not turn out as Calhoun had predicted—

[1] 6 *The Works of John C. Calhoun* 309–11 (R. K. Crallé ed. 1857).

Negro supremacy, he said in his 1849 address, would force the whites to flee the very homes of their ancestors and leave the South "to become the permanent abode of disorder, anarchy, poverty, misery, and wretchedness"[2]—that was because of the extreme nature of the Radical Republican program. The measures taken during Reconstruction, in the traditional view, were bound to result in a reaction in the opposite direction once southerners regained control over their own destiny. Reconstruction was seen as an aberration in American constitutional history. It was, wrote Sir Henry Maine soon after it ended, "a Revolutionary period of several years, during which not only the institutions of the Southern States, but the greater part of the Federal institutions were more or less violently distorted to objects not contemplated by the framers of the Constitution."[3] This language has been echoed by more recent writers, even those who have contributed to the changed climate of opinion on Reconstruction. "Frankly revolutionary in mood," concedes C. Vann Woodward, "Thaddeus Stevens and his followers overrode constitutional restraints right and left."[4]

The time has come for a reassessment of the constitutional implications of Reconstruction. In making it, we must start with the Holmes admonition that "the great ordinances of the Constitution do not establish and divide fields of black and white."[5] The constitutionality of the Reconstruction measures cannot be determined through a mechanical approach. The truth of the matter was stated by Senator John Sherman just before Lee's surrender, when he referred to "the difficulties which will spring up, after the war—questions as hard to determine as it was originally to make the Constitution."[6] The legal and practical problems confronting congressional leaders in 1865–1868 were fully as difficult as those which faced the men of 1787.

Reconstruction can be considered a patent violation of the Constitution only if we ignore the fact that it posed issues which the Framers had neither foreseen nor provided for in the document they drafted. The picture of congressional imposition of military government and law is one of constitutional transgression only to one who loses sight of the realities which the defeated South presented. Without a doubt, the Constitution establishes a wall of separation between civil and military affairs; throughout our history "the Court has viewed the separation

---

[2] *Id.* at 311.

[3] H. Maine, *Popular Government* 245 (1886).

[4] *C.V. Woodward, Reunion and Reaction: The Compromise of 1877 and the End of Reconstruction* 14 (1956).

[5] Dissenting, in Springer v. Philippine Islands, 277 U.S. 189, 209 (1928).

[6] Quoted in *H.M. Hyman, The Radical Republicans and Reconstruction, 1861–1870,* at lxiv (1967).

and subordination of the military establishment as a compelling principle."[7] Yet that is true only in states which are not in an actual theater
of military operations and in which the civil courts are open and
functioning.[8] Ever since the Mexican war, a different rule has been
applied with regard to territory occupied by American forces; there the
prevailing principle has been that of military conquest, with government set up by the occupying forces, though subject to ultimate
congressional control.[9]

What happens, however, if the occupied territory consists of states
which have sought to secede and have been prevented from doing so by
federal force? Such a situation plainly was not considered by the
Framers, who intended the Union to be perpetual and indissoluble.
"The Constitution," declared the Supreme Court in 1869, "in all its
provisions, looks to an indestructible Union."[10] Nor were there constitutional provisions for the legal status of the defeated states after their
attempt at secession had been suppressed.

How to deal with these unprecedented constitutional problems? The
one thing clear to the Republican leaders was that the constitutional
clock could not simply be turned back to 1860. That had, of course,
become the "southern" theory of Reconstruction—that with the end of
the war, all affairs should revert to their previous condition[11] —but
even the hero of Atlanta could not be allowed to erase what had
happened between Sumter and Appomattox. By 1865 the North had
come to recognize the truth of Elizur Wright's statement that "the
general facts . . . make a restoration of the state [of affairs] before the
war equivalent to defeat."[12]

One other thing should be plain by now: however much men may
disagree on the merits of the congressional Reconstruction measures,
those who sponsored them sincerely believed them to be within the
confines of the Constitution. Like most Americans of the time, they
both revered the Constitution and believed in its adequacy.[13] The
victorious outcome of the war only reinforced these attitudes. In the
words of a Williams College lecturer in 1865, "We at the North, all
learned that there was in our [Constitution and] Government a power
of which we never before dreamed."[14] It was widely felt that the

7 Warren, C.J., in *The Great Rights* 106 (E. Cahn ed. 1963).

8 *Ex parte* Milligan, 4 Wall. 2 (U.S. 1866).

9 P. 77 *supra.*

10 Texas v. White, 7 Wall. 700, 725 (U.S. 1869).

11 *See* E.L. McKitrick, *Andrew Johnson and Reconstruction* 97–98 (1960).

12 E. Wright, The Programme of Peace, by a Democrat of the Old School 18 (1862), quoted
in *H.M. Hyman, New Frontiers of the American Reconstruction* 25 (1966).

13 *See id.* at 20 *et. seq.*

14 Charles Demond, quoted in *id.* at 22.

Constitution was adequate to dealt with the problem of reconstituting the nation. "Adequacy for the nation's war needs led seamlessly to competency to cope with the needs of the post-battle period that was not quite peace."[15]

We should not be misled on this point by the extreme language so frequently used by the Radical leaders themselves. "I am not a Chinese to be swathed by traditions," typically declared Charles Sumner in the Senate, "I break all bands and wrappers when the occasion requires." [16] In practice, nevertheless, he and his colleagues strove to adapt their Reconstruction theories to constitutional scruples. The older picture of the postbellum struggle between president and Congress as one between constitutionalists and revolutionists is a distortion of history. "No one can read the debates of 1866 to 1868 in the *Globe* without being forcibly impressed with the fact that the overwhelming number of so-called Radical Reconstruction leaders . . . staged their arguments within an essentially conservative constitutional frame."[17]

RECONSTRUCTION THEORIES

"Who looking at the matter dispassionately," asked Sir James Fitzjames Stephen in 1873, "can fail to perceive the vanity and folly of the attempt to decide the question between the North and the South by lawyers' metaphysics . . . about the meaning of the Constitution and the principles by which the written documents ought to be interpreted?"[18] To Americans of the time, on the contrary, the whole approach to be followed in Reconstruction depended upon the legal position of the defeated states and, in particular, their relationship to the Union from which they had attempted to secede.

During the war Lincoln adopted a flexible attitude to the question of status and to Reconstruction itself. He was not irrevocably bound even to his Ten Per-Cent Plan, saying, "it must not be understood that no other possible mode would be acceptable."[19] He articulated this refusal to be "inflexibly committed to any single plan of restoration"[20] on later occasions as well.[21] In his last public address, on April 11, 1865, he stated that he was "considering . . . to make some new announce-

---

15 *Id.* at 34.

16 11 *The Works of Charles Sumner* 66 (1874).

17 A.H. Kelly, quoted in *Hyman, supra* note 12, at 52.

18 J.F. Stephen, *Liberty, Equality, Fraternity* 168 (R. White ed. 1873).

19 7 *The Collected Works of Abraham Lincoln* 56 (R.P. Basler ed. 1953).

20 *Id.* at 433.

21 8 *id.* at 404–5.

ment to the people of the South."[22] In the same address, delivered by candlelight to a throng in front of the White House, he referred to "the question whether the seceded States, so called, are in the Union or out of it." On this point, he declared, "I have *purposely* forborne any public expression." The question had not yet become practically material: "As yet, whatever it may hereafter become, that question is bad, as the basis of a controversy, and good for nothing at all—a merely pernicious abstraction."[23]

To Lincoln, the important thing was to get on with the job of "doing the acts necessary to restoring the proper practical relations between these states and the Union." Once that was done, the theorists could be left to determine whether the southern states were "brought . . . from without, into the Union" or only given "proper assistance, they never having been out of it."[24] What he was doing, in his last statement on the matter, was warning against formalizing a problem that had not yet crystallized[25] because "any discussion of it, while it thus remains practically immaterial, could have no effect other than the mischievous one of dividing our friends."[26]

At the time of the northern victory, however, when the status of the defeated states became translated from the realm of the "practically immaterial" to that of pressing, practical politics, Lincoln's approach to Reconstruction was not as different from that of the Radical leaders as has commonly been supposed.[27] In explaining his pocket veto of the Wade-Davis bill, he stated that he was "fully satisfied with the system for restoration contained in the bill as one very proper plan."[28]

The truth is that we do not know what approach Lincoln would have followed once the war was completely ended, and it is sheer speculation to assume that he would have reacted to southern conduct during the early Reconstruction period exactly as his successor did. What we do know is that presidential Reconstruction in the hands of Andrew Johnson provoked an unprecedented impasse between the legislative and executive branches. The Radical leaders could scarcely accept the two constitutional foundations upon which Johnson based his Reconstruction policy: 1) presidential, rather than congressional, power over Reconstruction; and 2) the conception that the southern states had

---

22 *Id.* at 405.

23 *Id.* at 402–3.

24 *Id.* at 403.

25 *See McKitrick, supra* note 11, at 106.

26 8 *Lincoln, supra* note 19, at 403.

27 H. Belz, *Reconstructing the Union* 293–311 (1969).

28 *Lincoln, supra* note 19, at 433.

only had "their life-breath . . . suspended"[29] and that it could be speedily restored by presidential action.

Johnson's restoration of the southern states to their former status on his own authority was bound to be contested by congressional leaders. They rejected the claim that Reconstruction authority existed elsewhere than in the legislative department. Even during the war Lincoln's establishment of governments in occupied territory was not left unchallenged. Sumner's famous Senate resolutions in 1862 declared that such territory "falls under the exclusive jurisdiction of Congress."[30] As the war ended, the Radical leaders became more insistent in this claim: "It is for Congress, in such way as it shall think best, to regulate their return to the Union, whether in time or manner."[31] The nub of the Radical claim was stated, with characteristic pithiness, by Thaddeus Stevens early in 1867: "Though the President is Commander-in-Chief, Congress is his commander; and, God willing, he shall obey."[32]

Even more fundamental was the Radical refusal to accept the Johnsonian conception of the postwar task as that of bringing about a prompt restoration of the South to the Union. The president, said Stevens, "preferred 'restoration' to 'reconstruction.' He chooses that the slave States should remain as nearly as possible in their ancient position."[33] Though there were differences of detail and degree between the various theories advanced by different Radical spokesmen— from the extreme "conquered provinces" theory of Stevens to the somewhat more moderate ones of "state suicide" espoused by Charles Sumner or "forfeited rights" of Samuel Shellabarger—they all refused to accept the view that the southern states needed only the restoration of "loyal" governments.

However they were phrased, the Radical Reconstruction theories meant in practice that the rebel states would be treated (in George W. Julian's phrase) "as outside of their constitutional relations to the Union, and as incapable of restoring themselves to it except on conditions to be prescribed by congress."[34] The southern states could no longer be considered in the same relationship to the Union as other states. On the contrary, "such States and their people ceased to have any of the rights or powers of government as States of this Union."[35]

---

29 *See McKitrick, supra* note 11, at 102.

30 6 *Sumner, supra* note 16, at 302.

31 7 *id.* at 539.

32 *Cong. Globe,* 39th Cong., 2d Sess. 252.

33 House of Representatives, June 13, 1866, quoted in 1 *B. Schwartz, Statutory History of the United States: Civil Rights* 282 (1970).

34 Quoted in *K.M. Stampp, The Era of Reconstruction: 1865 to 1877,* at 87 (1966).

35 *Cong. Globe,* 39th Cong., 1st Sess. 142.

The assumption was that the Civil War had wiped away the southern states as states and left a constitutional vacuum to be filled by Congress. "It is absolutely self-evident," wrote Representative Shellabarger early in 1866, "that here a thing is still looked at as, and called 'a state' which has no government or no republican one."[36] It was for Congress to decide the conditions upon which the southern states were to be reconstructed as full states of the Union. "The Southern states have ceased to be states of the Union—their soil has become National territory"[37] —subject, as such, to congressional power.

SUPREME COURT THEORY

In the 1869 case of *Texas* v. *White*[38] the Supreme Court stated its position on the constitutional basis of Reconstruction. In that case, it will be recalled from the discussion in Chapter VI,[39] the Supreme Court upheld, in strong language, the indissoluble nature of the Union. From a constitutional point of view, the attempted secession of a state like Texas was ruled "absolutely null . . . utterly without operation in law."[40] Texas remained a state, with its obligations as a member of the Union unimpaired. The fact that secession was legally void did not mean that it had never happened, however, and that "the governmental relations of Texas to the Union remained unaltered."[41] There was a difference between the constitutional existence of a state itself and the existence within it of a government competent to represent it in its relations with the nation. When the war ended there was no such government in Texas, and it became the duty of the United States to provide for the reestablishment of such a government. The president had initial authority in the matter, since as commander-in-chief he could institute governments in areas occupied by federal forces. However, "the action of the President must . . . be considered as provisional";[42] presidential power was ruled subject to the overriding authority of Congress to provide for lawful governments in the southern states.

The answer given to the question of Reconstruction in *Texas* v. *White* is one that has been repeated in more recent cases involving

---

36 Quoted in *McKitrick, supra* note 11, at 114.

37 Letter from John Jay to Charles Sumner, Feb. 12, 1862, quoted in *J.M. McPherson, The Struggle for Equality: Abolitionists and the Negro in the Civil War and Reconstruction* 238 (1964).

38 7 Wall. 700 (U.S. 1869).

39 P. 133 *supra.*

40 7 Wall. at 726.

41 *Id.* at 727.

42 *Id.* at 730.

occupied territory, particularly those growing out of the war with Spain and World War II.[43] Those cases confirm the overriding congressional power to establish governments in areas occupied by American forces. Under them, too, the military power of the president to govern such areas continues only until it has been terminated by congressional action.[44]

Texas v. *White* supports both the Radical claim of overriding Reconstruction authority in Congress and the constitutionality of the congressional Reconstruction measures. The Supreme Court recognized that it was for Congress to provide for governments in the defeated states to fill the vacuum which existed after the southern defeat. As for the southern states' relation to the Union, "All admit that, during this condition of civil war, the rights of the State as a member, and of her people as citizens of the Union, were suspended."[45] After Appomattox, it was the duty of Congress to re-establish the broken relationship. While the president could act as commander-in-chief, the governments set up by him had to yield when Congress exercised its authority.

Just as important was the source of the congressional power: "authority was derived from the obligation of the United States to guarantee to every state in the Union a republican form of government."[46] *Texas* v. *White* followed Chief Justice Taney in *Luther* v. *Borden*[47] in holding that the power to carry out the Republican Guaranty Clause "resides in Congress."[48] Under *Luther* v. *Borden* and the later cases,[49] legislative action to enforce the Guaranty Clause presents a political, rather than a judicial, question. What this means is shown by *Georgia* v. *Stanton*,[50] where an action was brought to enjoin enforcement of the Reconstruction acts. "It seemed to the Court that the only constitutional claim that could be presented was under the Guaranty Clause, and Congress having determined that the effects of the recent hostilities required extraordinary measures to restore governments of a republican form, this Court refused to interfere with Congress' action at the behest of a claimant relying on that very guaranty."[51]

---

43 *See* Dooley v. United States, 182 U.S. 222 (1901); Madsen v. Kinsella, 343 U.S. 341 (1952).

44 *See* Dooley v. United States, 182 U.S. 222, 234 (1901).

45 7 Wall. at 727.

46 *Id.* at 727–28.

47 7 How. 1 (U.S. 1849).

48 7 Wall. at 730.

49 *See* B. Schwartz, *Constitutional Law: A Textbook* 55 (1972).

50 Georgia v. Stanton, 6 Wall. 50 (U.S. 1868).

51 Baker v. Carr, 369 U.S. 186, 225 (1962).

In substance, the Supreme Court adopted the constitutional position upon which congressional Reconstruction was based. The framers of the Wade-Davis bill had expressly relied on *Luther* v. *Borden*. According to Davis himself, that case meant that "it is the exclusive prerogative of Congress—of Congress, and not of the President—to determine what is and what is not the established government of the State."[52] As another member of the House Committee on Reconstruction put it, "The question of the recognition of a government in one of the revolted States . . . is a political one, and is to be decided by Congress, not by the Executive or the judiciary."[53] The same approach was followed by Representative Shellabarger in a speech on January 8, 1866, which outlined what became the basic Republican Reconstruction theory.[54] In *Texas* v. *White* the Supreme Court placed its imprimatur upon this approach. That one may disapprove of some or all of the Radical Reconstruction measures should not obscure this fact. To characterize Reconstruction as a constitutional aberration is an exercise in rhetoric, not in law—certainly not in the law laid down by the Supreme Court.

CONGRESSIONAL RECONSTRUCTION

"I was a Conservative in the last session of this Congress," announced Thaddeus Stevens at the opening of the second session of the Thirty-Ninth Congress in December, 1866, "but I mean to be a Radical henceforth."[55] The congressional session that followed, as well as the new Congress that met in March, 1867, was dominated by Stevens' spirit. "A Radical party caucus," wrote Gideon Welles, "decides in relation to the course to be pursued on all important questions. . . . A majority of them follow Stevens."[56]

The 1866 election had given the Republicans an overwhelming majority in both houses. This majority the congressional leaders used to remake the Reconstruction process in the legislative image. The governments instituted under the presidential plan of Reconstruction were swept aside, and Congress itself assumed control over the re-establishment of southern governments. But that is exactly what Congress had the authority to do, under *Texas* v. *White*. One may criticize the details of congressional Reconstruction while still recognizing that, constitu-

52 Quoted in *Belz, supra* note 27, at 207.
53 *Id.*
54 *Cong. Globe*, 39th Cong., 1st Sess. 145.
55 Quoted in *J.G. Randall* and *D. Donald, The Civil War and Reconstruction* 592 (1961).
56 3 *The Diary of Gideon Welles* 41 (H. Beale ed. 1960).

tionally speaking, these were matters for Congress itself to determine. Nor, in considering the merits of the congressional program, should we lose sight of the point noted a decade ago by an English observer: "The true fact about congressional Reconstruction was that it became law by a succession of two-thirds votes in both Houses of Congress, and that in mid-passage the Republicans won a resounding electoral victory. This kind of sustained solidarity is exceptional in American political history."[57] Most members of Congress were prepared to follow the Radical leaders because they had come to feel that drastic measures were needed to deal with the results of President Johnson's laissez-faire Reconstruction program. Rather than permit an unreconstructed South "to substitute a degrading peonage for slavery and make a mockery of the moral fruits of northern victory,"[58] the congressional majority decided upon the drastic measure of military rule.

The basic statute in the congressional Reconstruction program was the First Reconstruction Act of March 2, 1867.[59] Its two principal features were the imposition of military rule and the complete reorganization of government. It declared that "no legal State governments or adequate protection for life or property" existed in the ten "rebel States." Those states were then divided into five military districts, each under the command of an army general. These commanders were given broad powers "to protect all persons in their rights of person and property, to suppress insurrection, disorder, and violence, and to punish . . . all disturbers of the public peace." To make such powers effective, they were authorized to make arrests, conduct trials in military courts,[60] and use federal troops to preserve order.

Without a doubt, the Reconstruction Act was a drastic measure, but its severity should not be exaggerated. The South was not to be subjected indefinitely to such treatment: instead, Congress imposed a period of limited military probation, designed to curb acts of rebellion and to guarantee political rights for the freedmen. It was a very partial political probationary period, imposed upon a very limited segment of the population, and even that disability was virtually removed in 1872.[61] Rarely, if ever, has there been a milder occupation in a country in which a rebellion has been crushed.

Writing of the Reconstruction Act in 1902, John W. Burgess asserted, "There was hardly a line in the entire bill which would stand the test of the Constitution." This assertion appears wide of the legal mark. As

---

[57] *W.R. Brock, An American Crisis: Congress and Reconstruction, 1865–67,* at vii (1963).

[58] Woodward, in *Hyman, supra* note 12, at 131.

[59] 14 Stat. 428 (1867).

[60] Though no death sentence could be executed without presidential approval.

[61] *Compare* Kelly, in *Hyman, supra* note 12, at 56.

Burgess himself concedes, "There can be no question in the mind of any sound political scientist and constitutional lawyer that Congress was in the right, logically, morally, and legally, in insisting upon brushing aside the results of executive Reconstruction in the winter of 1867, and beginning the work itself from the bottom up." If Congress had the power to brush aside the governments set up during presidential Reconstruction, it surely had the power to set up governments in their place. Perhaps, as Burgess contends, Congress should have set up "regular Territorial civil governments."[62] The choice, however, was within the discretion of Congress, and that body could reasonably conclude that a probationary period under military rule was necessary. That an immediate transition to civil government might have been a wiser choice does not affect the legality of the congressional action.

The decision of the Supreme Court in *Ex parte Milligan*[63] does not really alter the constitutional picture. The Court went out of its way to lay down limitations upon resort to martial law and use of military tribunals to punish civilians, which led Thaddeus Stevens to assert that the *Milligan* decision, "although in terms perhaps not as infamous as the Dred Scott decision, is yet far more dangerous in its operation."[64] But it was the exercise of military jurisdiction in Indiana—a loyal state not in an actual theater of war, in which the civil courts were functioning—that called forth restrictive language from the Court. Military jurisdiction, it said, "can never be applied to citizens in states which have upheld the authority of the government, and where the courts are open."[65] This reasoning did not necessarily apply to states whose attempt to secede had been overcome by force and which Congress had not yet provided with lawful governments, entitling them to resume their full place in the Union. Justice Davis, himself the author of the Court's opinion, indicated that *Milligan* did not necessarily imply the unconstitutionality of Reconstruction. In a letter early in 1867, he noted that there was "not a word said in the opinion about reconstruction, & the power is conceded in insurrectionary States."[66]

[62] *J.W. Burgess, Reconstruction and the Constitution* 113, 111 (1902).

[63] 4 Wall. 2 (U.S. 1866).

[64] *Cong. Globe*, 39th Cong., 2d Sess. 251.

[65] 4 Wall. at 121.

[66] Quoted in *S. Kutler, Judicial Power and Reconstruction Politics* 67 (1968). The entire Davis letter is contained in *C. Fairman, Reconstruction and Reunion* 232–34 (1971).

RECONSTRUCTION IN OPERATION

By now historians find only hyperbole in the sanguinary similes[67] which used to characterize accounts of the "tragic era"[68] of Reconstruction. We now know enough about what the Radical Republicans tried to accomplish to appreciate the idealistic ends which motivated them, particularly their attempts to place the emancipated race upon a plane of more than formal equality. However, we are not required to gloss over the questionable aspects of Radical Reconstruction in operation. The imposition by Congress of military governments upon the defeated South may have been consistent with the Constitution. One may nevertheless doubt whether the military rule had to be as all-pervasive and free of civilian control as it was.

The Reconstruction Act, Andrew Johnson's veto message declared, "places all the people in the ten States therein named under the absolute domination of military rulers."[69] Johnson himself sought to soften the impact of military rule by relying on the opinion of his attorney general that the authority of the military commanders was not "all comprehensive" and ruling that they had no power to remove state officers or to promulgate laws in defiance of civil governments in the states.[70] Johnson's effort was overruled by passage of the Third Reconstruction Act.[71] It declared that governments in the South were "subject in all respects to the military commanders of the respective districts." Military commanders were given the express authority to suspend or remove any civil officer and to appoint another in his place, and, in a direct rebuff to the attorney general's ruling, the act stated that no district commander "shall be bound in his action by any opinion of any civil officer of the United States." This provision supplemented the Army Appropriation Act of 1867,[72] which provided that military orders of the president and the secretary of war were to be issued only through the general of the army, who could not be relieved from command or transferred from Washington without his own or the Senate's consent. These laws must be considered of doubtful constitu-

---

[67] *Compare* Cardozo, J., dissenting, in Jones v. Securities and Exchange Commission, 298 U.S. 1, 33 (1936).

[68] *C.G. Bowers, The Tragic Era: The Revolution after Lincoln* (1929).

[69] Andrew Johnson, Veto Message, Mar. 2, 1867, 6 *J.D. Richardson, A Compilation of the Messages and Papers of the Presidents 1789–1897*, at 500 (1896–99).

[70] 12 *Op. Att'y Gen.* 182, 186 (1867).

[71] 15 Stat. 14 (1867).

[72] 14 Stat. 485, 486–87 (1867).

tionality; they directly usurped the military powers conferred upon the president by the Constitution.[73]

Congress intended the military commanders to exercise control over all aspects of civil government in the occupied areas. Civil officials, from the governor down, were replaced by military appointees; military tribunals were used to convict offenders; state jury systems were modified; state laws were superseded by military decrees; state court decisions were set aside or suspended, even in cases involving purely private rights (such as those between creditors and debtors). Even the decisions of federal courts were obstructed.[74] The objectives sought by the military commanders were often commendable (as reflected in measures prohibiting the manufacture and sale of liquor or abolishing imprisonment for debt and otherwise righting the balance between debtors and creditors), yet that hardly affects the all-pervasive nature of their authority.

It should, however, be realized that in the congressional program military rule was not an end but a means, imposed temporarily to ensure the creation of reconstructed governments which would become full partners in the Union. The First Reconstruction Act itself was framed upon the premise that military rule would be used to re-establish state governments in the occupied South. It provided that the military commanders were to enroll all qualified voters without regard to race or color (though excluding those barred from office by the proposed Fourteenth Amendment), who were then to vote for delegates to state constitutional conventions. The conventions were to frame new constitutions, which were to contain provisions for Negro suffrage and disqualification of former Confederate leaders. When such constitutions were ratified by popular vote, new state governments could be set up under them. When these steps were taken in a state, the new legislature ratified the Fourteenth Amendment, and that amendment itself had become part of the federal Constitution, "said State shall be declared entitled to representation in Congress."[75]

Historians have disagreed in their evaluations of the state governments established under the Reconstruction acts. During the immediate post-Reconstruction period, the general theme—set by Bryce, Dunning, and Rhodes—was one of extreme censure, if not vituperation: "Such a Saturnalia of robbery and jobbery has seldom been seen in any civilized country, and certainly never before under the forms of free self-government."[76] The state governments set up under Radical rule

[73] *See Burgess, supra note 62, at 129.*

[74] *See W.A. Dunning, Essays on the Civil War and Reconstruction 154–68 (1910).*

[75] Reconstruction Act §9, 14 Stat. at 429.

[76] 2 *J. Bryce, The American Commonwealth 498 (1916).*

were portrayed as the very nadir of the governmental process. More recent historians, who look upon the Reconstruction process with a more favorable eye, have swung the pendulum in the opposite direction. They assert that the positive accomplishments of state governments established under the Reconstruction acts outweigh the deficiencies which prior historians had stressed. The constitutions written and the governments set up under them have been termed "by far the most democratic the South had ever known."[77] Certainly, the efforts of those governments to extend full civil and political rights to Negroes did constitute a basic step forward in American constitutional development.

The crucial aspect of Reconstruction in operation was the effort to ameliorate the lot of the Negro. "Like Nemesis of Greek tragedy, the central problem of America after the Civil War . . . was the black man."[78] The war had put an end to slavery, but it had not settled the status of the emancipated race. Lincoln himself declared in 1864 that "the restoration of Rebel States to the Union must rest upon the principle of civil and political equality of both races."[79] Before the Reconstruction acts went into effect, it was far from clear that this principle would prevail in the South. "The great danger there is local oppression—local ruffianism—depriving the individual Citizen on account of color . . . of the Commonest rights."[80] The Radical leaders rightly placed their primary emphasis upon the securing of political rights for the Negro, particularly the right to vote. "From the possession of political rights," Wendell Phillips declared, "a man gets means to clutch equal opportunities. . . . Give a man his vote, and you give him . . . arms to protect himself."[81] Without the ballot, the Negro was "only a recent chattel, awaiting your justice to be transmuted unto manhood."[82]

Yet, if Negro suffrage was (in Frederick Douglass' phrase) "the *only solid,* and *final solution* of the problem before us,"[83] its attainment in practice presented serious problems: "if you expect the recent slavemaster to confer suffrage without distinction of color, you will find the proposition a delusion and a snare."[84] On the other hand, to compel Negro suffrage in the South involved difficult constitutional questions.

[77] *Stampp, supra* note 34, at 184–85.

[78] *W.E.B. Du Bois, Black Reconstruction in America 1860–1880,* at 237 (1935).

[79] 7 *Lincoln, supra* note 19, at 102.

[80] Letter from Rutherford B. Hayes to Friedrich Hassaurek, Apr. 8, 1866, Charles Hamilton, Auction No. 16, Item 301 (1966).

[81] Quoted in *McPherson, supra* note 37, at 240.

[82] 10 *Sumner, supra* note 16, at 134.

[83] Quoted in *McPherson, supra* note 37, at 240.

[84] 10 *Sumner, supra* note 16, at 121.

A constitutional amendment would, of course, have wholly solved the problem—at least from a legal point of view. But public hostility to Negro voting in the North made such an amendment impractical for the time being, and the Radical leaders felt they had to force the issue through congressional action alone. They did so by providing in the Reconstruction acts that the reconstitution of southern governments was to be on the basis of suffrage without regard to race.

The requirement of Negro suffrage can be considered unconstitutional only if one assumes that the occupied areas were full "states" at the time the requirement was imposed. Congress has the authority to fix voting qualifications only in federal elections; it is for the states themselves to determine who may vote in state elections.[85] State authority in this respect may have been limited by the Fifteenth, Nineteenth, and Twenty-Sixth Amendments. Before the Fifteenth Amendment, nevertheless, there was no constitutional basis for Congress to dictate general voter qualifications to the states. However, the rights of the southern states as members of the Union had been suspended. It was for Congress to re-establish state governments and to determine the conditions upon which they should be recognized as states within Article IV's Republican Guaranty Clause. Even Burgess, who characterized the congressional imposition of Negro suffrage as "a monstrous thing" and "a great wrong to civilization," conceded that, legally speaking, once the South was brought "under the exclusive jurisdiction of the central Government, Congress certainly had, and has, the power to create the electorate in such territory at its own discretion."[86] Congress could impose conditions on the southern states, including suffrage, just as it has imposed comparable conditions upon territories for admission to statehood. Even if, on the basis of Supreme Court decisions, such conditions were no longer binding once full statehood was attained,[87] the legality of the Negro suffrage requirement was by then rendered academic by ratification of the Fifteenth Amendment.

CURBING THE EXECUTIVE

"I wish currently," wrote Senator John Sherman in a letter of April 19, 1866, "to prevent a breach between Congress & the President for I see no occasion for it," yet he was finding himself more and more isolated.

---

85 Oregon v. Mitchell, 400 U.S. 112 (1970).

86 *Burgess, supra* note 62, at 133.

87 *See* Coyle v. Smith, 221 U.S. 559, 567 (1911).

The president's veto of the civil rights bill a month earlier had convinced most congressional leaders that compromise was now virtually impossible. Even Sherman saw that his role as a moderate was becoming increasingly untenable: "I do think the stubborn will of the President & the dogmatic obstructions of a few men in Congress will break us up. Perhaps in standing between I may lose the good opinion of both." [88]

Even a friendly study of the Radical Republicans entitles its chapter on the impeachment of President Johnson "The Radicals Blunder." [89] From a constitutional point of view, the same can be said of the extreme attempts to restrict presidential power during 1867 and 1868. When the congressional leaders realized that the break with Johnson was irreparable, they secured enactment of laws limiting the president's pardoning power[90] and restricting his authority over the armed forces.[91] These laws were of questionable constitutionality.[92] Then came the Tenure of Office Act of March 2, 1867.[93] It provided that the consent of the Senate was necessary for the removal, as well as the appointment, of all civil officers. Johnson had vetoed the law as an encroachment upon his constitutional prerogative,[94] but his veto was speedily overridden.

The Tenure of Office Act severely undermined presidential power. "It was designed to transfer control of the public service from the President to the Senate, and thus to strike a vital blow both to executive power and to the capacity of a President to maintain a coordinate position with the legislative branch."[95] Chapter II described the so-called decision of 1789, in which the first Congress declared that the power to remove department heads was vested in the president alone, and Jackson's use of the removal power to confirm the position of the president as administrative chief. Now, in the heat of the congressional struggle with Andrew Johnson, these precedents were ignored. The Tenure of Office Act meant a reversal of both the decision of 1789 and the theory and practice of decades.[96]

Writing from London, Judah P. Benjamin declared that Johnson "is

[88] John Sherman, Senate Chamber, Apr. 19, 1866, Charles Hamilton, Auction No. 16, Item 302 (1966).

[89] *H.L. Trefousse, The Radical Republicans: Lincoln's Vanguard for Racial Justice* ch. 11 (1969).

[90] *See,* e.g., 15 Stat. 14, 16 (1867).

[91] 14 Stat. 485, 486 (1867).

[92] United States v. Klein, 13 Wall. 128 (U.S. 1872); and *Burgess, supra* note 62, at 129.

[93] 14 Stat. 430 (1867).

[94] *Richardson, supra* note 69, at 492.

[95] *L.D. White, The Republican Era, 1869–1901: A Study in Administrative History* 28 (1958).

[96] *See id.*

apparently cowed by the overbearing violence of the Radicals and dare not act in accordance with his judgment."[97] Johnson was, nevertheless, bound to resist enforcement of the new law if he hoped to preserve the essential prerogatives of his office. He therefore attempted to remove Secretary of War Stanton from office even though the Senate had refused its consent. This attempt became the principal charge in the impeachment proceedings against him.

In fairness to the Radical leaders, it must be said that the constitutional case against the Tenure of Office Act was not as clear in 1867–1868 as it is a century later. Johnson was legally right in his refusal to comply with the Tenure of Office Act, and the Radical leaders were wrong in their contention that Stanton's removal was an impeachable act, because the 1867 statute itself was unconstitutional. But the law has been clear on the matter only since the 1926 *Myers* case, where the Supreme Court expressly affirmed that "the Tenure of Office Act of 1867, in so far as it attempted to prevent the President from removing executive officers who had been appointed by him by and with the advice and consent of the Senate, was invalid."[98]

On February 21, 1868, Johnson formally removed Stanton from office and designated General Lorenzo Thomas as secretary of war *ad interim.*[99] Three days later the House resolved "that Andrew Johnson, President of the United States, be impeached of high crimes and misdemeanors in office"[100] and set up a committee of seven "to prepare and report articles of impeachment."[101] In a proceeding essentially criminal in nature, first to decide upon impeachment and then to gather the evidence to justify the charge was most unusual.[102] Articles of impeachment were prepared by the committee, upon which (in the words of one member) "we may safely go to the Senate and the country for the final judgment of guilty." Eleven articles were adopted by the House on March 2 and 3,[103] and the trial itself began in the Senate on March 5. It continued in that chamber until May 26, with the crucial vote on the eleventh article taking place on May 16.

As Georges Clemenceau (then a young reporter in this country) wrote at the time, "The black cloud has finally broken. The President called upon the lightning and the lightning came."[104] The impeach-

[97] Letter from Judah P. Benjamin to Mr. Mason, Oct. 25, 1866, Charles Hamilton, Auction No. 31, Item 78 (1968).

[98] Myers v. United States, 272 U.S. 52, 176 (1926).

[99] *Richardson, supra* note 69, at 621.

[100] *Cong. Globe,* 40th Cong., 2d Sess. 1400.

[101] *Id.* at 1402.

[102] *Compare Stampp, supra* note 34, at 150.

[103] *Cong. Globe,* 40th Cong., 2d Sess. 1544.

[104] G. Clemenceau, *American Reconstruction, 1865–1870,* at 151 (1928).

ment of Andrew Johnson was one of the most dramatic events in our constitutional history. The failure of the Senate to vote him guilty (albeit by the slenderest of margins) was of great constitutional importance: he may have escaped conviction by only a single vote, but the decisive fact is that he did escape! [105] Had the impeachment succeeded, it would have destroyed the separation between executive and legislative departments intended by the Framers. "Once set the example," declared Senator Lyman Trumbull, in explaining his vote for Johnson, "of impeaching a President for what, when the excitement of the hour shall have subsided, will be regarded as insufficient cause, . . . and no future President will be safe who happens to differ with a majority of the House and two-thirds of the Senate on any measure deemed by them important, particularly if of a political character." [106] Kenneth Stampp differs with Trumbull's estimate of the dimensions of the threat, [107] but to one familiar with the history of impeachment in Britain, Trumbull was not exaggerating. Impeachment would have become a political process, and something like the executive dependence that prevails in a parliamentary system might well have been established in ours.

The trial also settled some important questions concerning the nature of the impeachment process itself. The Radical leaders insisted from the beginning that impeachment was, in Charles Sumner's phrase, "a political proceeding before a political body with a political purpose." [108] "We claim and respectfully insist," declared Benjamin F. Butler in his opening address for the prosecution, "that this tribunal has none of the attributes of a judicial Court. . . . we are in the presence of the Senate . . . convened as a constitutional tribunal, to inquire into and determine whether Andrew Johnson . . . is longer fit to retain the office of President." [109] Throughout, the prosecutors addressed the Chief Justice, who presided, as "Mr. President." Counsel for the president, on the other hand, insisted throughout on the judicial nature of the proceeding. "Mr. Chief Justice," began former Justice Curtis in his presentation for the defense, "I am here to speak to the Senate . . . sitting in its judicial capacity as a court of impeachment, presided over by the Chief Justice for the trial of the President." [110]

[105] *Compare E.S. Corwin, The President: Office and Powers* 25 (4th ed. 1957).

[106] 3 *Trial of Andrew Johnson, President of the United States, Before the Senate of the United States, on Impeachment by the House of Representatives for High Crimes and Misdemeanors* 328 (1868).

[107] *Stampp, supra* note 34, at 153-54.

[108] Quoted in *D. Donald, Charles Sumner and the Rights of Man* 334 (1970). *See,* similarly, Thaddeus Stevens, *Cong. Globe,* 40th Cong., 2d Sess. 1399.

[109] 1 *Johnson, supra* note 106, at 90.

[110] *Id.* at 377.

The nature of the impeachment proceeding was of great practical importance. If the prosecution was correct, it meant that "the judgment is political and nothing more." [111] If that was the case, the Senate was, as Butler urged, "bound by no law. . . . You are a law unto yourselves, bound only by the natural principles of equity and justice, and that *salus populi suprema est lex*." [112] Impeachment could be used by Congress to replace the president with one of its own members. "The very first task . . . ," declared Wendell Phillips at Cooper Union, "is to impeach the Rebel at the White House. . . . What is the advantage; Then *we* run the machine." [113] If, as counsel for the defense contended, the impeachment trial was judicial in nature, then it follows that the Senate, acting as a court, could only convict if the president were proved guilty of "Treason, Bribery, or other high Crimes and misdemeanors." [114] On the face of it, the constitutional language providing for conviction on these charges seems limited to criminal offenses. Johnson's impeachment was based upon a different theory. As Stevens put it in moving the impeachment resolution, "it is [not] necessary to prove a crime as an indictable offense, or any act *malum in se*." [115]

The Tenure of Office Act itself provided that any violation of its provisions "shall be deemed . . . a high misdemeanor," [116] but this was a mere figure of speech. The articles of impeachment charged Johnson not with any indictable offense but with failure to carry out certain laws and with making public utterances, especially those attacking Congress. This, in the argument of the managers of the proceeding, was enough. An impeachable offense, they urged, "may consist of a violation of the Constitution, of law, of an official oath, or of duty, by an act committed or omitted, or, without violating a positive law, by the abuse of discretionary powers from improper motives or for an improper purpose." [117] Johnson's acquittal represents the rejection of this view, at least so far as the impeachment of executive officers is concerned. Curtis, in his argument in Johnson's defense, stated what may be taken as the prevailing law: "when the Constitution speaks of 'treason, bribery, and other high crimes and misdemeanors,' it refers to, and includes only, high criminal offenses against the United States,

---

[111] 12 *Sumner, supra* note 16, at 324.

[112] 1 *Johnson, supra* note 106, at 90.

[113] Quoted in *McPherson, supra* note 37, at 369.

[114] Article II, § 4.

[115] *Cong. Globe*, 40th Cong., 2d Sess. 1399.

[116] § 9, 14 Stat. at 432.

[117] 1 *Johnson, supra* note 106, at 147 (italics omitted).

made so by the law of the United States existing when the acts complained of were done." [118]

THE ERA OF THE OATH

To one who remembers all too vividly the "cold war" era of emphasis on individual loyalty, a particularly interesting aspect of the Civil War and postbellum period was the pervasive use of loyalty tests. Perhaps they were inevitable in a time of civil conflict, when the fear of treason was the dominant sentiment. "Treason is rife in every dwelling..," wrote John Fiske to his mother in 1862: "I hear treason and nothing else talked all the time." [119] In such an environment, stress upon loyalty to the exclusion of virtually everything else is scarcely surprising. As one of the Radical leaders put it, "We are learning to draw the line between treason and loyalty." [120]

Before Sumter, Americans took it for granted that public servants were loyal to the United States. As soon as hostilities began, that assumption gave way. Two weeks after Sumter fell, Lincoln's attorney general recommended that "all the employees of the Departments— from the head secretary to the lowest messenger, be required to take anew the oath of allegiance." [121] But the simple oath to defend the Constitution (which was contained in the first statute enacted by the first Congress) [122] was soon deemed inadequate to ensure loyalty. In August, 1861, Congress passed a law prescribing a new and more elaborate oath for government employees. They were required to swear to "support, protect, and defend" the Constitution and the federal government and to declare their "loyalty to the same, any ordinance, resolution, or law of any State Convention or Legislature to the contrary notwithstanding." [123] The swearing process was duly repeated a second time in all federal offices. [124] This new loyalty oath itself was soon believed to be insufficient. On July 2, 1862, Congress enacted into law the so-called "ironclad oath" of loyalty. [125]

---

[118] *Id.* at 109. What has been said is true so far as executive officers are concerned. It does not fully apply to federal judges, for the reasons stated in 1 B. *Schwartz, A Commentary on the Constitution of the United States: The Powers of Government: Federal and State Powers* 115 (1963).

[119] Quoted in *H.M. Hyman, Era of the Oath* 1 (1954).

[120] George Julian, quoted in *id.* Introduction.

[121] *The Diary of Edward Bates* 187 (1933).

[122] 1 Stat. 23 (1789).

[123] 12 Stat. 326 (1861).

[124] *See Hyman, supra* note 119, at 2.

[125] 12 Stat. 502 (1862).

That oath became the very backbone of the Radical system of disenfranchisement and disqualification for office during the war and in the 'Reconstruction period. [126] All persons (except the president) "elected or appointed to any office . . . under the government of the United States, either in the civil, military, or naval departments" were required to take the ironclad oath. The oath was in two parts. The affiant had to swear that he had never voluntarily borne arms against the United States or given any voluntary aid to those engaged in armed hostilities against the Union, and that he had not held office under or yielded voluntary support to any government hostile to the United States. The second part of the oath was a pledge to support and defend the Constitution and bear true faith and allegiance to it in future.

Lincoln, like the congressional leaders, relied on the oath technique as the basic test to determine loyalty, [127] but he was much milder than the legislators with regard to the oath that should be imposed. "On principle," he wrote, "I dislike an oath which requires a man to swear he has *not* done wrong. It rejects the Christian principle of forgiveness on terms of repentance. I think it is enough if the man does no wrong *hereafter*." [128] In accordance with this view, the famous oath he prescribed in his December 8, 1863, Proclamation of Amnesty and Reconstruction [129] required only an undertaking "henceforth" to support and defend the Constitution and the Union, as well as to acquiesce in emancipation.

Lincoln's approach was adopted by his successor. Johnson's most important amnesty proclamation, that of May 29, 1865, [130] contained, as a condition of amnesty, an oath essentially similar to Lincoln's—a pledge "henceforth" to support the Constitution and the Union, together with all laws and proclamations concerning emancipation. Johnson's second amnesty proclamation, on September 7, 1867, [131] also contained this oath.

During Lincoln's presidency, the conflict between congressional and presidential policies on loyalty oaths remained dormant; during Reconstruction it became an actuality. President Johnson based his exercise of the amnesty power (itself the basis of presidential Reconstruction) upon the milder Lincolnian loyalty oath; the Radical leaders insisted upon the ironclad oath as the fundamental test. "I have ceased to hope

[126] *See Hyman, supra* note 119, at 23.

[127] For early examples, *see* 4 Lincoln, *supra* note 19, at 22 (Sept. 15, 1861); 5 *id.* at 86 (Jan. 1, 1862).

[128] 7 *id.* at 169.

[129] *Id.* at 54.

[130] *Richardson, supra* note 69, at 310.

[131] *Id.* at 547.

anything that justice or humanity demands," wrote Judah P. Benjamin in October, 1866, "from the men who now seem to have uncontrolled power over public affairs in the U.S." [132] The ironclad oath had become the fulcrum upon which the Reconstruction process turned. The Supplemental Reconstruction Act (March 23, 1867) [133] prescribed an oath of past loyalty comparable to the ironclad oath for all who sought to register as voters; all registration officials were required to take the ironclad oath itself. The Third Reconstruction Act (July 19, 1867) required that "all persons hereafter elected or appointed to office in said military districts" should take the ironclad oath. [134] The final step was a law of 1869 requiring the military commanders in Virginia, Texas, and Mississippi (which were still unreconstructed) to remove all officials who could not take the ironclad oath and to replace them with persons who could. [135]

The loyalty oath did not remain confined to the federal government. Instead (as those familiar with the revival of the technique in our own day well realize[136]), such techniques for determining loyalty have a tendency to spread until they infect virtually every element of society. "Loyalty," stated James Russell Lowell in April, 1865, "has hitherto been a sentiment. . . . Now for the first time it is identical with patriotism and has its seat in the brain." [137] That being the case, it was inevitable that the states, too, would become increasingly concerned with the question of which of their "people . . . were true at heart to the Union, and what part were tainted with treasonable sympathies and wishes." [138] A number of states outside the reconstructed South made wide use of the loyalty oath technique both among their own officials and people outside government. [139]

The first people usually required to take loyalty oaths are public employees; concern with loyalty, however, soon extends to other areas. By mid-1862, oaths of loyalty to the Union were required of government contractors, [140] shipmasters, [141] claimants before federal agen-

---

[132] Letter from Judah P. Benjamin to Mr. Mason, Oct. 25, 1866, Charles Hamilton, Auction No. 31, Item 78 (1968).

[133] 15 Stat. 2 (1867).

[134] § 9, 15 Stat. at 16.

[135] 15 Stat. 344 (1869).

[136] *See* 4 B. Schwartz, *A Commentary on the Constitution of the United States: Rights of the Person* 363–64 (1968).

[137] Quoted in *Hyman, supra* note 119, at 13.

[138] Nathaniel Hawthorne, *Chiefly about War Matters, Atlantic Monthly* 61 (July, 1862).

[139] Among the states which enacted loyalty oath statutes were California, Kansas, Kentucky, Maryland, Minnesota, Missouri, Nevada, New York, Tennessee, and West Virginia.

[140] *See* 13 *Op. Att'y Gen.* 390 (1871).

[141] 12 Stat. 610 (1862).

cies, [142] pensioners, telegraphers, and passport applicants. [143] Congress imposed the ironclad oath upon attorneys seeking to practice in the federal courts, [144] as well as a comparable oath upon federal jurors. [145] In addition (as we have seen), the Reconstruction laws required Southern voters to take such an oath.

State extensions of the loyalty oath requirement beyond the field of public service went just as far. A number of states required loyalty oaths of all voters, as well as attorneys, jurors, and litigants. Perhaps the most far-reaching use of the oath was in Missouri, [146] where it was required in order to practice any profession, including law, medicine, and the ministry, as well as to teach or hold corporate office. At the end of the war the Missouri oath was incorporated into the state's Constitution. The wartime loyalty system was to be perpetuated to bar from public and professional life all who could not swear to an oath even more restrictive than the federal ironclad oath.

"It is unfortunate," wrote Clemenceau in 1867, "that the Republicans have not in all cases shown good judgment in their Reconstruction measures. One of the principal tests of loyalty . . . is the oath. But the Anglo-Saxons have always abused the oath. . . . It does not in the least hamper a rogue who becomes as accustomed to taking an oath as a dealer in church furniture to handling a pyx." [147] Even more important is the impact of the requirement upon honorable men. As Lincoln put it with regard to the Tennessee loyalty oath, "I have found that men who have not even been suspected of disloyalty, are very averse to taking an oath of any sort as a condition to exercising an ordinary right of citizenship." [148]

More fundamental is the question whether the oath technique can possibly attain its purpose of fostering loyalty. The observer who has lived through a second "era of the oath" has more than a "modest doubt" about what the oath technique accomplishes apart from indicating the malaise of the society in which it is employed. While the Decii are rushing with devoted bodies on the enemies of Rome, what need is there of preaching patriotism? When loyalty is made a principal object of the state's concern, it has already become less than all-transcendent.

---

142 *Id.*

143 *See Hyman, supra* note 119, at 20–21.

144 13 Stat. 424 (1865).

145 12 Stat. 430 (1862).

146 *See Hyman, supra* note 119, at 97.

147 *Clemenceau, supra* note 104, at 84–85.

148 *Lincoln,* supra note 19, at 284.

JUDICIAL NADIR?

The traditional view of the Supreme Court during the Civil War and Reconstruction has been that it played a more subdued role than at any other time in its history—that it had been weakened, if not impotent, ever since the *Dred Scott* decision: [149] "Never has the Supreme Court been treated with such ineffable contempt, and never has that tribunal so often cringed before the clamor of the mob." [150] This view has recently been challenged by Stanley I. Kutler, who asserts that "the Court in this period was characterized by forcefulness and not timidity, . . . by boldness and defiance instead of cowardice and impotence, and by a creative and determinative role with no abdication of its rightful powers." Kutler's study is scholarly and full of suggestive insights. One may wonder, nevertheless, whether his attempt to change the accepted picture completely is justified. The postbellum Court may have played a more important role than the traditional view admitted; all the same, the historical evidence does not support the Kutler conclusion that "the Supreme Court under Salmon P. Chase was of only 'little less importance' than that under John Marshall." [151]

The Kutler case for judicial activism during Reconstruction is based upon the increasing use by the Chase Court of the power to hold laws of Congress unconstitutional. From 1865 to 1873 ten congressional acts were voided, a statistic which, Kutler points out, must be compared with two judicial vetoes in the previous seventy-six years. [152]

Two things should be noted before accepting his conclusion, however. First, the Chase Court was exercising a review power which had already been confirmed in both law and practice. By the postbellum period, there was no doubt of the legal power of the courts to review constitutionality. The Supreme Court may have exercised the power over congressional acts so rarely before the Civil War, but it was exercised in many cases by state courts and was accepted without question by the leading text writers and other legal commentators. Even the critics of *Dred Scott* did not dispute the power of judicial

---

[149] *See Kutler, supra* note 66, at 1–6.

[150] *Bowers, supra* note 68, at v.

[151] *Kutler, supra* note 66, at 6.

[152] *See id.* at 114. Kutler cites as the two previous decisions invalidating congressional acts Marbury v. Madison, 1 Cranch 137 (U.S. 1803) and the Dred Scott case. Like most commentators he overlooks Hodgson v. Bowerbank, 5 Cranch 303 (U.S. 1809), where a section of the Judiciary Act was declared unconstitutional.

review; their strictures were directed to the merits of the Court's decision on constitutionality.

In the second place, it should be recognized that, of the ten cases cited by Kutler, seven were of little practical importance and received scant notice either at the time or from constitutional historians since then. [153] This cannot be said of *Hepburn* v. *Griswold*, [154] where the Chase Court made its boldest assertion of review authority, yet even there the decision was limited in its effect. It applied only to contracts entered into before 1862, and, even more important, it was overruled by the Supreme Court the next year. [155] Reargument of the issue was granted only three months after the case had been decided. The promptness of the Court in allowing reargument "had the effect of apprising the country that the decision was not fully acquiesced in, and of obviating any injurious consequences to the business of the country by its reversal." [156] Certainly the *Legal Tender Cases* focused attention upon the Court's review function, but their main immediate impact was in their demonstration of the manner in which the Court could be "packed" by new appointments to secure a desired decision. [157]

The remaining two cases arose out of the congressional Reconstruction program. The significance of *United States* v. *Klein* [158] as a limitation upon congressional control over Supreme Court jurisdiction has been demonstrated by this writer. Its impact at the time was nevertheless highly limited; it invalidated a statute which had been scarcely noted when it was passed by Congress. In addition, its practical effect was, in large part, nullified by a later decision. [159] The other case dealing with an aspect of Reconstruction was *Ex parte Garland*. [160] The decision there held invalid the ironclad oath which Congress had required for admission to practice in the Supreme Court. In the com-

---

[153] Gordon v. United States, 2 Wall. 561 (U.S. 1865); Reichart v. Felps, 6 Wall. 160 (U.S. 1868); The Alicia, 7 Wall. 571 (U.S. 1869); United States v. Dewitt, 9 Wall. 41 (U.S. 1870); The Justices v. Murray, 9 Wall. 274 (U.S. 1870); Collector v. Day, 11 Wall. 113 (U.S. 1871); United States v. Railroad Company, 17 Wall. 322 (U.S. 1873). Of these, only Collector v. Day was of great potential importance, but it had no immediate effect because the federal income tax at issue expired a few months after the decision. *Compare Fairman, supra* note 66, at 1435, which treats Collector v. Day as not belonging among the decisions holding an act of Congress unconstitutional. It may also be doubted that United States v. Railroad Company belongs among such decisions, since it turned on statutory interpretation, though the constitutional issue was dealt with by way of *obiter. Compare id.* at 1435–36.

[154] 8 Wall. 603 (U.S. 1870).

[155] Legal Tender Cases, 12 Wall. 457 (U.S. 1871).

[156] Bradley, J., concurring, *id.* at 570.

[157] *See* p. 227 *infra.*

[158] 13 Wall. 128 (U.S. 1872). *See Schwartz, supra* note 49, at 18–19.

[159] Hart v. United States, 118 U.S. 62 (1886) (Congress need not appropriate funds to satisfy claims of pardoned persons).

[160] 4 Wall. 333 (U.S. 1867).

panion case of *Cummings* v. *Missouri,* [161] the Missouri oath required to practice any profession (in this case, that of a Catholic priest) was ruled unconstitutional. In both cases, the oaths were ruled unconstitutional "as bills of attainder on the ground that they were legislative acts inflicting punishment on a specific group: clergymen and lawyers who had taken part in the rebellion and therefore could not truthfully take the oath." [162] In addition, since they imposed a penalty for an act not so punishable at the time it was committed, they also violated the prohibition against *ex post facto* laws.

Under *Cummings* and *Garland,* it is clear that much of the loyalty oath program was unconstitutional. The imposition of disqualifications upon those who could not swear to their past loyalty to the Union comes directly within the reach of the Supreme Court decisions. Yet only two months after *Cummings* and *Garland,* Congress (as already seen) prescribed an oath of past loyalty for all voters in the reconstructed South and, a few months later, required the ironclad oath of all officeholders in the South. Despite the Supreme Court's categorical condemnation, these oath requirements were continued during the entire congressional Reconstruction program, [163] nor did the high bench censure affect the use of the ironclad oath in the federal government, both for civil servants and in other cases. Four years after *Cummings* and *Garland,* Benjamin F. Butler declared, "I hope the iron-clad oath will never be repealed—ay, even after every disability is removed from every rebel. . . . I roll it as a sweet morsel under my tongue." [164] It was not, indeed, until 1884 that it was finally repealed. [165]

Against the cases cited by Kutler must be placed *Ex parte McCardle,* [166] which stands virtually alone as an example of congressional control over the functioning of the Supreme Court. A Mississippi newspaper editor was arrested and held for trial by a military commission. He petitioned for a writ of habeas corpus in the federal circuit court, challenging the validity of the First Reconstruction Act's provision authorizing the military detention and trial of civilians. The writ was denied by the circuit court, and an appeal was taken to the Supreme Court under the statute authorizing appeals from circuit court

[161] 4 Wall. 277 (U.S. 1867).

[162] United States v. Brown, 381 U.S. 437, 447 (1965). In addition, the law at issue in Garland was held an invalid infringement upon the presidential power of pardon.

[163] For other instances in which Garland and Cummings were flouted, see *Fairman, supra* note 66, at 246–47.

[164] *Cong. Globe,* 41st Cong., 3d Sess. 886.

[165] 23 Stat. 21 (1884).

[166] 7 Wall. 506 (U.S. 1869).

decisions in all cases involving detentions in violation of the Constitution or federal laws. [167] The high bench unanimously decided that it had jurisdiction to hear the appeal. [168] The case was thoroughly argued upon the merits and taken under advisement by the justices. Congressional leaders feared that the Court would seize the occasion presented by *McCardle* to invalidate the military governments authorized by the Reconstruction Act. "Should the Court in that case, as it is supposed they will, pronounce the Reconstruction laws unconstitutional, the military governments will fall and the whole Radical fabric will tumble with it." [169]

To avoid this danger, the Radical leaders considered various maneuvers. The most extreme was embodied in a bill passed by the House early in 1868, [170] which required a two-thirds vote of the justices before any act of Congress could be ruled unconstitutional. That bill, said Gideon Welles, "is a scheme to change the character of the Supreme Court." [171] It ultimately died in the Senate, as did a bill introduced by Senator Lyman Trumbull forbidding the Court to take jurisdiction in any case arising out of the Reconstruction acts. [172] Congress then passed a law repealing the statute authorizing an appeal to the Supreme Court from circuit court judgments in habeas corpus cases and prohibiting the Court's exercise of any jurisdiction on appeals which had been or which might be taken. [173] The *McCardle* case was reargued on the question of the authority of Congress to withdraw jurisdiction from the Supreme Court over a case which had already been argued on the merits. The effect of the relevant statute was plain: it withdrew jurisdiction over the appeal. It is quite clear, therefore, the Court concluded unanimously, "that this court cannot proceed to pronounce judgment in this case, for it has no longer jurisdiction of the appeal." [174]

If the Court had been able to decide the merits in *McCardle*, the decision might well have been in petitioner's favor—that, at any rate, was what Chief Justice Chase and Justice Field told two of their contemporaries. [175] But the whole point of *McCardle* is that Congress

[167] 14 Stat. 385, 386 (1867).

[168] *Ex parte* McCardle, 6 Wall. 318 (U.S. 1868).

[169] *Welles, supra* note 56, at 314.

[170] *Cong. Globe,* 40th Cong., 2d Sess. 489.

[171] *Welles, supra* note 56, at 258.

[172] *Cong. Globe,* 40th Cong., 2d Sess. 1204, 1428.

[173] 15 Stat. 44 (1868).

[174] 7 Wall. at 515.

[175] *See Fairman, supra* note 66, at 494; *Hughes, Salmon P. Chase: Chief Justice,* 18 *Vand. L. Rev.* 568, 591 (1965).

was able to prevent a decision on the merits. "The Judges of the Supreme Court," Gideon Welles plaintively wrote, "have caved in, fallen through, failed, in the McCardle case." [176] The *McCardle* law is the only instance in American history in which Congress has rushed to withdraw the appellate jurisdiction of the Supreme Court for the purpose of preventing a decision on the constitutionality of a particular statute. That law, in the pithy phrase of a newspaper, "put a knife to the throat of the *McCardle* Case." [177] And the *McCardle* decision itself permitted Congress to do just that. "Congress," wrote former Justice Curtis, "with the acquiescence of the country, has subdued the Supreme Court." [178]

[176] *Welles, supra* note 56, at 320.
[177] Quoted in 3 *C. Warren, The Supreme Court in United States History* 199 (1924).
[178] *Id.* at 205.

CHAPTER EIGHT

Reconstruction and Equal Rights

EQUALITY AND THE CONSTITUTION

On June 26, 1857, Abraham Lincoln replied to the contention of Stephen A. Douglas that the Declaration of Independence, in declaring "that all men are created equal," was only "speaking of British subjects on this continent being equal to British subjects born and residing in Great Britain." Lincoln emphatically rejected this interpretation. The authors of the Declaration, he said, "intended to include *all* men. . . . They meant to set up a standard maxim for free society, which should be familiar to all, and revered by all; constantly looked to, constantly labored for, and even though never perfectly attained, constantly approximated, and thereby constantly spreading and deepening its influence, and augmenting the happiness and value of life to all people of all colors everywhere."[1]

In emphasizing the concept of equality as a central theme of the Declaration of Independence Lincoln echoed what has always been a driving force in American history, despite the fact that the Framers of the Constitution did not repeat the unqualified assertion of the Declaration of Independence. Nowhere in the basic document is there any guarantee of equality or even any mention of that concept. Yet, whatever may have been the Framers' intent, their work disseminated the ideals of Liberty and Equality throughout the world. "What Archi-

[1] 2 *The Collected Works of Abraham Lincoln* 405–7 (R.P. Basler ed. 1953).

medes said of the mechanical powers," wrote Tom Paine in his *Rights of Man,* "may be applied to Reason and Liberty. 'Had we,' said he, 'a place to stand upon, we might raise the world.' The revolution of America presented in politics what was only theory in mechanics."[2]

The concept of equality, however, could scarcely complete its triumphant march while the institution of slavery not only existed but was protected by the Constitution. "Liberty and Slavery—opposite as Heaven and Hell—are both in the Constitution," and the Constitution itself was "a compromise with Slavery—a bargain between the North and the South."[3] While that bargain persisted, an express guarantee of equality would have only been hypocritical. With the Civil War, the situation completely changed. "The bond of Union being dissolved," Jefferson Davis himself conceded, "the obligation of the U.S. Govt. to recognize property in slaves, as denominated in the compact, might be reecognized as thereby no longer binding."[4] William Lloyd Garrison (who had earlier committed the Constitution to the fire) could now fervently support the Union. When charged with inconsistency, he replied: "Well, ladies and gentlemen, when I said I would not sustain the Constitution, because it was a 'covenant with death and an agreement with hell,' I had no idea that I would live to see death and hell secede."[5]

When slavery was abolished and the American system repudiated the heresy that "all men are created equal, except Negroes,"[6] it was no longer inconsistent with reality for the Constitution to contain an express guarantee of equality. It came with ratification of the Fourteenth Amendment in 1868. That amendment and the other postbellum additions to the Constitution made equality regardless of race a fundamental constitutional principle.

It was the congressional leaders who elevated the concept of equality to the constitutional plane. "What is Liberty without Equality?" asked Charles Sumner in 1866. "One is the complement of the other. . . . They are the two vital principles of republican government."[7] Whatever we may think of the Reconstruction congresses, they first made equality an express constitutional principle. In doing so, they at last gave specific effect to the great theme announced in the Declaration of

---

[2] *T. Paine, Rights of Man* 155 (Heritage Press ed. 1961) (italics omitted).

[3] Frederick Douglass, quoted in *S. Lynd, Class Conflict, Slavery, and the United States Constitution* 155 (1967).

[4] Jefferson Davis, Notes for W.T.W., Charles Hamilton, Auction No. 31, Item 83 (1968).

[5] Quoted in *J.M. McPherson, The Struggle for Equality: Abolitionists and the Negro in the Civil War and Reconstruction* 100 (1964).

[6] *Lincoln, supra* note 1, at 323.

[7] 10 *The Works of Charles Sumner* 236 (1874).

Independence itself. "In securing the Equal Rights of the freedman, . . . we shall perform the early promises of the Fathers [who] solemnly announced the Equal Rights of all men."[8]

One may go further and say that the history of civil rights in this country really begins with the amendments added to the Constitution during Reconstruction. Not only (as already stressed) did they make the concept of equality a constitutional one; they made it possible for Congress to enact civil rights legislation under the power vested in it to enforce the amendments "by appropriate legislation."

The postbellum amendments themselves constituted the first changes in the organic text in over sixty years. From a legal point of view, the changes were fundamental, for they made for a nationalization of civil rights that was completely to transform the constitutional system. The protection of life, liberty, and property now became a national responsibility—federalizing, as it were, the vindication of individual rights throughout the land.

THE CIVIL RIGHTS ACT OF 1866

The cornerstone of the Reconstruction program with regard to the Negro was, of course, the Thirteenth Amendment. The very notion of civil rights could scarcely have practical meaning until there was a constitutional guarantee of freedom in its most elementary sense. To the congressional leaders, however, abolition alone did not mark the end of the struggle against slavery: "While the Legislatures of the South retain the right to pass laws making any discrimination between black and white, slavery still lives there."[9] Freedom had been made a constitutional principle, but it was still only a "paper" freedom.[10] "It leaves the letter in the Constitution, but it takes away the powers by which that letter is made a living soul."[11]

The goal to be attained was thus not mere emancipation but (as Wendell Phillips declared in an 1865 speech) "'absolute equality before the law; absolute civil equality'; and I shall never leave the negro until, so far as God gives me the power, I achieve it."[12] While the congressional leaders may not have intended to go as far as the fiery abolitionist, an essential part of the Radical program was the protection of

---

8 *Id.* at 128.

9 Frederick Douglass, quoted in *McPherson, supra* note 5, at 305.

10 *Compare id.* at 133.

11 *Sumner, supra* note 7, at 279.

12 Quoted in *McPherson, supra* note 5, at 304.

Negro rights. The first measure seeking to give effect to this aim was the Civil Rights Act of 1866.[13]

From a historical point of view, this law is important primarily because of the part it played in making the breach between Andrew Johnson and the Radical congressional leaders irrevocable. Johnson's veto of the act marked the point of no return, so far as further cooperation between the legislative and executive branches was concerned. Constitutionally speaking, the chief significance of the act is that it was the first congressional effort to provide broad protection in the field of civil rights. As such, it was the precursor of the Fourteenth and Fifteenth Amendments and of the civil rights statutes subsequently enacted by Congress.

The purpose of the act as explained by Lyman Trumbull, chairman of the Senate Judiciary Committee, in his address introducing the proposed legislation, was to carry into effect the Thirteenth Amendment by destroying the discrimination against the Negro that existed in the laws of the southern states, particularly the Black Codes enacted since emancipation.[14] In this way, the new statute would "provide for the real freedom of their former slaves."[15] The heart of the bill, said Trumbull, was in its first section, which provided that citizens of every race and color have the same right "as is enjoyed by white citizens" to contract, sue, take and dispose of property, bring actions and give evidence, and to benefit from all laws for the security of person and property. This provision was intended to "secure to all persons within the United States practical freedom."[16]

The opposition to Trumbull's bill is of interest chiefly because of the claim of unconstitutionality raised against it—a claim voiced even by members of the Republican Party who favored federal protection of civil rights. Foremost among these was Representative John A. Bingham of Ohio, whose views are of particular significance because of the crucial role he was to play in the drafting of the Fourteenth Amendment. When the bill came before the House, Bingham, in a strong speech, asserted that Congress had no power to enact such a law on the ground that "the care of the property, the liberty, and the life of the citizen, under the . . . Federal Constitution, is in the States, and not in

[13] 14 Stat. 27 (1966).

[14] 1 *B. Schwartz, Statutory History of the United States: Civil Rights* 107 (1970). This work contains the important portions of the congressional debates on the postbellum amendments and civil rights legislation. References to these debates in this chapter will, so far as possible, be to this work (cited as *Schwartz*), since it is more readily available in libraries than the original *Congressional Globe*.

[15] *Schwartz* 99.

[16] *Id.* at 106. Trumbull's bill also provided that there should be no discrimination on account of race, but this general prohibition was removed in the House.

the Federal Government."[17] The evils which the bill sought to remedy, he argued, should be dealt with by constitutional amendment—thus indicating that his drafts of section 1 of the Fourteenth Amendment were intended to give constitutional validity to the principles laid down in the bill. Trumbull himself recognized the existence of strong constitutional doubts about his bill. He asserted that, since any encroachment upon a citizen's liberty was "a badge of servitude" and hence within the prohibition of the Thirteenth Amendment, which Congress had the express authority to enforce,[18] the bill was valid. Opponents remained unconvinced.

During the congressional debates, an important change was made in section 1 of the Trumbull proposal: a citizenship clause was added, making persons born in this country United States citizens.[19] Its purpose was to remove the doubts about the Negro's citizenship status that persisted because of the *Dred Scott* decision.

Despite the objections of Republicans like Bingham, the bill passed both houses overwhelmingly. It was vetoed by President Johnson, in large part because, he asserted, Congress lacked constitutional power to confer citizenship and abrogate discriminatory state laws. Practically speaking, the veto had no effect; it was speedily overridden by both houses, and the bill became law in early April, 1866. However, the doubts raised by its congressional opponents had made a deep impression. They led the congressional advocates of federal enforcement of civil rights to settle the matter by constitutional amendment, and section 1 of the Civil Rights Act was ultimately recast as section 1 of the Fourteenth Amendment.

HOUSING DISCRIMINATION

What makes the history of the 1866 Civil Rights Act particularly pertinent today is the 1968 Supreme Court decision in *Jones* v. *Alfred H. Mayer Co.*[20] In that case, the Court held that section 1 of the 1866 Act contains a broad prohibition of racial discrimination in the sale or rental of property and, as such, forbids a private development company to refuse to sell a home to someone because he is a Negro. It is fair to say that the *Jones* decision not only revives the previously obscure 1866 Civil Rights Act (which even in its own day had virtually been consigned to legal oblivion) but interprets that statute in a manner

[17] *Id.* at 143.
[18] *Id.* at 108.
[19] *Id.* at 100.
[20] 392 U.S. 409 (1968).

which had never been urged before, much less accepted by, any court. Only two months before the *Jones* decision, Congress finally took what it thought was the momentous step of enacting the "first" federal fair housing law in the Civil Rights Act of 1968.[21] With *Jones,* however, Congress and the country learned that the effort on Capitol Hill to work out the boundaries of fair housing had been redundant, for the nation already had such a law in the federal statute book and one which, unlike the 1968 act, contained no exemptions.

The goal sought by the Court in *Jones*—elimination of racial discrimination which "herds men into ghettos and makes their ability to buy property turn on the color of their skin"[22] —is so desirable that it may seem a mere cavil to wonder whether it should be attained by judicial reliance upon a half-hidden statute which had almost never before been invoked. If it was intended to have this effect, it is astounding that it was not used when its purpose was fresh in the minds of those who passed the law. Both the legislative history of the 1866 Civil Rights Act and the situation with which it was intended to deal indicate that it had two main purposes: to make Negroes citizens and to give them the citizen's right to make contracts, bring actions, and own property. Before the Thirteenth Amendment, slaves could not own property, and after emancipation the southern states enacted Black Codes to perpetuate this disability. This was the "incident of slavery" which the 1866 statute was aimed at, relying for its enforcement on the Thirteenth Amendment.

In an unpublished 1866 letter, Rutherford B. Hayes dealt with a misconception similar to that upon which the *Jones* decision is based. Writing to an Ohio newspaper publisher, he declared, "I know it [the 1866 act] is grossly misrepresented and greatly misunderstood in Ohio. *The Commercial* speaks of it as if it gives increased and unheard of rights as privileges to negroes—as if it would compel the schools to receive negro children, the hotels negro guests &c &c &c now please to note what I say. It undertakes to secure to the negro no right which he has not enjoyed in Ohio since the repeal of the Black Laws in 1848–9."[23] The "same right . . . as is enjoyed by white citizens to . . . purchase property" was intended only to mean the same legal right, the same capacity granted by law[24] It was not contemplated that the ex-slave was being given a legal right to compel an unwilling seller to

---

[21] 82 Stat. 73 (1968).

[22] 392 U.S. at 442–43.

[23] Letter from Rutherford B. Hayes to Friedrich Haussaurek, Apr. 8, 1866, Charles Hamilton, Auction No. 16, Item 301 (1966).

[24] *Compare Henkin, Foreword: On Drawing Lines,* 82 *Harv. Law Rev.* 63, 85 (1968). The quoted language is from section 1 of the 1866 act.

convey—a thing no citizen could compel in 1866 and which was completely alien to the individualist law of that day.

In addition, it is not at all clear that the Thirteenth Amendment was intended to go as far as *Jones* v. *Alfred H. Mayer Co.* assumes. In the congressional debate on the amendment there were suggestions of an intent to abolish not only the institution of slavery itself but also "the necessary incidents of slavery,"[25] but no one expressed anything like the *Jones* view that the amendment could be used to reach private discriminations in the sale of property.[26] During the ratification process, the governor of South Carolina wrote President Johnson that his state feared that section 2 of the amendment "may be construed to give Congress power of local legislation over the negroes." Secretary of State Seward replied that the state's objection was "querulous and unreasonable, because that clause is really restraining in its effect, instead of enlarging the powers of Congress."[27] South Carolina then ratified the amendment, stating the qualification "that any attempt by Congress towards legislating upon the political status of former slaves, or their civil relations, would be contrary to the Constitution of the United States as it now is, or as it would be altered by the proposed amendment." Alabama and Florida also ratified "with the understanding that it does not confer upon Congress the power to legislate upon the political status of freedmen." Mississippi stated an even broader qualification, ratifying with the condition that the amendment "shall not be construed as a grant of power to Congress to legislate in regard to the freedmen."[28]

While not legally binding, the qualifications stated, as well as Seward's interpretation for the executive, are indicative of the intent of those who ratified the Thirteenth Amendment. They are certainly far narrower than the 1968 Supreme Court holding. So far as can be seen, the Court itself was unaware of this aspect of the amendment's history when it decided the *Jones* case.

[25] Senator James Harlan, quoted in *Schwartz* 74.

[26] *See* the contrary expressions collected in *C. Fairman, Reconstruction and Reunion* 1157–59 (1971).

[27] *E. McPherson, A Political Manual for 1866 and 1867*, at 23 (1867). Seward was doubtless wrong in interpreting section 2 as a restraint, but his reply does show that the executive view on the scope of the Thirteenth Amendment was a narrow one.

[28] The South Carolina, Alabama, and Florida qualifications are contained in *id.*, at 21–25. For the Mississippi qualification, see *L. Cox* and *J.H. Cox, Politics, Principle, and Prejudice, 1865–1866*, at 170 (1963).

THE FOURTEENTH AMENDMENT

Early History

The landmark enactment during the Reconstruction period was the Fourteenth Amendment, which deals specifically with civil rights in its key first section. It has its origins in the resolution offered by Thaddeus Stevens on December 4, 1865, when the Thirty-Ninth Congress convened for its first session, to create a joint committee of nine representatives and six senators to "inquire into the condition of the States which formed the so-called Confederate States of America, and report whether they, or any of them, are entitled to be represented in either House of Congress."[29] This measure was adopted on December 13 and brought into being the Joint Committee on Reconstruction (known to its friends as the Committee of Fifteen, to its enemies as the "Directory" or the "Star Chamber"[30]), vested with authority "to report at any time, by bill or otherwise."

The Joint Committee interpreted its broad mandate to include the drafting of constitutional amendments. Amendments submitted at the committee's third meeting, on January 12, 1866, by Representatives John A. Bingham and Stevens[31] sought to ensure the newly emancipated Negro equality with the white in the operation of the laws. The Bingham draft is of particular interest both because of his key role as "the Madison of the first section of the Fourteenth Amendment"[32] and the fact that it contained the first use of the phrase "equal protection" in a proposed constitutional provision. On February 3 Bingham moved a new draft as a substitute amendment: "The Congress shall have power to make all laws which shall be necessary and proper to secure to the citizens of each state all privileges and immunities of citizens in the several states (Art. 4, Sec. 2); and to all persons in the several States equal protection in the rights of life, liberty and property (5th Amendment)."[33] This measure was accepted by the committee and reported to both houses of Congress. After three days debate in the House, it was evident that the Bingham draft could not secure the

---

[29] *Schwartz* 186.

[30] *See* the speech of Senator Hendricks in *id.* at 268.

[31] The Bingham proposal read: "The Congress shall have power to make all laws necessary and proper to secure to all persons in every state within this Union equal protection in their rights of life, liberty and property." The Stevens proposal read: "All laws, state or national, shall operate impartially and equally on all persons without regard to race or color."

[32] Black, J., dissenting, in Adamson v. California, 332 U.S. 46, 74 (1947).

[33] *Schwartz* 190.

necessary two-thirds majority, and its further consideration was deferred. This proposal was never considered again, though it did reappear a few weeks later, phrased differently, as section 1 of the Fourteenth Amendment.

Unlike the Fourteenth Amendment itself, the Bingham proposal was framed in terms of a grant of power to Congress to secure the privileges and immunities of citizenship and equal protection for all persons. Had this proposal been adopted, subsequent controversy over the reach of the Fourteenth Amendment would have been avoided because it would not, of its own force, have restricted state action—thus the need for judicial interpretation of the scope of the amendment, in the absence of congressional action would have been eliminated. In addition, the power given to Congress would not have been limited to "state action" but could have reached individual discriminatory action. Under the broad grant to Congress in the Bingham resolution, there could have been no decision such as that in the 1883 *Civil Rights Cases*.[34]

Bingham's speeches indicate some confusion on the crucial question of the force of the Bill of Rights upon the states. He seems to assert that its provisions had always been binding but that Congress had not been given the power to force the states to observe them.[35] Such an assertion was plainly inaccurate, in view of the holding in *Barron* v. *Mayor of Baltimore*[36] that the Bill of Rights is a limitation only upon the federal government. Nor is it clear whether Bingham, in referring to "this immortal bill of rights,"[37] was talking, in the precise legal sense, of the first eight amendments and their specific provisions. Note too how the draft amendment progressed from a provision intended only to protect the emancipated Negro to one whose broad language covered all persons in the United States.

The legislative scene now shifts to the Joint Committee on Reconstruction. It had done nothing on the subject of civil rights since its vote to approve Bingham's ill-fated proposal. On April 21 Thaddeus Stevens reopened the subject with a draft amendment ("one not of his own framing") which had been submitted to him by Robert Dale Owen, son of the English reformer, who had come to this country before the Civil War.[38] The Owen draft covered most of the matters

[34] 109 U.S. 3 (1883), holding that the reach of the Fourteenth Amendment did not include private, as opposed to state, action.

[35] *Schwartz* 194, 211–13, 248–50.

[36] 7 Pet. 243 (U.S. 1833).

[37] *Schwartz* 194.

[38] "Section 1. No discrimination shall be made by any state, nor by the United States, as to the civil rights of persons because of race, color, or previous condition of servitude.

Section 2. From and after the fourth day of July, in the year one thousand eight hundred and seventy-six, no discrimination shall be made by any state, nor by the United States, as to

dealt with by the Fourteenth Amendment. Its key first section was, however, framed only in terms of racial discrimination—a step backward from the Bingham drafts. Bingham himself then moved to add a new Fifth section "No state shall make or enforce any law which shall abridge the privileges or immunities of citizens of the United States; nor shall any state deprive any person of life, liberty or property without due process of law, nor deny to any person within its jurisdiction the equal protection of the laws." This contains, for the first time, the language of section 1 of the Fourteenth Amendment (except for its clause defining citizenship). After twice declining to recommend Bingham's new proposal, the committee accepted it on April 28 as section 1 of the recommended Fourteenth Amendment.[39]

At last the committee was able to report the essential text of what was to become the Fourteenth Amendment. As far as its crucial first section was concerned, the draft Bingham finally induced it to accept marked a real advance over earlier proposals. It was no longer a mere grant of power to Congress but a self-executing provision barring the states from restricting civil rights. There was now a Privileges and Immunities Clause—with all the uncertainties inherent in that vague phrase. The equal protection requirement was retained, and the protection of life, liberty, and property was secured by a Due Process Clause copied out of the Bill of Rights.

Congressional Debate

The proposed Fourteenth Amendment, with the crucial first section in its final form (except for the definition of citizenship), was debated first in the House and then the Senate. In considering the debate, we should note that much of it focused upon provisions that are of little concern a century later, sections 2, 3 and 4, especially upon their

---

the enjoyment by classes of persons of the right of suffrage, because of race, color, or previous condition of servitude.

Section 3. Until the fourth day of July, one thousand eight hundred and seventy-six, no class of persons, as to the right of any of whom to suffrage discrimination shall be made by any state, because of race, color, or previous condition of servitude, shall be included in the basis of representation.

Section 4. Debts incurred in aid of insurrection or of war against the Union, and claims of compensation for loss of involuntary service or labor, shall not be paid by any state nor by the United States.

Section 5. Congress shall have power to enforce by appropriate legislation, the provisions of this article."

[39] *Schwartz* 217–18. Bingham specifically indicated that he sought to protect person and property from state power by using the phraseology of the Fifth Amendment. *See Bickel, The Original Understanding and the Segregation Decision,* 59 *Harv. L. Rev.* 5 (1955).

punitive intent vis-à-vis the southern states.[40] In operation, the key provision of the Fourteenth Amendment has been section 1.[41] Those parts of the debate devoted to this section are of crucial importance to an understanding of the impact its sponsors actually intended. It was the subject of speeches by Stevens, James A. Garfield, and Bingham.

To Stevens, the great object of section 1 was *discrimination,* its goal to ensure that "the law which operates upon one man shall operate *equally* upon all." To Garfield, already one of the leaders of the House, it was intended to give permanence to the Civil Rights Act of 1866 by incorporating its provisions "in the eternal firmament of the Constitution."[42] Garfield's approach summarizes the main theme of almost all the speakers who supported the proposed amendment: the constitutional question was to be settled by including the rights established by the 1866 act within the protection of the new amendment.

The participants in the House debate did not even consider the question of whether the proposed section would make the Bill of Rights binding upon the states (one of the concerns of later constitutional lawyers). The one possible exception was Representative Bingham, who argued that it would supply "that great want of citizen and stranger, protection by national law from unconstitutional State enactment." As an example, Bingham referred to the fact that, "contrary to the express letter of your Constitution, 'cruel and unusual punishments' have been inflicted under State laws within this Union upon citizens"[43] — an argument which implies that the Eighth Amendment was already binding upon the states and that the new amendment would give Congress power to repress any such state action inconsistent with the Constitution. If Bingham believed that the states had always been bound by a Bill of Rights provision like the Eighth Amendment, his whole approach was based upon a legal misconception.

Critics asserted that an amendment designed to clarify the rights of citizenship should itself make clear who were citizens. The Senate agreed, and added to section 1 an opening sentence defining citizenship. The addition was made without debate as one of the changes agreed

[40] Thus Stevens, sponsoring the amendment in the House, declared, "The second section I consider the most important in the article," Schwartz 223.

[41] "All persons born or naturalized in the United States and subject to the jurisdiction thereof, are citizens of the United States and of the State wherein they reside. No State shall make or enforce any law which shall abridge the privileges or immunities of citizens of the United States; nor shall any State deprive any person of life, liberty, or property without due process of law; nor deny to any person within its jurisdiction the equal protection of the laws." For a good summary of the Fourteenth Amendment debate, *see J. ten Brock, Equal under Law* ch. 12 (1969).

[42] *Schwartz* 222, 229.

[43] *Id.* at 249–50.

upon in a Republican caucus. Its purpose was to lend constitutional sanction to the status of the Negro as citizen, and thus hammer the last nail in the coffin of the by-then thoroughly discredited *Dred Scott* decision.

The key speech in the Senate debate was the introductory address of Senator Jacob Howard, who was called upon to substitute for Senator William P. Fessenden (the ailing committee chairman). His speech contains the only specific assertion that the aim of the new provison was to make the Bill of Rights binding upon the states. The "privileges and immunities" guaranteed by the amendment, he said, included the privileges and immunities spoken of in Article IV, section 2, as well as "the personal rights guaranteed and secured by the first eight amendments." "The great object of the first section of this amendment is, therefore," he added, "to restrain the power of the States and compel them at all times to respect these great fundamental guarantees."[44]

The recent controversy over whether the Fourteenth Amendment makes the Bill of Rights binding upon the states[45] has turned on the scope of its Due Process Clause. As other senators (notably Reverdy Johnson, perhaps the ablest lawyer in the Chamber) pointed out,[46] the term "privileges and immunities" itself was far from clear, and it was difficult, if not impossible, to say what the effect of the new Privileges and Immunities Clause would be. Certainly no participant in the congressional debates hinted that the Due Process Clause would have the drastic impact that has since been claimed for it.

Senator Howard's opinions are worth consideration, but his assertion that the amendment was intended to make the Bill of Rights binding upon the states was concurred in by no other senator. On the contrary, the majority, particularly those with impressive legal backgrounds such as Luke Poland (former chief justice of Vermont), Reverdy Johnson, and John B. Henderson, took the opposite view.[47] They asserted either that the new Privileges and Immunities Clause secured nothing beyond what was intended by Article IV, section 2, or that its effect was uncertain.

Ratification

The congressional debate on the Fourteenth Amendment ended in June, 1866, with overwhelming votes in its favor in both houses. Then came the ratification process itself. It has been characterized as "most

[44] *Id.* at 261.

[45] As exemplified by the opinions in Adamson v. California, 332 U.S. 46 (1947).

[46] *Schwartz* 280.

[47] *Id.* at 272–76. See also the summary of their views by Representative Farnsworth in 1871, *id.* at 318–19.

unusual, if not contrary to constitutional principles."[48] The southern states, acting through the governments established under presidential Reconstruction, originally rejected the amendment. They were replaced by the governments set up under the Reconstruction acts, and the First Reconstruction Act provided that no state could be restored until its legislature had ratified the amendment and it had become part of the Constitution.[49] The new legislatures, confronted with the choice of ratifying or being denied recognition as states of the Union, all voted approval (six of them before the amendment was declared adopted).

It cannot be denied that there were anomalies in the Fourteenth Amendment ratification process. First, there was the question of whether the southern legislatures could legally ratify an amendment in 1868. There was an inconsistency in the congressional view that the southern states were still out of the Union for every purpose except that of the highest of state functions—ratifying changes in the fundamental law of the Union. In addition, the First Reconstruction Act was based on the notion that the seceded states could not qualify as members of the Union until after they had performed an act which only members could do, namely, ratify a constitutional amendment.[50]

There was also the constitutional question posed by the fact that, early in 1868, two legislatures (Ohio and New Jersey) voted to revoke their earlier ratifications. On July 9, Congress adopted a resolution requesting the secretary of state to communicate a list of the states which had ratified.[51] This posed a dilemma for Secretary Seward (who had doubts about the validity of the southern ratifications as well as the effect of the two revocations). The result was a curious proclamation on July 20 in which he announced that the amendment had been ratified by twenty-nine state legislatures, including "newly established bodies avowing themselves to be and acting as the legislatures" of six southern states. He then certified that, if the Ohio and New Jersey ratifications were still effective, the amendment had become valid.[52] On the following day, Congress adopted a resolution that three-fourths of the states had ratified and that the amendment was therefore a part of the Constitution and should be duly promulgated as such by the secretary of state.[53] Accordingly, on July 28, 1868, Seward issued a proclamation certifying that the Fourteenth Amendment was valid "to all intents and purposes as a part of the Constitution."[54]

48 J.B. James, *The Framing of the Fourteenth Amendment* 192 (1956).
49 14 Stat. at 429.
50 *Compare J.G. Randall* and *D. Donald, The Civil War and Reconstruction* 634 (1961).
51 *Cong. Globe,* 40th Cong., 2d Sess. 3857.
52 15 Stat. 706 (1868).
53 *Cong. Globe,* 40th Cong., 2d Sess. 4295.
54 15 Stat. 708, 711 (1868).

The white South has consistently attacked the Fourteenth Amendment as a Force Bill, steamrollered through the southern states as part of Radical Reconstruction. From a constitutional point of view, this position must be rejected. Regardless of irregularities in the ratification process, it must now be considered a part of the Constitution, for it was declared duly ratified in accordance with the established forms. As the Supreme Court put it in the leading case on the matter, with regard to the resolution and proclamation of ratification by Congress and the secretary of state, "This decision by the political departments of the Government as to the validity of the adoption of the Fourteenth Amendment has been accepted."[55]

One may go further and say that, regardless of the manner of its ratification, the amendment has been accepted without question as part of the supreme law of the land by most Americans. More than that, its provisions have accorded with the felt need for equal justice among all men. By now it is built into the conscience of the nation. In Sumner's phrase soon after its adoption, "It has already taken its place in the immortal covenants of history. . . . As well attempt to undo the Declaration of Independence, or suspend the law of gravitation."[56]

Corporate Protection

One of the key questions that has concerned constitutional historians has been whether the framers of the Fourteenth Amendment intended to include corporations within the scope of its protection. A decade and a half after it was adopted, Roscoe Conkling, a former member of the committee which drafted it, implied, in argument before the Supreme Court, that he and his colleagues, in framing the Due Process and Equal Protection clauses, had deliberately used the word "person" in order to include corporations.[57] "At the time the Fourteenth Amendment was ratified . . . ," he averred, "individuals and joint stock companies were appealing for congressional and administrative protection against invidious and discriminating State and local taxes."[58] The implication was that the committee had taken cognizance of such appeals and had drafted its text to extend the organic protection to

---

[55] Coleman v. Miller, 307 U.S. 433, 449–50 (1939).

[56] 12 *Sumner, supra* note 7, at 531.

[57] *See* Black, J., dissenting, in Connecticut General Life Ins. Co. v. Johnson, 303 U.S. 77, 87 (1938). The argument in question occurred in San Mateo County v. Southern Pac. R.R. Co., 116 U.S. 138 (1885).

[58] Quoted in *Graham, 'The Conspiracy Theory' of the Fourteenth Amendment,* 47 *Yale L. J.* 371 (1938). The Conkling argument to such effect is not contained in the law reports.

corporations: "The men who framed . . . the Fourteenth Amendment *must have known* the meaning and force of the term 'persons.' "[59]

Most historians reject the Conkling insinuation.[60] From a purely historical point of view, it is clear that Conkling, influenced by the advocate's zeal, overstated his case.[61] Yet, even if his argument on the real intent of the draftsmen was correct, that alone would not justify the inclusion of corporations within the word "person." As a member of the highest bench has put it, "a secret purpose on the part of the members of the committee, even if such be the act, . . . would not be sufficient to justify any such construction."[62] After all, what was adopted was the Fourteenth Amendment and not what Roscoe Conkling or the other members of the drafting committee thought about it.[63]

What stands out to one concerned with the meaning of the amendment is the deliberate use in its Equal Protection and Due Process clauses of the same language employed in the Fifth Amendment. It is surely reasonable to assume that, when Bingham in his draft deliberately used that language,[64] he intended to follow the same approach as his predecessors with regard to the applicability of the new safeguard. By the middle of the nineteenth century, the corporate entity had become an established part of the economy. If corporate "persons" were to be excluded from the new constitutional protections, it is difficult to see why the unqualified generic term "persons"[65] was employed.

It must be emphasized that corporate personality antedated the Fourteenth Amendment. Its protection had, by the time of the postbellum amendments, become a vital concern of the law. The end of the Civil War saw a vast expansion in the role of the corporation in the economy,[66] but even before that conflict, the corporate device was recognized as an indispensable adjunct of the nation's growth. This realization had already led to decisions favorable to the corporate personality.[67] When the ultimate protection of person and property

[59] Quoted in *id.* at 378.

[60] The best-reasoned rejection of the Conkling thesis is to be found in the Graham article, referred to in the two prior notes. *See also* E.S. Corwin, *Liberty against Government: The Rise, Flowering, and Decline of a Famous Juridical Concept* 191–93 (1948). It should, however, be noted that earlier writers, following the lead of *C.A. Beard* and *M.R. Beard, Rise of American Civilization* 111–13 (1927), tended to follow the Conkling view.

[61] *See Bickel, supra* note 39.

[62] Black, J., dissenting, in Connecticut General Life Ins. Co. v. Johnson, 303 U.S. 77, 87 (1938).

[63] *Compare R.J. Harris, The Quest for Equality: The Constitution, Congress and the Supreme Court* 40 (1960).

[64] *Schwartz* 305–6.

[65] Which, in the Fifth Amendment, has always been construed to include corporations.

[66] *See H.U. Faulkner, Economic History of the United States* ch. 9 (1938).

[67] Especially Bank of Augusta v. Earle, 13 Pet. 519 (U.S. 1839), p. 23 *supra.*

was transferred by the Fourteenth Amendment from the states to the nation, the judicial trend in favor of the corporation also became a national one. The role of the corporate person in the post-Civil War economy made the use of the amendment to safeguard such persons a natural development, whatever may have been the subjective goals of its framers.

Incorporation of the Bill of Rights

The Fourteenth Amendment revived the constitutional question that had been laid to rest in 1833, when *Barron* v. *Mayor of Baltimore* [68] ruled that the Bill of Rights placed restraints only on the federal government, not the states. The amendment plainly made for some nationalization of civil rights, but how far did it go in that direction? More specifically, was it intended to make the whole Bill of Rights binding upon the states? In many ways, the most provocative legislative statements on the purpose of the framers of the Fourteenth Amendment were made in 1871, five years after its passage, in a House debate on a bill to enforce it. Of particular interest in the debate—which Garfield rightly characterized as "historical"—is a lengthy address by Bingham explaining why he changed the form of his draft amendment from the affirmative version he first introduced (giving Congress the power to secure equal protection) to the negative version ultimately adopted (prohibiting the states from abridging privileges and immunities or denying due process or equal protection). He said that he relied specifically on the statement in *Barron* v. *Mayor of Baltimore* that, had the draftsmen of the Bill of Rights intended them to limit the states, they "would have imitated the framers of the original Constitution." Bingham said that he did imitate the original Framers in their drafting of Article I, section 10, which contained express limitations upon state power. Imitating their example "to the letter," he recast his proposal so that it began, "no State shall. . . ."[69] This change has been of the greatest consequence, for it converted the Fourteenth Amendment from a grant authorizing Congress to protect civil rights to a self-operative prohibition which could be enforced by the courts without congressional action. The amendment could thus develop into the Great Charter of civil rights that it has since become, which would have been impossible if it had remained only a delegation of legislative power.

What was it, according to Bingham, that the states were now prohibited from doing? His answer was given in terms of the Bill of Rights: "the privileges and immunities of citizens of the United States, as

[68] *Supra* note 36.
[69] *Schwartz* 321.

contradistinguished from citizens of a State, are chiefly defined in the first eight amendments."[70] And it is these eight articles, which were never limitations upon the states, that were now made so by the Fourteenth Amendment. This statement is far from conclusive, however. What was adopted by Congress and submitted for ratification was Bingham's proposal, not his speech — certainly not a speech made years after the event. Perhaps Garfield was unfair when he declared, "My colleague can make but he cannot unmake history,"[71] but his retort goes to the heart of the matter. Never in the 1866 debates did Bingham refer specifically to the incorporation of the Bill of Rights in the new amendment, though there were confused hints to this effect in some of his speeches at the time, nor (apart from Senator Howard) did any speaker in those debates remotely support the view he now expressed. As Congressman John B. Storm put it in response, "If the monstrous doctrine now set up as resulting from the provisions of that Fourteenth Amendment had ever been hinted at that Amendment would have received an emphatic rejection at the hands of the people."[72]

The Supreme Court has steadily refused to follow the view that the Bill of Rights is incorporated *in toto* into the Fourteenth Amendment. In recent years the argument for incorporation has been made most forcefully by Justice Black. His noted dissent in *Adamson* v. *California*[73] asserts categorically that those who sponsored and favored the amendment intended its first section to make the Bill of Rights applicable to the states. His opinion has yet to command a majority of the Supreme Court. The Court has followed a rule of selective incorporation, under which only those rights secured by the Bill of Rights which may be considered fundamental are included within the Due Process Clause. In recent years, the tendency has been to consider as "fundamental" more and more of the rights protected by the first eight amendments, and this process may ultimately render the whole issue academic.

THE FIFTEENTH AMENDMENT

The Fourteenth Amendment gave Negroes citizenship, but it did not expressly give them the franchise. To eliminate state power to restrict the franchise on racial grounds Congress passed the Fifteenth Amendment, which specifically prohibits both the federal government and the

70 *Id.* at 305–6.
71 *Id.* at 323.
72 *Id.* at 294.
73 332 U.S. 46 (1947).

states from denying or abridging the right of United States citizens to vote "on account of race, color, or previous condition of servitude." It had its origins in some of the proposals considered by the Joint Committee on Reconstruction. An early version of the Fourteenth Amendment had provided for striking down state laws "whereby any distinction is made in *political* or civil rights or privileges, on account of race, creed or color."[74] This proposal was voted down in the committee. Another approach—a prospective guarantee of suffrage—was taken in the draft amendment introduced by Stevens on April 21, 1866. Under it, after 1866, no discrimination was to be made by the federal government or any state "as to the enjoyment by classes or persons of the right of suffrage, because of race, color, or previous condition of servitude."[75] This proposal was adopted by the Joint Committee but opposed by more moderate congressional Republicans, who felt that Negro suffrage tied to the party program would be a handicap in the coming elections. The committee retreated, and the Fourteenth Amendment ultimately reported and voted by Congress contained no express reference to the right of suffrage.[76]

Congressional debate on the Fifteenth Amendment started in January, 1869, with proposals reported by the House and Senate judiciary committees. The Senate draft used almost exactly the language that ultimately became the Fifteenth Amendment, with the important difference that it protected the right to vote and to hold office, while the version finally passed guarantees only the right to vote. It was opposed by two principal groups in Congress. Those hostile to any constitutional protection of the right of suffrage attacked it, and moderates in this group focused their attack upon the alleged invasion of states' rights that would be involved. The more extreme group denied the authority to amend the Constitution in this respect—an argument that seems without any constitutional basis in view of the almost unrestrained reach of the amending power under Article V. Relatively few congressmen attacked it on the grounds of Negro inferiority, which is surprising when we reflect that the Negro was a slave less than a decade earlier.

More influential than the opponents of any amendment were those who felt that the proposal did not go far enough, and who sought a broad guarantee of universal male suffrage, rather than one limited to those denied the right to vote on racial grounds. Led by Bingham, they

[74] *Schwartz* 188 (emphasis added).

[75] *Id.* at 216.

[76] Except in its second section, which provides for indirect enforcement of the right to vote through congressional power to reduce the representation of states in which the right is abridged. The congressional power thus granted has, however, never been exercised and the Fourteenth Amendment has had no practical impact upon the right of suffrage.

sought to substitute an amendment prohibiting any state from denying the vote to a United States citizen except on the grounds of sex, age, residence, or past criminal record. Such an amendment, introduced in both houses, was overwhelmingly defeated. The proponents of universal male suffrage then tried another substitute (reminiscent of Bingham's early version of the Fourteenth Amendment) which gave Congress power to abolish any state restrictions upon the right to vote. This, too, was defeated and the attempt to impose a uniform rule of universal male suffrage abandoned.

The universal suffragists urged, as one of them put it, that "the question before us is not one of negro suffrage. It is the question of suffrage in itself."[77] To others, however, the sole issue was that of Negro suffrage; they urged that the provision should be worded only to make the Negro a voter. Under a substitute amendment citizens of African descent were given the same right to vote as other citizens. The proposal, supported by senators from the Pacific Coast because it eliminated the problem of Chinese suffrage, was opposed on the ground that, if the principle was correct, it should not be restricted to one race. As one senator put it, "Why a distinction against the descendants of other countries?"[78]

Each house voted approval of its own committee's version. A conference committee then recommended that the Senate version be adopted, with deletion of the words "or hold office," and its report was concurred in overwhelmingly by both houses in February, 1869. The Fifteenth Amendment became part of the Constitution on March 30, 1870.

Of particular interest today is a substitute amendment offered in the Senate prohibiting discrimination in voting "on account of race, color, nativity, property, *education,* or religious belief."[79] This would have outlawed all educational qualifications, including literacy tests. It was actually passed by the Senate, which feared that the South might still be able to disenfranchise the Negro by the imposition of educational tests, but the House rejected it and the Senate acquiesced. It can be argued that the congressional rejection of this substitute amendment indicates a legislative intent not to have the Fifteenth Amendment affect state power to impose such qualifications, including literacy tests. If that is true, that intent has been frustrated by the Voting

[77] Senator Willard Warner, *Schwartz* 393.

[78] Senator William M. Stewart, *id.* at 369. For a good summary of the congressional debates on the Fifteenth Amendment, *see* W. Gillette, *The Right to Vote: Politics and the Passage of the Fifteenth Amendment* ch. 2 (1965).

[79] *Schwartz* 408 (emphasis added).

Rights Act Amendments of 1970,[80] which override state literacy requirements, and by the Supreme Court decision upholding congressional power to enact such provisions.[81] It may be doubted, however,
whether those who wrote and voted the Fifteenth Amendment realized
the extent to which their command of racial equality in the electoral
process would be thwarted by state literacy tests. One familiar with the
use of those tests to frustrate the Fifteenth Amendment will conclude
that the Supreme Court is correct in holding that the congressional
authority to enforce the amendment includes the power to proscribe
literacy tests because they unduly lend themselves to racially discriminatory application.

CIVIL RIGHTS STATUTES, 1870–1871

From a legal point of view the amendments added to the Constitution
during the post-Civil War period have two aspects. In the first place,
they contain self-executing prohibitions protecting civil rights, which
lay down rules of decision to be enforced by the courts. The Thirteenth
Amendment of its own force outlaws all forms of slavery and involuntary servitude; the Fourteenth Amendment strikes down all "state
action" which denies due process or equal protection; the Fifteenth
Amendment puts an end to all state attempts to restrict the franchise
on racial grounds. It is the self-executing aspect of the amendments that
has made possible the many cases brought directly under them.

But the framers of these amendments recognized that direct judicial
enforcement of their prohibitions alone might not be enough to secure
the goal of civil equality for the Negro. Hence they provided for
legislative as well as judicial enforcement. Each of the amendments
contains an express grant to the Congress of authority to enforce its
provisons "by appropriate legislation." These enforcement clauses have
been the constitutional source of the civil rights statutes enacted by
Congress from Reconstruction to our own time.

The statutes enacted during Reconstruction, like the amendments
upon which they were based, had several goals. The first was to ensure
enforcement of the Fifteenth Amendment, for it was seen that
protection of the right to vote was the key to equal rights. Negro voting
was secured by express criminal prohibitions and by setting up independent federal enforcement machinery. In addition, these laws provided

---

[80] 84 Stat. 314 (1970).
[81] Oregon v. Mitchell, 400 U.S. 212 (1970).

sanctions to deter infringements upon the other civil rights guaranteed by the Constitution or federal law and provided for equality in public accommodations.

To the constitutional historian, certain things stand out in the legislative history of the Reconstruction civil rights laws. The congressional effort was extended from official to private action in the first of the post-Fourteenth and Fifteenth Amendment laws—the Enforcement Act of 1870.[82] As originally passed in the House, that measure, intended to protect the right to vote, dealt only with official action; there was nothing in it to reach action by private individuals to prevent Negroes from voting. The Senate substituted a stronger version not limited to official action; its key section was aimed at "any person" who sought to prevent or obstruct any citizen from exercising his right to vote.

Of particular significance in the Senate debate was the action of Senator John Pool in sponsoring, as an amendment, what became sections 5, 6, and 7 of the 1870 act. His address explaining his action constitutes the sole legislative explanation of the only portions of the Enforcement Act that are still on the statute book.[83] The sections he introduced went further than either the House bill or the original Senate version in dealing with the problem of non-official action (individual or mob) aimed at preventing Negroes from exercising constitutional rights. In the form in which they were finally adopted, they made it an offense for "any person" to prevent or hinder anyone in the exercise of the right of suffrage guaranteed by the Fifteenth Amendment or for two or more persons to conspire together, or go in disguise, to injure, oppress, or intimidate any citizen in the free exercise or enjoyment of any right or privilege guaranteed him by the Constitution or federal laws.

The theory offered by Senator Pool in support of his sections was as interesting as it was far-reaching. The rights secured by the Fourteenth and Fifteenth Amendments could be abridged either by positive legislation or by acts of omission. The former was reached directly by the constitutional provisions; the latter was not. If a state should fail to act to prevent private individuals from contravening the rights of citizens under the amendments, it was the duty of Congress "to supply that omission, and by its own laws and by its own courts to go into the States for the purpose of giving the amendment vitality there."[84] In

[82] 16 Stat. 140 (1870).

[83] Pool's sections 5 and 6, having survived later revisions and repeals, are now contained, with some changes, in the *Federal Criminal Code,* 18 U.S.C. § 241, and have increasingly been used to protect civil rights in recent years.

[84] *Schwartz* 479.

this approach, Congress might act directly against private individuals who were able to violate constitutional rights because of the failure of state officials to protect those rights. What gives the Pool theory such significance is the recent tendency of the Supreme Court to expand drastically the "state action" which the Fourteenth and Fifteenth Amendments alone may reach[85] —a trend that may culminate one day in the acceptance of the Pool view in the matter.

The Pool position (under which "state inaction" is equated with the "state action" called for by the Fourteenth and Fifteenth Amendments) was restated during the debate on the Ku Klux Act of 1871,[86] both by Senator Pool himself[87] and, even more explicitly, by Congressman John Coburn.[88] The Ku Klux Act sought to deal with the rising tide of terrorism in the southern states, led by the Ku Klux Klan. As the Supreme Court has pointed out, "The Act, popularly known as the Ku Klux Act, was passed by a partisan vote in a highly inflamed atmosphere. It was preceded by spirited debate which pointed out its grave character and susceptibility to abuse."[89]

While section 1 of the Ku Klux Act, by its terms, applied only to persons who violated constitutional rights under color of state law, section 2 imposed its criminal sanctions upon "any person" who so acted, regardless of whether his action was connected with the action of the state in which the violation took place. Opponents of the measure could thus contend that the law went beyond the constitutional language, which was limited to "state action" alone. The Pool-Coburn argument the other way (as noted) proceeded upon the theory that state failure to act to protect constitutional rights furnished a sufficient basis for congressional action.

The remarks made during the Ku Klux Act debate by Senator Trumbull on the Privileges and Immunities Clause of the Fourteenth Amendment are of particular interest. According to him, that clause "did not extend the rights and privileges of citizenship one iota."[90] In substance, Trumbull's view was an anticipation of the basic holding in the matter two years later in the *Slaughter-House Cases.*[91] In view of the criticism to which the Supreme Court decision there has been subjected, it is most pertinent to note that the same interpretation of

---

[85] Decisions illustrating such expansion are Evans v. Newton, 382 U.S. 296 (1966), and United States v. Guest, 383 U.S. 745 (1966).

[86] 17 Stat. 13 (1871).

[87] *Cong. Globe,* 42nd Cong., 1st Sess. 608, 459.

[88] *Schwartz* 619.

[89] Collins v. Hardyman, 341 U.S. 651, 657 (1951).

[90] *Schwartz* 636.

[91] 16 Wall. 36 (U.S. 1873).

the effect of the Privileges and Immunities Clause was given in 1871 by the man who headed the Senate Judiciary Committee when the Fourteenth Amendment was passed.

A word should also be said about another of the Reconstruction civil rights laws, the so-called Force Act of 1871.[92] It was enacted to supplement the Enforcement Act of 1870 by supplying independent enforcement machinery which would ensure the right to vote in all congressional elections through the appointment of federal officials to supervise the election process. In effect, the statute provided for the supersession of the normal state electoral process by federal officers.

Congressional action on the Force Act dramatically illustrates the steamroller tactics which the Radical leadership at times employed. Despite the far-reaching nature of the measure, only one day was devoted to its consideration in each house. The haste with which Congress acted is shown by the refusal of the majority to accept even amendments correcting obvious misprints in the bill.[93] In the words of a leading Democratic senator, "the fiat of caucus has gone forth that this bill is to be passed."[94]

Until recently, we might have considered the Force Act as an extreme measure which could rarely, if ever, be justified in a constitutional system such as ours. In our own day, too, however, Congress has seen fit to provide for a comparable supersession of state by federal authority in the electoral process in the Voting Rights Act of 1965 and the Voting Rights Act Amendments of 1970. In some ways, the 1965 and 1970 statutes are even more sweeping than their 1871 predecessor, yet the abuses which called them forth were not nearly as great as those which existed in the post-Civil War period.

THE CIVIL RIGHTS ACT OF 1875

The Civil Rights Act of 1875[95] was the most important of the post-Civil War statutes designed to ensure equal rights for the Negro. As such, it constituted the culmination of the postbellum Republican program and a decade of efforts to place the ideal of racial equality upon the legal plane. One may go further and see in the 1875 law the last victory for the egalitarian ideal of the Reconstruction period. From 1875 to the middle of the next century, there were to be no further legal gains for racial equality. On the contrary, the civil rights legislation

---

[92] 16 Stat. 433 (1871).

[93] *See Schwartz* 577.

[94] Senator Allen G. Thurman, quoted in *id.* at 548.

[95] 18 Stat. 335 (1875).

enacted during the Reconstruction decade was soon to be virtually emasculated by both Congress and the Supreme Court.

To the present-day observer, the Civil Rights Act of 1875 is of particular interest, for it provides the historical nexus between the Fourteenth Amendment and the Civil Rights Act of 1964.[96] The goal of equality in public accommodations, which Congress sought to attain by enactment of the 1964 statute, was what had been intended by the 1875 law. The legislative history of the 1875 law demonstrates that the legislators of the post-Civil War period were intimately concerned with many of the key problems that are still with us in the field of civil rights: integration versus segregation (particularly in education), legal versus social equality, and the crucial question of whether an ideal such as racial equality can be achieved by legislative action, especially in a society opposed to practical implementation of that ideal.

The key figure in the enactment of the 1875 Civil Rights Act was Senator Charles Sumner. Whatever may be said against Sumner, he was, throughout his career, a sincere believer in the cause of equal rights. Well before emancipation, he gave substance to Whittier's encomium, "He saw a brother in the slave,—/With man as equal man he dealt." His crucial position in the history of the act is not affected by the fact that he died in March, 1874, a year before it became law. As the sponsor of the measure in the House pointed out, the bill was originated by Sumner and he regarded it as his main legacy to his country.[97] On his death bed, he is said to have told Judge Ebenezer R. Hoar, then a congressman from Massachusetts, "You must take care of the civil-rights bill,—my bill, the civil rights bill,—don't let it fail!"[98]

Sumner's efforts to secure legislative implementation of racial equality go back to the war period itself, when he was the very "lion of the anti-slavery cause."[99] During the postwar decade he led the congressional struggle to secure legal equality for the freedmen. He felt, however, that the measures which had been enacted prior to the 1875 statute were scarcely adequate to attain this goal. As he put it in an 1870 speech, "it remains that equal rights shall be secured in all the public conveyances, and on the railroads. . . . All schools must be opened to all, without distinction of color." [100] Enactment of federal

---

[96] 78 Stat. 241 (1964).

[97] *Schwartz* 727.

[98] 4 *E.L. Pierce, Memoir and Letters of Charles Sumner* 598 (1893); *D. Donald, Charles Sumner and the Rights of Man* 586 (1970).

[99] *B. Catton, This Hallowed Ground* 82 (1961). For a detailed account of Sumner's efforts, see *Donald, supra* note 98, chs. 2, 4, and 5.

[100] *Schwartz* 657–58.

legislation to secure the rights referred to remained the dominant theme of Sumner's life in the four years that followed.

In 1870, he introduced the first version of what was to become the 1875 Civil Rights Act—a bill to prohibit discrimination by railroads, steamboats, public conveyances, hotels, restaurants, licensed theaters, public schools, juries, and church organizations or cemetery associations "incorporated by national or State authority." Though it did not get out of committee, Sumner reintroduced it in subsequent sessions and succeeded in securing its passage by the Senate (though in weakened form) in 1872. The House refused to pass the bill, and Sumner's illness during the next session left it without the necessary leadership. He returned for what was to be his final effort in the first session of the Forty-Third Congress. This time the growing demand for a civil rights law was supported by President Grant's recommendation in his 1873 Annual Message of a statute "to better secure the civil rights which freedom should secure, but has not effectually secured, to the enfranchised slave." [101] The Republicans, by now committed to civil rights legislation, still had an overwhelming majority in both houses.

It was a bill introduced by Sumner in December, 1873, that reached the statute book. It is ironic that the crucial catalyst leading to Senate enactment was the death of Sumner himself in March, 1874. Only two months later the Senate passed his bill virtually as originally introduced, with the exception of a clause covering discrimination in churches. The speedy Senate passage was intended as a memorial to the dead senator. In the House no action was taken before adjournment. The measure was recommitted to the House Judiciary Committee, with instructions that it not be reported at that session.

It remained for the second session of the Forty-Third Congress to complete passage. To its advocates that session appeared to be their last chance because more than half the Republican members of the House had been defeated in the 1874 election. As it turned out, the bill was passed by a lame-duck House on February 3, 1875; ninety of the one hundred and sixty Republicans who voted for it had been defeated in the election. In the House debate, its opponents constantly stressed the election results as evidence of the overwhelming popular support for their position. The House did not pass the version of the bill which the Senate had voted. Instead, it approved a draft reported by its Judiciary Committee. With two exceptions, the House bill was substantially similar to the Sumner bill passed by the Senate, so that the Senate was able to vote the House bill on February 27, 1875, with comparatively

---

[101] 7 *J.D. Richardson, A Compilation of the Messages and Papers of the Presidents 1789–1897,* at 255 (1896–99).

little debate. The exceptions referred to were the cemetery and school provisions, which had been removed by the House.

To the student of civil rights in the mid-twentieth century, certain features of the 1874–1875 debate are especially pertinent. The discussion of the constitutional issues is relevant because of the striking down by the Supreme Court of the key public accommodations provisions of the 1875 act in the *Civil Rights Cases.* [102] Critics of the Court, especially in recent years, have contended that this decision amounted to virtual judicial usurpation, that the justices emasculated the post-Civil War amendments to nullify the broad remedial intent of their framers. The congressional debate on the 1875 civil rights law demonstrates that such a view is unfounded. There is ample indication in the debates that a substantial number of legislators considered the bill before them unconstitutional, many of them [103] for the very reason later stated by the Supreme Court—i.e., that it sought to reach individual, rather than state, action. These constitutional discussions also bear directly upon recent developments in the field of civil rights. In the Senate debate in February, 1875, Senator Matthew H. Carpenter (one of the outstanding lawyers of the day) stated that Congress might try to accomplish the public accommodation purposes of the 1875 act under its commerce power. "Such provision in regard to theaters," he asserted, "would be somewhat fantastic as a regulation of commerce."[104] In 1964, the Congress did enact a Civil Rights Act based upon the commerce power of the very type which Senator Carpenter had termed "fantastic" in 1875, [105] and, as Carpenter also prophesied, [106] such a statute was actually upheld by the Supreme Court. [107]

Even more interesting are those portions of the debate dealing with discrimination in education. The very problems that have become so important since the landmark decision in *Brown* v. *Board of Education* [108] —integration versus segregation, the threat of the South to close down the public school system rather than have "mixed" schools, and the claim that all that is really needed is "separate but equal" facilities for the two races—appear here. The sharpest controversy arose over the original Sumner bill's prohibition of racial discrimination not only in public accommodations but also in all "common schools

---

[102] *Supra* note 34.

[103] Notably Senators Allen G. Thurman and James K. Kelly. *See Schwartz* 671–76, 703–7.

[104] *Id.* at 764.

[105] 78 Stat. 241 (1964).

[106] *Schwartz* 764.

[107] Heart of Atlanta Motel v. United States, 379 U.S. 241 (1964).

[108] 347 U.S. 483 (1954).

and public institutions of learning or benevolence supported in whole or part by general taxation." Though a strong effort was made to strike out this prohibition in the Senate, it was defeated, and the bill as passed by the upper chamber in 1874 contained the provision drafted by Sumner.

The situation was different when the House considered the bill a year later. Public opposition (as shown by the 1874 election results) led it to strike out the clause prohibiting racial discrimination in educational institutions, as well as the one covering cemeteries. The actual vote on the amendment to strike out the school provisions was overwhelmingly in favor. The consensus against the school prohibition was now so great that no effort was made in the Senate to reinsert it in the bill. Instead, as noted, it speedily passed the House bill.

The debate on the proposed prohibition of racial discrimination in schools is directly relevant to the intent of those who wrote the Fourteenth Amendment with regard to segregation in education. One who has read it cannot help but conclude that the Congress that sat less than a decade after the Fourteenth Amendment was sent to the states for ratification did not think that the amendment had the effect of prohibiting school segregation. If it had, the whole debate would have been irrelevant, since integration would have been constitutionally required, regardless of any congressional provision in the matter. It is fair to say that no participant in the congressional debate took such a view (which was, of course, that ultimately taken by the Supreme Court in *Brown* v. *Board of Education*).

This does not necessarily mean that the decision in *Brown* was wrong. The Court there was interpreting the Constitution to meet society's needs in 1954—needs which were not necessarily the same as those of 1875. Only those who would make the Constitution as inflexible as the laws of the Medes and Persians will object to such constitutional construction. Stability and change are the twin sisters of the law and together make the Constitution a document enduring through the ages.

FIRST AND SECOND RECONSTRUCTION

It has become all but a constitutional cliché that the Reconstruction statutes did not succeed in their goal of securing equality in civil rights for the Negro, in part because of decisions of the Supreme Court. [109] It can scarcely be denied that the Court's decisions nullified some of the

[109] Notably in the Slaughter-House Cases, p. 227 *infra,* and the Civil Rights Cases, *supra* note 34.

key measures of the Reconstruction Congress, notably the 1875 Civil Rights Act. Yet the decisions themselves were but an indication of the general disenchantment with the Reconstruction program. Two decades after Appomattox, most of the nation was all too willing to forgive and forget; the civil rights laws that were not invalidated by the Court either were repealed by Congress itself [110] or became dead letters on the statute book.

By the turn of the century, "equal protection" had become a mere slogan for the Negro. The Thirteenth Amendment abolished slavery itself, and the Fifteenth Amendment struck from state laws all provisions overtly limiting suffrage to whites, but the incidents of slavery remained, in a system of discrimination against the former slave, and devices (such as the "white primary") defeated the intent of the Fifteenth Amendment. The situation was described to James Bryce by a leading southern politician: "We like the Negro, and we treat him well. We mean to continue doing so. But we vote him." [111] With regard to the Fourteenth Amendment, the situation was, if anything, worse. The failure of the Reconstruction statutes to implement the amendment's guarantee of equality led directly to "the familiar system of racial segregation in both public and private institutions which cuts across the daily lives of Southern citizens from the cradle to the grave." [112] Jim Crow replaced equal protection, and legally enforced segregation became the dominant fact in southern life.

The paradoxical result was that, though the post-Civil War amendments did work a veritable constitutional revolution, they had little immediate impact upon civil rights. As restraints upon state power, their effect was almost entirely confined to the economic sphere. When, toward the end of the century, the Supreme Court came over to the view that the Fourteenth Amendment (and especially its Due Process Clause) was intended to work an essential change in the organic framework, its decisions all but limited the change to the area of property rights. The limitation was understandable in an era of explosive industrial expansion, which so drastically altered the whole social and economic fabric. In such an era, it was not unnatural for the dominant emphasis to be placed upon the proper relationship between government and business. The Fourteenth Amendment was converted into a veritable Magna Carta for Business, rather than the Great Charter for civil rights which had been intended.

All this has, of course, changed in our own day, when the amend-

110 Especially by 28 Stat. 36 (1894).

111 2 *J. Bryce, The American Commonwealth* 279 (1916).

112 *To Secure These Rights, Report of the President's Committee on Civil Rights* 79 (1947).

ment has been revived as a charter for vigorous civil rights action by both judicial and legislative branches. Yet one familiar with the history of Reconstruction cannot help having a feeling of *déjà vu* as he contemplates the recent spate of congressional civil rights legislation. He wonders why the postbellum civil rights effort ultimately failed and whether that failure is destined to be repeated in this century. "Popular governments," wrote John Jay, "must be influenced by popular opinion, and popular opinion must be *created* not commanded. It is a kind of *creation* too which can proceed but slowly, because often opposed by Prejudices, Ignorances, clashing Interests, and . . . illfounded Jealousies." [113]

The history of the Reconstruction attempts to secure equal rights supports the validity of the Jay observation. So far as we can tell a century later, the 1866–1875 civil rights laws were not a result of popular demand; they were steered through Congress by the Republican leadership in the face of what was at first public apathy and later a widespread desire to forget and forgive the defeated South. Without public understanding and support, it was inevitable that the congressional momentum would soon lose force. With regard to the 1957–1968 civil rights statutes, on the other hand, the Congress has not led so much as followed the nation. The recent laws have been induced by popular opinion, created (in Jay's terms) from below, not commanded from above, and have had the popular backing which was lacking in the Reconstruction period. There is also the vital factor of judicial support. Whether rightly or wrongly, much of the Reconstruction legislation was frustrated by decisions of the Supreme Court. Here, too, the situation today is different. From the first cases heard under the recent statutes, the Court has indicated that it would look at those laws with anything but a hostile eye.

Yet, with all that has been said, one cannot help but note a malaise in the civil rights field, both in Congress and the nation, which makes one wonder whether we are not, in fact, living through a second Reconstruction period. There are increasing signs, on and off Capitol Hill, that the nation has begun to lose its pressing concern with civil rights. In this field particularly, such a loss of momentum may well foreshadow a demise of governmental activity comparable to that which occurred after 1875. If the history of the postbellum period shows anything, it is that it is not enough for the formal law to ban discrimination. Only continuing efforts to translate the legal "ought" into the "is" of practical reality can ultimately affect the structure of racial bias.

[113] Letter from John Jay to Rev. Dr. Price, Aug. 24, 1785, Parke-Bernet Galleries, Sale No. 2643, Item 234 (1968).

CHAPTER NINE

The Constitution in the Gilded Age

FROM PERSONAL TO PROPERTY RIGHTS

Early in 1871, General Sherman (then commanding general of the army) unburdened himself to an old comrade in arms. "The truth is," he declared, "politics have again gradually but surely drawn the whole country into a situation of as much danger as before the Civil War—The Army left the South subdued—broken and humbled. The Party then in power, forgetful of the fact that sooner or later the People of the South must vote, labored hard to create voters out of Negroes and indifferent material, and when at last these States became reconstructed . . . the prejudices of the past resumed Control. And now the Negro Governments . . . have been swept aside." "The memories of the War are fading fast," he lamented.[1]

The glory of the war years—the sincere, if often ruthless, idealism of Reconstruction—were being replaced by purely economic concerns. The era of Gettysburg and Appomattox gave way to that of the Crédit Mobilier and the Whiskey Ring. "I once heard a man say," affirmed Justice Holmes in a Memorial Day address, " 'Where Vanderbilt sits, there is the head of the table. I teach my son to be rich.' He said what many think. . . . The man who commands the attention of his fellows is the man of wealth. Commerce is the great power."[2]

---

[1] William T. Sherman to E.O.C. Ord, Mar. 18, 1871, Charles Hamilton, Auction No. 27, Item 262 (1968).

[2] *The Mind and Faith of Justice Holmes* 18 (M. Lerner ed. 1954).

Certainly there was a sharp shift in the constitutional center of gravity in the post-Reconstruction period, and that, in turn, meant a change in legal emphasis with regard to the basic rights which the Constitution protects. Concern with vindication of civil rights (which had dominated the Reconstruction era) receded. The headlong industrialization of the period inevitably raised new problems for the law and the constitutional history of the nation after Appomattox must largely be written in terms of the reaction of the legal order to the new economy. If, before the Civil War, the major constitutional theme was the nation-state problem, in the period that followed the dominant concern became the relationship between government and business.

The key constitutional provision of the new industrial era was that Fourteenth Amendment which was the most significant of the legal changes imposed as part of the price of southern defeat. Its Due Process Clause was to serve as the Great Charter for the protection of the private enterprise that was so transforming society. Due process as the great bulwark of private property did not develop fully until the last decade of the century. During the period to which this chapter is devoted, it had not yet been converted into the cornerstone of American constitutionalism. The first decisions under the Fourteenth Amendment manifested a restrictive attitude toward its effect, but they were only the first steps in the interpretation of the new amendment. The dissents delivered in them ultimately served as the foundation upon which due process was to be elevated to the foremost place in the organic pantheon. Before dealing with the constitutional protection of property rights under the post-Civil War Constitution, however, we should take note of the condition of the political departments during the period.

PRESIDENCY

The post-Civil War period saw the highest office sink to perhaps its lowest point in our history. "The degradation of the presidency," we are told, "came to its climax in Johnson's impeachment."[3] Nor did Johnson's narrow escape restore authority or prestige either to that unhappy incumbent or to the office itself. "The Administration . . . ," confided Gideon Welles to his *Diary,* "has fallen away and become feeble."[4] Under Johnson's successor, the situation was, if anything, worse. "The progress of evolution from President Washington to Presi-

[3] *L.D. White, The Republican Era, 1869–1901: A Study in Administrative History* 23 (1958).

[4] 3 *The Dairy of Gideon Welles* 514 (H. Beale ed. 1960).

dent Grant," declared Henry Adams, "was alone evidence enough to upset Darwin." The Grant administration "outraged every rule of ordinary decency;"[5] no other came to a close in such paralysis and discredit.[6]

Though Grant did display some political skills (as in his dealings with Charles Sumner[7]), his concept of the presidency was essentially a negative one. He adopted the theory of executive power enunciated by a leading Republican legislator: "The executive department . . . should be subordinate to the legislative department. The President should obey and enforce the laws, leaving to the people the duty of correcting any errors committeed by . . . Congress."[8] In accepting the Republican nomination, Grant had stated that he considered the president a "purely administrative officer."[9] Henry Adams noted in 1870, "His own idea of his duties as President may perhaps best be described as that of the commander of an army in time of peace . . . as it was the duty of every military commander to obey the civil authority without question, so it was the duty of the President to follow without hesitation the wishes of the people as expressed by Congress."[10]

After his retirement, Grant summed up his view on the matter with the remark that "an Executive depends on Congress."[11] The stalemate between the political departments that existed at the end of Johnson's term was replaced by congressional dominance. At the very outset of his administration, Grant announced that he would not enforce his policy against the legislative will: "all laws will be faithfully executed, whether they meet my approval or not."[12] This meant an immediate resolution of the bitter struggle over Reconstruction in favor of Congress. Grant readily conceded that "it was the work of the legislative branch. . . . My province was wholly in approving their acts which I did most heartily."[13]

To ensure effective control over administration, the president is given the twin constitutional weapons of appointment and removal, with the latter (as we have already stressed) being particularly crucial to the

---

[5] H. Adams, *The Education of Henry Adams* 266, 280 (1931).

[6] A. Nevins, *Hamilton Fish* 811 (1937).

[7] See D. Donald, *Charles Sumner and the Rights of Man* chs. 12–13 (1970). *See also* W.B. Hesseltine, *Ulysses S. Grant: Politician* (1935).

[8] 1 J. Sherman, *Recollections of Forty Years in the House, Senate and Cabinet* 447 (1895).

[9] Quoted in *White, supra* note 3, at 23.

[10] *Adams, The Session*, 111 *North Am. Rev.* 33–34 (1870).

[11] 2 J.R. Young, *Around the World with General Grant* 46 (1903).

[12] 7 J.D. Richardson, *A Compilation of the Messages and Papers of the Presidents 1787–1897*, at 6 (1896–99).

[13] *Id.* at 400.

president's role as administrative chief. On the exercise of these vital powers, Grant deferred almost completely to Congress: "The President very rarely appoints, he merely registers the appointments of members of Congress."[14] Senators and congressmen, Garfield wrote in 1877, had "become the dispensers, sometimes the brokers of patronage"[15] and successfully asserted the right to dictate local appointments.[16] The situation "has virtually resulted in the usurpation, by the Senate, of a large share of the appointing power . . . [and] has resulted in seriously crippling the just powers of the executive."[17] "These two departments," complained John Sherman in an 1871 Senate speech, "should be as distinct and marked as if they were separated by a broad river." Instead, "the power claimed by Senators and members to interfere in appointments does create a constant source of irritation between the legislative and executive departments."[18]

As far as the removal power was concerned, Grant entered office burdened by the incubus of the Tenure of Office Act. He asked for its repeal, but Congress refused to concur.[19] As Garfield said, in refusing to vote for repeal, "never by my vote shall Congress . . . allow to any one man, be he an angel from Heaven, the absolute and sole control of appointments to and removals from office in this country."[20] Grant was not the man to defy the legislative will, in the manner of his unfortunate predecessor. With a minor modification, the act remained a limitation upon the removal power throughout his administrations, but its outright repeal would not really have made any difference, in view of the continuing deference of the President to congressional leaders. "The mere repeal of the Tenure-of-Office Bill "cannot at once restore [the Presidency's] prestige," Henry Adams wrote, "or wrest from Congress the initiative which Congress is now accustomed to exercise. The Senate has no idea of abandoning its control of power."[21]

The presidency has never sunk lower in prestige. The Whig theory of the presidency temporarily prevailed, though the party which originated it had disappeared from the political scene decades earlier. Less than ten years after the Wade-Davis manifesto was issued, the conception of the highest office it urged—that the duty of the president is to obey and execute the laws, not to take any part in making them—had

14 *Young, supra* note 11.

15 *J.A. Garfield, A Century of Progress,* 90 *Atlantic Monthly* 61 (1877).

16 *See* Senator John Sherman, *Cong. Globe,* 41st Cong., 3d Sess. 293.

17 *Garfield, supra* note 15.

18 *Sherman, supra* note 16.

19 The act was not, indeed, repealed until 24 Stat. 500 (1887).

20 2 *T.C. Smith, The Life and Letters of James Abram Garfield* 444 (1925).

21 *Adams, The Session,* 108 *North Am. Rev.* 615 (1869).

all but taken over the field. Capitol Hill had become the vital place of action in the system.

CONGRESS: CONTROL AND CORRUPTION

In his *Congressional Government,* Woodrow Wilson assumed that Congress was the central and predominant power in the constitutional structure and that the presidency had been reduced to an ineffectual office. Since Lincoln's death, there had been no president who spoke for the nation and could cope with the overriding power of Congress.[22] In essence, the government was controlled by a congressional oligarchy which "held President Grant in the hollow of its hand."[23] This characterization by a more recent observer may sound extreme, but listen to the comment of a leading federal legislator at the time: "The most eminent Senators . . . would have received as a personal affront a private message from the White House expressing a desire that they should adopt any course in the discharge of their legislative duties that they did not approve. If they visited the White House, it was to give, not to receive advice."[24]

Congressional initiative and control of policy were generally in the Senate and (to a lesser degree) the House.[25] Once again, the situation was summed up by Henry Adams: "So far as the President's initiative was concerned, the President and his Cabinet might equally well have departed . . . to distant lands. Their recommendations were uniformly disregarded. Mr. Sumner, at the head of the Senate, rode rough-shod over their . . . policy and utterly overthrew it. . . . Mr. Conkling then ousted Mr. Sumner from his saddle, and headed the Senate in an attack upon the Executive."[26] Conkling's arrogance vis-à-vis President Grant has become well-nigh proverbial.

Nor did Capitol Hill rest content with reducing the presidency to this impotent stance. There were strong movements to impose further constitutional limitations upon the president, in the form of calls for a single-term amendment and for attendance of Cabinet members upon Congress. The former (a revival of an oft-repeated proposal by President Jackson) received support from Horace Greeley and other leaders and may have influenced Hayes's renunciation of any intention to seek a

[22] *Compare* W. Lippman, Introduction to *W. Wilson, Congressional Government: A Study in American Politics* 7, 8, 12 (1956 ed.).

[23] *W. Binkley, The Man in the White House: His Powers and Duties* 69 (1958).

[24] 2 *G.F. Hoar, Autobiography of Seventy Years* 46 (1879).

[25] *White, supra* note 3, at 41.

[26] *Adams, supra* note 10, at 41.

second term in his letter accepting the presidential nomination. The latter was strongly urged by Garfield in 1864, as well as by others in the 1870s, and was to receive the weighty support of a leading Senate committee in the 1880s.[27] Both proposals, of course, came to naught. Had they been adopted, they could have worked a transformation of the executive department, making impossible the renaissance of presidential power that was to become the outstanding feature of the twentieth-century Constitution. Our system might have evolved along the lines of Cabinet government on the British model (such as Woodrow Wilson was to favor in his early writings)—with "the Cabinet to be in the proper sense of the word a ministry."[28]

The failure of these proposals helped prevent the post-Civil War relapse into congressional supremacy from becoming a fixed feature of the constitutional system, but even more important was the inadequacy of Congress itself. "If not good law there was worldly wisdom in the maxim attributed to Napoleon that 'The tools belong to the man who can use them.' "[29] Presidential weakness may have opened the door to a permanent Capitol Hill Signory; yet only Congress itself could prevent the power available from slipping through its fingers. Henry Adams might declare that the United States had a "government of the people, by the people, for the benefit of Senators,"[30] but neither House was effective enough to give substance to Adams' remark, except in the pejorative sense. Though Congress was now the paramount power in the federal troika, undue concentration of authority in the legislature, as is so often the case, meant only headless government.

Even more than in the prewar period, the federal legislature was tainted by the pall of corruption. "It could probably be shown by facts and figures," said Mark Twain, "that there is no distinctly native American criminal class except Congress."[31] Even discounting the inevitable humorist's hyperbole, the Twain remark widely mirrored popular feeling. Almost every account of the Congress of the day, whether by contemporaries or later writers, reaches the same dreary conclusion on the mean moral climate that prevailed on Capitol Hill. "Admitted corruption" (to use the 1873 term of the scientist Simon Newcomb[32]) —with its inevitable counterpart of a "loss of public confidence in the

[27] *See White, supra* note 3, at 106–9.

[28] *Jacob D. Cox* (a leading advocate of the plan), *Civil Service Reform,* 112 *North Am. Rev.* 112 (1871).

[29] Jackson, J., concurring, in Youngstown Sheet & Tube Co. v. Sawyer, 343 U.S. 579, 654 (1952).

[30] Quoted in *J. Garraty, The New Commonwealth, 1877–1890,* at 235 (1968).

[31] *Mark Twain, Pudd'nhead Wilson's New Calendar,* ch. 8.

[32] *Newcomb, The Session,* 117 *North Am. Rev.* 200 (1873).

[Congress] which should alarm every thinking man"[33] —cast a gloom over the legislative department.

Morally speaking, the situation was equally bad at the other end of Pennsylvania Avenue. The Grant era stands unique in the comprehensiveness of its rascality:[34] "Corruption infested the executive departments as rats infest some slovenly warehouse."[35] Not until Teapot Dome (if even then) was executive morality to reach such a low ebb. The moral chaos of Grant's administration furnished the opportunity for wholesale use of congressional investigatory authority, and for the first time the potential inherent in the legislative power of inquiry was revealed. From 1869 to 1877 Congress undertook some thirty-seven investigations into charges of maladministration.[36] The high-water mark was reached in the last two years of Grant's second term, when the Democrats obtained control of the House. In addition to inquiries into corruption, in 1876 Congress passed a resolution authorizing its standing committees to conduct investigations of executive agencies within their jurisdiction.[37] A joint committee was also set up in 1869 to inquire into economies and administrative improvements; a special Senate committee in 1875 was to examine the Executive "with a view to the reorganization of the Departments."[38]

Though Congress kept the initiative through its investigatory power, it really did no more than uncover malfeasances. The legislative department was ill-constituted for the governmental leadership that had been left wanting by the presidential vacuum. Congress may have (as Woodrow Wilson was shortly to put it) "virtually taken into its own hands all the substantial powers of government,"[39] but its own ineffectiveness rendered its domination of the constitutional system at most a temporary phenomenon. It was in this sense that Bryce displayed acute perception when he remarked, "The weakness of Congress is the strength of the President."[40] The need for leadership made it inevitable that there would ultimately be a constitutional shift in favor of the presidency.

[33] *Id.* at 199.
[34] *Nevins, supra* note 6, at 638.
[35] *Nevins, Abram S. Hewitt* 291 (1935).
[36] *Harris, Congressional Control of Administration* 255 (1964).
[37] 4 *Cong. Record* 414.
[38] *See White, supra* note 3, at 86.
[39] *Wilson, supra* note 22, at 49.
[40] 2 *J. Bryce, The American Commonwealth* 908 (1916).

FROM TANEY TO CHASE

During the Civil War and Reconstruction (as already indicated), the Supreme Court was anything but the master of the Constitution.[41] In the main, control of the constitutional machine was concentrated in the legislative department, and the high bench could play only a minor part. When Chief Justice Taney died in 1864, the age of giants on the bench ended. Now it was the turn of the political jobbers and manipulators. Not for more than half a century would a man of true stature again sit in the Court's central chair.

Lincoln himself was frank about the political considerations which governed his choice of Taney's successor. "We wish," he said, "for a Chief Justice who will sustain what has been done in regard to emancipation and the legal tenders. . . . Therefore, we must take a man whose opinions are known."[42] Such a man Lincoln thought he had found in Salmon P. Chase, his former secretary of the treasury and a leader of the Republican Radicals. Chase was appointed to Taney's vacant seat on December 6, 1864.

The Supreme Court historian declares, of Chase's appointment, that "it was of inestimable value to the country to have at the head of the Court not only a great lawyer, but a great statesman."[43] One familiar with Chase's legal career can only be amazed at this characterization.[44] Regardless of what history may think of Chase as a statesman, he was anything but a "great lawyer." A recent biography concedes "his modest qualifications for the position" of chief justice,[45] and Chase himself tells us that when he applied in 1829 to Judge Cranch of the District of Columbia Circuit Court for admission to the Bar, Cranch was so skeptical of his professional attainments that he agreed to admit him only after Chase explained that he did not intend to practice in Washington but expected to go to the "western country."[46] He was able, after some years, to build up a practice at the Cincinnati bar. A recent account terms his practice "a most distinguished and lucrative" one,[47] but an advertising circular sent out by Chase himself in 1839 indicates that it was largely that of a glorified collection agent,[48] and

41 *Compare* 1 *id.* at 254.

42 2 *G.S. Boutwell, Reminiscences of Sixty Years in Public Affairs* 29 (1902).

43 3 *C. Warren, The Supreme Court in United States History* 135 (1924).

44 Yet it was repeated by so astute an historian as *Nevins, supra* note 6, at 659–60.

45 *T.G.* and *M.R. Belden, So Fell the Angels* 138 (1956).

46 E. Wambaugh, in 5 *Great American Lawyers* 344 (W.D. Lewis ed. 1908).

47 *Hughes, Salmon P. Chase: Chief Justice*, 18 *Vand. Law Rev.* 568, 572 (1965).

48 Circular, "S. P. Chase, Attorney, Solicitor and Counsellor of Cincinnati, Ohio," attached to letter to John H. James, Dec. 14, 1839 (in author's possession).

his political ambitions soon interfered even with that practice. Spending more and more time on politics, he all but gave up his legal work in the decade and a half before his appointment.

Noting Chase's probable appointment, Gideon Welles wrote, "The President sometimes does strange things, but this would be a singular mistake."[49] The Welles assessment proved accurate, and not primarily because of Chase's lack of learning. More important was the overriding fact that (as Lincoln is said to have put it) Chase "had the Presidential maggot in his brain, and he never knew anybody who once had it to get rid of it."[50] Certainly, Chase did not get rid of his ambition merely because of his appointment to the highest judicial position. As chief justice "He loved power as though he were still a Senator"[51] and throughout his judicial career still nourished the hope that the presidential mantle would at last descend upon him. "In my judgment," wrote Morrison R. Waite (Chase's successor) in 1875, "my predecessor detracted from his fame by permitting himself to think he wanted the Presidency. Whether true or not it was *said* that he permitted his ambitions in that direction to influence his judicial opinions."[52] His confreres on the bench, like the rest of the country, felt that Chase's judicial actions were governed primarily by political considerations. The inevitable result was a decline in the leadership role of the chief justice himself.

THE *LEGAL TENDER CASES*

The position of the Supreme Court during Chase's tenure is shown by its two legal tender decisions. During the Civil War, the Congress had been forced to make substantial changes in the currency system. In three Legal Tender acts, it had provided for the issuance of $450 million in United States notes not backed in specie (the so-called greenbacks) and provided that such notes were to be legal tender at face value in all transactions. Though the Framers' strong distrust of paper money had led them to strike from the original constitutional draft an express congressional power to "emit bills on the credit of the United States," it was incontestable that the doctrine of implied powers articulated by Marshall authorized the federal government to issue paper obligations. The constitutional controversy arose over the congressional power to make its paper money legal tender.

[49] 2 *Welles, supra* note 4, at 187.
[50] Quoted in *Warren, supra* note 43, at 122.
[51] *Adams, supra* note 5, at 250.
[52] Quoted in *C.P. Magrath, Morrison R. Waite: The Triumph of Character* 281 (1963).

During the Civil War the Supreme Court astutely avoided deciding a case challenging the validity of the greenback laws. After the war, the issue could not be evaded. In *Hepburn* v. *Griswold,*[53] a bare majority of the Court ruled the Legal Tender acts invalid. It will be recalled that one of the main reasons why Lincoln appointed Chase as chief justice was to ensure a favorable decision on the constitutionality of the legal tender laws, for Chase, as secretary of the treasury, had been their chief architect. But the new chief justice disappointed the presidential expectation. Writing of Chase's attitude toward legal tender, Henry Adams comments, "As Secretary of the Treasury he had been its author; as Chief Justice he became its enemy."[54] It was Chase who delivered the majority opinion in *Hepburn* v. *Griswold.*

What in another judge might have been considered high moral courage was in Chase condemned as but another example of political jobbery. His act was interpreted not as an indication of judicial independence but as a bid for the Democratic nomination. Legally, too, the Chase opinion was a weak one. As the young Holmes put it in a contemporary comment, *Hepburn* v. *Griswold* "presented the curious spectacle of the Supreme Court reversing the determination of Congress on a point of political economy."[55]

When *Hepburn* v. *Griswold* was decided, the Court consisted of only seven members, who divided four to three. To deprive President Johnson of the opportunity of filling expected vacancies, Congress passed a law providing that no vacancy on the Court was to be filled until it was reduced to seven members.[56] With Grant's election, the situation was changed, and an 1869 statute raised the number of justices to nine and authorized the president to make the necessary appointments.[57] On the very day on which the decision adverse to the government was announced in *Hepburn* v. *Griswold,* Grant appointed two new justices (Strong and Bradley) who were known to support the constitutionality of the Legal Tender acts. After they took their seats, the Court permitted argument again on the validity of the greenback laws. This time, in the *Legal Tender Cases*[58] —decided only a year after *Hepburn* v. *Griswold*—Justices Strong and Bradley, plus the *Hepburn* dissenters, made up a new majority. Finally putting to rest the controversy over congressional authority, the Court ruled that the nation's fiscal powers

53 8 Wall. 603 (U.S. 1870).

54 *Adams, supra* note 5, at 250.

55 7 *Am. L. Rev.* 146 (1872).

56 14 Stat 209 (1866).

57 16 Stat. 44 (1869).

58 12 Wall. 457 (U.S. 1871).

included the authority to issue paper money vested with the quality of legal tender.

Historians today reject the charge that Grant "packed the Court" for the deliberate purpose of obtaining a reversal of *Hepburn* v. *Griswold*.[59] At the same time, it is clear that the president chose the new justices not only because he was convinced of their fitness but because he believed they would sustain the Legal Tender acts.[60] For years after the cases were decided there was strong criticism because of the coincidence of the change in constitutional interpretation with the change in Court personnel. The Court's action, a contemporary newspaper commented, "will greatly aggravate the growing contempt for what has long been the most respected . . . department of our government, its Judiciary."[61]

The legal tender decisions demonstrate the congressional predominance over the Court in the immediate post-Civil War period. Even if there was no specific intent to "pack" the Court to secure a favorable legal resolution of the greenback controversy, the eventual outcome was the same. Yet, even here, the picture is not entirely onesided. The very fact that the weighty issue of legal tender was accepted as a judicial issue to be resolved by the Supreme Court is ultimately more important than the political injury inflicted on the Court. As it turned out, the vote of one justice (however the new majority was really secured) decided a matter crucial to the economic life of the nation.

THE *SLAUGHTER-HOUSE CASES*

The fundamental role of the Supreme Court in the constitutional system, even in a period when the judicial power is essentially in repose, was also underscored by the 1873 decision in the *Slaughter-House Cases*.[62] Like so many landmark decisions rendered by the Court, its effect was scarcely noted at the time. "The decision," wrote a newspaper reporter the day after it was announced, "was given to an almost empty Courtroom . . . and has as yet attracted little attention outside of legal circles, although the Judges of the Court regard the case as the most important which has been before them since the Dred Scott decision."[63]

[59] *See C. Fairman, Reconstruction and Reunion* 1395 (1971).
[60] *Nevins, supra* note 6, at 306.
[61] Quoted in *Warren, supra* note 43, at 247.
[62] 16 Wall. 36 (U.S. 1873).
[63] Quoted in *Warren, supra* note 43, at 261.

In 1869 the Louisiana legislature passed a statute which incorporated the Crescent City Live-Stock Landing and Slaughter House Company and gave it the exclusive right to slaughter livestock in the New Orleans area. The law, voted amid charges of widespread bribery, put one thousand butchers out of business. They brought an action challenging "The Monopoly" (the popular name for the new corporation) as violative of the Fourteenth Amendment. "The banded butchers are busted. Matt"[64] —in this telegram the noted lawyer Matthew H. Carpenter announced his victory in the *Slaughter-House Cases*. But it was not only the plaintiff butchers who were "busted" by the high-bench decision. The *Slaughter-House* opinion virtually emasculated section 1 of the Fourteenth Amendment itself. Had the Court's restrictive interpretation not ultimately been relaxed, the amendment could scarcely have come to serve as the legal instrument for the protection of property rights, particularly those of corporations.

The congressional debates on the Fourteenth Amendment indicate that its framers (particularly Representative John Bingham, who drafted most of section 1, and Senator Jacob Howard, who opened the Senate debate) placed particular stress upon the clause prohibiting the states from abridging "the privileges and immunities of citizens of the United States." It is possible, indeed, that the privileges and immunities to be protected included all the rights covered in the first eight amendments, with the Privileges and Immunities Clause intended to make the Bill of Rights binding upon the states. If that was the intent of the draftsmen, it was soon frustrated. The clause was all but read out of the amendment by the *Slaughter-House Cases,* where the Court found crucial decisional significance in the difference in language between its Citizenship Clause and its Privileges and Immunities Clause. The opinion of Justice Miller stressed the fact that, while the first sentence of the amendment makes all persons born or naturalized in this country both "citizens of the United States and of the State wherein they reside," the next sentence protects only "the privileges or immunities of citizens of the United States" from state abridgement. The distinction was intended to leave the fundamental rights of life and property untouched by the amendment; they remained, as always, with the states.

Under *Slaughter-House,* the Privileges and Immunities Clause did not transform the rights of citizens of each state into rights of national citizenship enforceable as such in the federal courts. It only protected against state encroachment those rights "which owe their existence to

[64] Quoted in *Fairman, supra* note 59, at 1349.

the Federal Government, its national character, its Constitution, or its laws."[65] Rights which antedate, and thus do not owe their existence to, that government are privileges and immunities of state citizenship alone. Earning a living is such a right. Hence, the Louisiana law in *Slaughter-House* was not violative of the clause.

If the *Slaughter-House* decision rendered the Privileges and Immunities Clause "a practical nullity"[66] within five years after it became part of the Constitution, what of the amendment's Due Process Clause, upon which the *Slaughter-House* butchers had also relied? The opinion adopted the limited view that the Fourteenth Amendment was intended only to protect the Negro in his newly acquired freedom. That being the case, the Due Process Clause was all but irrelevant in considering the constitutionality of the law which conferred upon "The Monopoly" the exclusive right to slaughter livestock. Referring to the Due Process Clause, the Court declared that "under no construction of that provision that we have ever seen, or any that we deem admissible, can the restraint imposed by the State of Louisiana upon the exercise of their trade by the butchers of New Orleans be held to be a deprivation of property within the meaning of that provision."[67] With the Due Process Clause inapplicable, the states were left almost as free to regulate the rights of property as they had been before the Civil War.

It would be erroneous to assume that the entire *Slaughter-House* Court was in favor of the restrictive interpretation of due process. Four justices strongly disputed the Court's casual dismissal of the Due Process Clause, foremost among them Justices Field and Bradley, who delivered vigorous dissents. In their view, the Fourteenth Amendment "was intended to give practical effect to the declaration of 1776 of inalienable rights, rights which are the gift of the Creator, which the law does not confer, but only recognizes."[68] From the rights guaranteed in the Declaration of Independence to due process was a natural transition in the Field-Bradley approach: "Rights to life, liberty, and the pursuit of happiness are equivalent to the rights of life, liberty and property. These are the fundamental rights which can only be taken away by due process of law."[69] A law like that in *Slaughter-House,* in the dissenting view, did violate due process: "In my view a law which prohibits a large class of citizens from adopting a lawful employment, or from

65 16 Wall. at 79.

66 *E.S. Corwin, The Constitution of the United States of America: Analysis and Interpretation* 965 (1953).

67 16 Wall. at 81.

68 *Id.* at 105.

69 *Id.* at 116.

following a lawful employment previously adopted, does deprive them of liberty as well as property, without due process of law "[70]

What the Field-Bradley dissents were doing was to urge adoption of a substantive due process approach similar to that used in Chief Justice Taney's ill-fated *Dred Scott* opinion.[71] Like Taney, the *Slaughter-House* dissenters rejected the limitation of due process to a procedural guarantee. They urged that it also contemplated judicial review of the substance of challenged state action. In their view a monopoly law which deprived the New Orleans butchers of their right to earn their living was an arbitrary violation of due process. Much of the substance of constitutional history in the quarter century following *Slaughter-House* involved the writing of the Field-Bradley dissents into the opinions of the Supreme Court,[72] but for over a decade after it was decided, *Slaughter-House* sharply restricted the reach of the Fourteenth Amendment and its Due Process Clause. "When this generation of mine opened the reports," says a federal judge who came to the bar at that time, "the chill of the Slaughter House decision was on the bar . . . the still continuing dissents of Judge Field seemed most unorthodox. The remark in another judgment,[73] that due process was usually what the state ordained, seemed to clinch the matter."[74]

WAITE AND THE *GRANGER CASES*

Three weeks after the *Slaughter-House* decision, Chief Justice Chase suddenly died. President Grant's attempts to find a successor were so ludicrous that they might be relegated to the realm of the comic but for the baneful effect they had on the Supreme Court's reputation. Charles Sumner is reported to have said, "We stand at an epoch in the country's life, in the midst of revolution in its constitutional progress . . . ; and I long for a Chief Justice like John Marshall, who shall pilot the country through the rocks and rapids in which we are."[75] Instead, Grant used the office as a political plum—a gift to be bestowed on those who had won his personal gratitude.[76] Only after he had failed in his stumbling efforts to appoint various associates of his did Grant choose Morrison

[70] *Id.* at 122.

[71] *See* p. 124 *supra.*

[72] *Compare Frankfurter, Mr. Justice Holmes and the Constitution, 41 Harv. L. Rev. 141* (1927).

[73] Referring to Walker v. Sauvinet, 92 U.S. 90, 93 (1876).

[74] *Hough, Due Process of Law—Today, 32 Harv. L. Rev. 226* (1919).

[75] Quoted by *Samuel Shellabarger,* in In Memoriam—Morrison Remick Waite, 126 U.S. 585, 599–600 (1888).

[76] *Magrath,* supra note 52, at 20.

R. Waite, a little-known Ohio lawyer, who was accepted by the Senate and the country with a collective sigh of relief. "The President," declared the *Nation,* "has, with remarkable skill, avoided choosing any first-rate man. . . . [But], considering what the President might have done, and tried to do, we ought to be very thankful."[77]

Waite himself was a competent legal craftsman, though scarcely endowed with the personality or prestige usually associated with the highest judicial office. "The touch of the common-place about him was, indeed, the key to his appointment. . . . Grant doubtless felt confident that the relative obscurity of Waite was the best assurance for his confirmation."[78] Certainly, Waite had nothing of the grand manner— the spark which made Marshall and Taney what they were. A humdrum, pedestrian lawyer, he remains (despite recent biographies) a dim figure in our constitutional history. "I can't make a silk purse out of a sow's ear," wrote Justice Miller a year after Waite's appointment. "I can't make a great Chief Justice out of a small man."[79]

Yet, if Waite was not a great chief justice, he may have been just what the Supreme Court needed after the turbulence of *Dred Scott,* the war, Reconstruction, and the political maneuverings of Chase and some of his colleagues. The Court's tarnished reputation was largely refurbished during his tenure, and at his death in 1888, it was ready to take its place again as a fully coordinate department of government.

During Waite's term the Supreme Court was first called upon to respond to the modern current of social legislation. His was the beginning of the epoch when due process served as the most fertile source of constitutional lawmaking, Before the trend toward due process as the basic restriction upon state power became established in the Supreme Court, that tribunal decided the 1877 *Granger Cases.*[80] "Judged by any standards of ultimate importance," says Justice Frankfurter, Waite's ruling in the *Granger Cases* "places it among the dozen most important decisions in our constitutional law "[81] It upheld the power of the states to regulate the rates of railroads and other businesses—a holding, never since departed from, which has served as the basis upon which governmental regulation in this country has essentially rested.

The *Granger Cases* arose out of the abuses that accompanied the post-Civil War growth of railroads. Highly speculative railroad building, irresponsible financial manipulation, and destructive competitive warfare resulted in monopolies, fluctuating and discriminatory rates—and

---

77 Quoted in *Warren, supra* note 43, at 283.

78 *Frankfurter, The Commerce Clause under Marshall, Taney and Waite* 76–77 (1964).

79 Quoted in C. *Fairman, Mr. Justice Miller and the Supreme Court* 373 (1939).

80 Munn v. Illinois, 94 U.S. 113 (1877), and its companion cases.

81 *Frankfurter, supra* note 78, at 83.

the inevitable public outcry. The grievances against the railroads were especially acute in the Midwest, where the farmer was dependent upon them for moving his crops, as well as on the grain elevators in which those crops were stored. The farmers' resentment led to the Granger movement, which swept through the Midwest in the early 1870s. The Grangers sought to correct these abuses through state regulation. They secured laws in Illinois, Wisconsin, Minnesota, and Iowa regulating railroads and grain elevators and limiting the prices they could charge. These were the laws at issue in the *Granger Cases*. In the principal case before the Court, an Illinois law fixed the maximum prices to be charged by grain elevators in Chicago; four companion cases involved state statutes regulating railroad rates.

The Court sustained all these laws against due process attacks on the ground that "property ... become[s] clothed with a public interest when used in a manner to make it of public consequence, and affect the community at large. When, therefore, one devotes his property to a use in which the public has an interest, he, in effect, grants to the public an interest in that use, and must submit to be controlled by the public for the common good, to the extent of the interest he has thus created." [82] Chief Justice Waite's opinion in the *Granger Cases* was greatly influenced by an outline prepared by the Court's leading legal scholar, Justice Bradley.[83] In particular, it was Bradley who called Waite's attention to the common law on the subject, especially Lord Hale's seventeenth-century statement that when private property is "affected with a publick interest, it ceases to be *juris privati*[84] only."[85] But the *Granger* opinion was more than a rehash of the Bradley outline. Waite articulated his opinion in language broad enough to transform the whole course of the law of business regulation. In the words of a contemporary, "Suffice it, that the decision itself in its general breadth and purpose has no precedent."[86]

Waite was only following the time-honored judicial technique of pouring new wine into old bottles. He read and expounded Lord Hale in the spirit of the industrial era. He tore a fragment from the annals of the law, stripped away its limited frame of reference, and re-created it in the image of the modern police power.[87] Under the *Granger* approach, for a business to be subject to regulation, it need only be one

---

[82] 94 U.S. at 126.

[83] *See Fairman, The So-Called Granger Cases,* 5 Stan. L. Rev. 592 (1953).

[84] Of private right.

[85] Sir Matthew Hale, De Portibus Maris, in *F. Hargrave, Collection of Tracts Relative to the Law of England* 77–78 (1787).

[86] Note, 25 *Am. L. Reg.* 545 (1877).

[87] *Compare Hamilton, Affectation with a Public Interest,* 39 *Yale L. J.* 1092, 1097 (1930).

which affects the community. "Waite's reference to property 'clothed with a public interest' surely meant no more than that the Court must be able to attribute to the legislature the fulfillment of a public interest."[88] In this sense, a business affected with a public interest becomes nothing more than one in which the public has come to have an interest.[89] This rationale becomes a means of enabling governmental regulatory power to be asserted over business far beyond what was previously thought permissible. As a member of the highest bench once pointed out, "There is scarcely any property in whose use the public has no interest."[90] The public is concerned about all business because it contributes to the welfare of the community.[91]

Waite's rationale did not really reveal its potential until over half a century later. In the years immediately following *Granger,* it was virtually neutralized by judicial adoption of the Field-Bradley notion of due process. It was revived when the due process current was reversed, starting in 1934.[92] Since that time, it has been the doctrine that has furnished the constitutional foundation for the ever-broader schemes of business regulation that have become so prominent a feature of the society today.

THE ELECTION CRISIS

Coming so soon after the traumatic experiences of civil conflict and Reconstruction, the disputed Hayes-Tilden election of 1876 might well have resulted in a permanent breakdown of the constitutional system—bringing about, in the contemporary terminology, the "Mexicanization" of American politics. That that result did not ensue is, after all, the most important thing to note in a constitutional survey. The nation was able to continue into its second century still basically faithful to its original organic structure.

A study published thirty years after the event asserts, "Few of the generation which has grown up since then will have any but the faintest conception of the gravity of the situation existing during the winter of 1876–77."[93] Such a comment is, of course, even more true today. It is all but impossible to appreciate the gravity of the crisis presented by

---

88 *Frankfurter, supra* note 78, at 86.

89 *See* Wolff Packing Co. v. Industrial Court, 262 U.S. 522, 536 (1923).

90 Brewer, J., dissenting, in Budd v. New York, 143 U.S. 517, 549 (1892).

91 *Supra* note 89.

92 Nebbia v. New York, 291 U.S. 502 (1934).

93 *P.L. Haworth, The Hayes-Tilden Disputed Presidential Election of 1876,* at 168 (1966 ed.).

the dispute. At the time, "more people dreaded an armed conflict than had anticipated a like outcome to the secession movement of 1860-61."[94] This sentiment was expressed in a letter from Senator Sherman to Hayes himself: "The same influence now rules . . . as did in 1860-61, and I feel that we are to encounter the same enemies that we did then."[95] Well might Chief Justice Waite, in a letter to a federal judge, characterize the situation as a "great trial."[96] As so often in our history, an essentially political controversy was converted into a legal battle, with the disputed issues argued and resolved in constitutional terms. Perhaps, ultimately, that is why the crisis could be settled without bloodshed. Justice Jackson's striking claim, "struggles over power that in Europe call out regiments of troops, in America call out battalions of lawyers,"[97] was given dramatic corroboration in this peaceful resolution.

Legally speaking, the conflict arose because of a lacuna in the Constitution with regard to the process of electing the president. Article II provides for the selection of presidential electors under state laws, for the casting of their votes, and for the certification of same to the president of the Senate. It then goes on, "The President of the Senate shall, in the Presence of the Senate and House of Representatives, open all the Certificates, and the Votes shall then be counted." But counted by whom? The president of the Senate (who in 1876–1877 was Thomas W. Ferry, a leading Republican), the two houses separately (leading to a deadlock, since the Senate had a Republican and the House a Democratic majority), or the houses jointly (in which case the Democratic House would outvote the Republican Senate)?

The Constitution did not answer these questions, which assumed critical importance in the face of conflicting electoral certificates from four states. The returning boards in Florida, Louisiana, and South Carolina (solidly Republican[98]) had certified the electors for Hayes, converting Tilden majorities by disallowing thousands of Democratic votes. The Democrats, claiming fraud, had conflicting certificates, certifying their electors, sent to Washington. In Oregon, where Hayes had received a clear majority, one of his electors was ineligible under the Constitution because he was a federal officer. The governor certified the other two Republican electors and the Democrat who had lost to

---

[94] *Id.* Abram S. Hewitt's *Secret History* reaches the same conclusion, *Nevins, supra* note 35, at 380.

[95] Quoted in *C.V. Woodward, Reunion and Reaction: The Compromise of 1877 and the End of Reconstruction* 120 (1956).

[96] Quoted in *Magrath, supra* note 52, at 289.

[97] *R.H. Jackson, The Struggle for Judicial Supremacy* xi (1949).

[98] Except in Florida, where there was one Democrat to two Republicans.

the ineligible official. The two Republican electors chose a third Republican to fill the vacancy and sent a certificate, accompanied by a certification of the election results by the Oregon secretary of state. In these circumstances, the crucial question was, of course, who counted the electoral votes, and it could not be decided by the normal political machinery. That the situation was finally resolved by extra-constitutional means may be attributed to the overwhelming popular desire, particularly in the South, for a peaceful solution.[99]

When the crisis was at its height, early in 1877, Chief Justice Waite wrote that "the good sense of the people is exerting its influence upon the leaders."[100] Two weeks later Congress set up an Electoral Commission to decide which of the disputed electoral votes to count.[101] It was to be composed of five senators and five congressmen, equally divided between the two parties, and four Supreme Court justices, designated by circuits. These four (two from each party) were then to select a fifth member of the Court, who would be the commission's key man, if, as was expected, the other fourteen members divided evenly along party lines. It was hoped that the partisan element in the commission's work would be neutralized by the selection of David Davis as the fifth justice (he was the only member of the Court not formally affiliated with either party). This expectation was frustrated by Davis' sudden election to the Senate by the Illinois legislature. That left only Republican members of the Court to choose from, and Justice Bradley, supposedly the least partisan among them, was chosen.

When it came time to decide the disputed returns, the Electoral Commission divided, in every instance, strictly along party lines. Justice Bradley's vote, added to those of the other Republicans, meant an 8-7 division in Hayes's favor on every disputed elector, and the Republican candidate was declared elected by the margin of one electoral vote. By then it was March 2, 1877—only two days before inauguration day.

The vital legal question before the electoral commission was that of whether it could properly go behind the returns certified by the relevant state officials. The Republican majority gave a negative answer on the disputed returns from Florida, Louisiana, and South Carolina. "It seems to me," declared Justice Bradley for the majority, "that the two Houses of Congress, in proceeding with the count, are bound to recognize the determination of the State board of canvassers as the act of the State, and as the most authentic evidence of the appointment

---

[99] After a northern Democrat made a fiery speech at a party caucus, a southerner arose and said, "Perhaps the gentleman is not aware of the conservative influence of a fifteen-inch shell with the fuse in process of combustion," *Woodward, supra* note 95, at 33.

[100] Quoted in *Magrath, supra* note 52, at 291.

[101] 19 Stat. 227 (1877).

made by the State." [102] This position appears valid and was, in fact, the one ultimately adopted when Congress, a decade later, finally provided a permanent procedure for counting the electoral vote. [103] Any other rule leaves it open for a majority in Congress—even though repudiated at the polls—to perpetuate its candidate in the highest office. It has, however, been claimed that the commission did not follow its own ruling when, in Oregon, it refused to accept the governor's certification of the one Tilden elector. Though a close question, it seems that the claim misconceives the nature of what the commission did in this case. Under the Oregon statutes it was the secretary of state who had the authority to canvass the returns, and his certificate as to those chosen was accepted in view of his exclusive authority under state law. [104]

Legally justified or not, a storm of controversy resulted from the Electoral Commission's rulings. In particular, Justice Bradley was subjected to vituperative attacks for allegedly changing his original opinion in favor of the Democrats after pressure from leading Republicans and railroad interests, to which he was supposedly beholden. The charge against Bradley's integrity severely tarnished the remaining career of one who (from the point of view of legal ability) was one of the best men ever to sit on the high tribunal. More important, as in every instance in which justices have performed non-judicial duties, the judicial descent into the political arena reflected unfavorably on the Supreme Court itself. According to Garfield, "All the judges, *save one,* were very sorry to be called to this commission." [105] The spectacle of the justices casting their votes on partisan lines cannot but have had a deleterious effect upon the Court's reputation. At the same time, it must be recognized that without them, it is doubtful that the Electoral Commission could ever have been approved—much less had its decision accepted by the country. Had they refused to serve, they would have upset the carefully worked-out compromise and plunged the country into a crisis which it might not have been possible to settle peacefully.

"Just at present," wrote Chief Justice Waite after the Electoral Commission had decided, "our judges are severely criticized, but I feel sure time will bring us out all right." [106] And so it turned out. With Henry Adams, the country "still clung to the Supreme Court, much as the churchman still clings to his last rag of Right. Between the Execu-

---

[102] Quoted in *A.C. McLaughlin, A Constitutional History of the United States* 707 (1935).

[103] 24 Stat. 373 (1887).

[104] There was also an Oregon statute permitting the electors to fill any vacancy in their ranks.

[105] Quoted in *Magrath, supra* note 52, at 293.

[106] *Id.* at 294.

tive and the Legislature, citizens could have no Rights; they were at the mercy of Power. They had created the Court to protect them from unlimited Power." [107] The need for an impartial umpire in a working federation was too great. For the balance properly to be kept, judicial power could not long be kept in repose.

Resolution of the dispute took place soon after the centennial of the nation. Writing at that time, Henry Adams mourned that "the system of 1789 had broken down, and with it . . . the fabric of . . . moral, principles. Politicians had tacitly given it up." [108] Adams was (as all too often) wide of the mark. The constitutional system set up a century earlier had endured the test of fire. Reconstruction and the bitterness it engendered was at last ended. For the first time since the war, it was governmental policy that "the flag should wave over states, not provinces, over freemen and not subjects." [109] The focus of constitutional concern could now shift from the great issues that had almost destroyed the nation to those more appropriate to a less troubled era.

[107] *Adams, supra* note 5, at 277.
[108] *Id.* at 280–81.
[109] Rep. Charles Foster, 5 *Cong. Rec.* 1708.

Index

SUBJECT INDEX

INDEX OF CASES

THE JOHNS HOPKINS UNIVERSITY PRESS

This book was composed in Baskerville text and
Caslon display type by The Composing Room from
a design by Victoria Dudley. It was printed
on 60-lb. Danforth paper
and bound in Holliston Roxite linen finish cloth
by The Maple Press Company.

Library of Congress Cataloging in Publication Data

Schwartz, Bernard, 1923–
 From confederation to nation.

 Includes bibliographical references.
 1. United States—Constitutional history.
I. Title.
KF4541.S35   342'.73'029   72-12353
ISBN 0-8018-1464-2